The Market System

Introduction to Economics Series
Kenyon A. Knopf, Editor

The Market System: An Introduction to Microeconomics
Fourth Edition
Robert H. Haveman and Kenyon A. Knopf

The National Economy: An Introduction to Macroeconomics
Gordon Philpot

International Economic Problems, Third Edition
James C. Ingram

The Economics of the Public Sector, Second Edition
Robert H. Haveman

Case Studies in American Industry, Third Edition
Leonard W. Weiss

The Market System

AN INTRODUCTION TO MICROECONOMICS

Fourth Edition

Robert H. Haveman
UNIVERSITY OF WISCONSIN, MADISON

Kenyon A. Knopf
WHITMAN COLLEGE

John Wiley & Sons

NEW YORK   CHICHESTER   BRISBANE   TORONTO

Library of Congress Cataloging in Publication Data:

Haveman, Robert H
    The market system.

    (Introduction to economics series)
    Includes bibliographical references and index.
    1. Microeconomics.   I.   Knopf, Kenyon A.,
joint author.   II. Title.
HB172.H38   1981   338.5   80-21972
ISBN 0-471-08530-8

Printed in the United States of America

10 9 8 7 6 5 4 3 2 1

Introduction to Economics Series

Teachers of introductory economics seem to agree on the impracticality of presenting a comprehensive survey of economics to freshmen or sophomores. Many of them believe there is a need for some alternative that provides a solid core of principles while permitting an instructor to introduce a select set of problems and applied ideas. This series attempts to fill that need and also to give interested readers a set of self-contained books that they can absorb with interest and profit, without assistance.

By offering greater flexibility in the choice of topics for study, these books represent a more realistic and reasonable approach to teaching economics than most of the large, catchall textbooks. With separate volumes and different authors for each topic, the instructor is not as tied to a single track as in the omnibus introductory economics text.

Underlying the Introduction to Economics Series is the pedagogical premise that students should be introduced to economics by learning how economists think about economic problems. The series contains books for use with any of several other books that apply theory to events and problems of the United States and the world economy. An approach of this kind offers a good beginning to the student who intends to move on to advanced work and furnishes a clearer understanding for those whose study of economics is limited to an introductory exposure. Teachers and students alike should find the books helpful and stimulating.

Kenyon A. Knopf, Editor

About the Authors

Robert Haveman is a Professor of Economics at the University of Wisconsin, Madison, where he has also been Director of the Institute for Research on Poverty. He has been a Professor of Economics at Grinnell College, Senior Economist on the Joint Economic Committee of the U.S. Congress, Research Professor at the Brookings Institution, Research Economist at Resources for the Future, Inc., and Fellow at the Netherlands Institute for Advanced Study. Professor Haveman's primary fields of interest are Public Finance, Human Resources Economics, and Environmental Economics. His books in these fields include: *The Economics of the Public Sector* (Wiley/Hamilton, 1976), *Public Expenditure and Policy Analysis* (co-edited with Julius Margolis), *The Economic Performance of Public Investments*, and *The Economics of Environmental Policy* with A. Myrick Freeman and Allen Kneese [Wiley/Hamilton, 1973]. Professor Haveman's current research involves the evaluation of alternative anti-poverty and income redistribution policies.

Kenyon A. Knopf is Provost, Whitman College where he also serves as Professor of Economics. Prior to that he was Professor of Economics at Grinnell College. He earned his Ph.D. in economics at Harvard.

He served for four years on the Committee on Economic Education of the American Economics Association where he was the principal member concerned with college-level economic education. He is a Public Interest Director for the District 12 Federal Home Loan Bank in Seattle that supervises the federal savings and loan institutions in eight western states.

Preface

Any text on economic theory that uses examples from the contemporary economy is destined to rapid obsolescence in a rapidly changing world. *The Market System* is no exception. As a result, even though the third edition is but three years old, several signs of its being outdated have appeared. In this fourth edition our primary aim is to up-date the applied material, retaining the structure of the more basic revision that was incorporated into the third edition.

All of the chapters of *The Market System* were completely revised in the third edition. There we emphasized changes that would make the analysis of a price or market economy more comprehensible to first- or second-year students. More technical analyses are placed in the appendixes to chapters 3 and 5. This enables instructors to have some flexibility in the level of analysis that they employ in their course, without loss of continuity in the text. Substantial effort was devoted to the style of presentation: our objective has been to delineate the basic principles of microeconomics in terms that are as clear, as concise, and as understandable as possible.

The most basic changes in the third edition were stimulated by the comments of some of the adopters of earlier editions. They felt that the theory could be made richer and more relevant if short examples of its applicability to real-life business and policy problems were also presented. In response we added several sections that describe some of the ways in which the theoretical concepts presented here have been applied in making more effective choices in both the public and private sectors. In chapter 3 we added a section that discusses the role of demand analysis in measuring the benefits of public outdoor recreation investments and the role of factor supply analysis in measuring the work disincentives of a national guaranteed income. Chapter 4 was supplemented by a new section that describes the role of supply and demand estimates in formulating public policy in the areas of energy, environmental pollution, and public investment. Chapter 5 presents and discusses the relevance of empirical studies of the price elasticity of demand. It also considers the Russian grain purchases in the 1970s and now the grain embargo to the Soviet Union in 1980. In chapter 6, the discussion of the money market is clarified by explicitly utilizing loanable funds language. Chapter 7 includes a new section on cartels, emphasizing the impact of the international oil producers' cartel. Price control in the Nixon administration is introduced as a deviation from price rationing of goods. Finally, chapter 8 adds material on benefit-cost analysis of water resources investments, public policy strategies for correcting spillover effects, and the evaluation of proposals that would impose irreversible impacts on future generations.

Throughout this new edition, we have tried to be fair in our treatment of both sexes; thus we have used examples that involve men and women. Occasionally, a "he" may have slipped by us, only because we did not wish to employ a grammatical device that would become clumsy. We hope that the spirit of fairness will be evident in all our discussions.

It is hoped that with these changes in the third and fourth editions, the book will be a better instrument both for understanding the basic functioning of a market system and for perceiving the importance of fundamental economic relationships in framing efficient public policy decisions.

Robert H. Haveman
Kenyon A. Knopf

Contents

1 | Economies and Economizing

The United Nations Secretariat classifies countries into market economies and centrally planned economies.[1] This book is about developed market economies, such as that of the United States, or Canada, or most of the countries of Western Europe. It is not a description of any of these economies; rather, it is a statement of the logic of a pure market economy. However, it is difficult to recognize the components of this logic in any existing market economy. Hence, we will also consider the ways in which real-world economies deviate from our description, and why they do so.

In the American economy millions of decisions are made about spending income at the same time that millions of other decisions are made about what work to do to produce goods and services in order to earn income. Amazingly, the two sets of decisions match up fairly well. Where they match poorly, there are forces at work which will lead them to match better. This would not be so remarkable if households produced a high proportion of what they consume, or if they purchased on special order from friends and neighbors. But this is not the case. Most production is for a vast number of unknown and unseen potential customers, in short, production is for impersonal markets.

People living in Chicago sleep peacefully at night oblivious to the fact that a fantastic array of decisions have been made and acted on, some of them years earlier, in order that the store shelves in the city

---

1. This book presents the logic of market relationships abstracted from dynamic change in an economy.

will be stocked in the morning. As a community, they do not fear famine, nor do they often experience gluts of some goods. The same is true for other communities in the United States. Yet there is no superior authority, no board of directors, seeing to it that all of the decisions mesh, that the system is orderly. The reconciling of these millions of individual decisions would be beyond human mental capacities and beyond the capability of the most sophisticated computer imaginable.

Our central concern is this observed economic order. What does produce order out of decentralized decision making in economic affairs? The answer is that the economic system possesses a very special mechanism to reconcile the many conflicting interests, to solve the problems of economic choice. We will call this mechanism the *market mechanism* and the system that embodies it the *market system*.

I.   THE LOGIC OF THE MARKET SYSTEM

All societies face the same basic economic questions of *what* goods and services to produce, *how* to produce them, and *for whom*. All societies make choices in answering these questions by means of a socioeconomic system. Many developed economies answer these questions through a market system, one in which the basic decisions are made, not by some central authority, but by individual producers and consumers. These producers and consumers are all striving to achieve their own goals, and in so doing, respond as best they can to the incentives which penalize or reward their activities. In a market system, the primary incentives are expressed in prices which are generated in markets.[2] In a market system, all goods are produced for exchange and exchanges are money transactions. All inputs and outputs have prices that are set in markets by the actions of a host of competitors, each seeking his own advantage.

Households spend their income to purchase the goods and services that they most desire from the businesses that produce them. Households are encouraged to buy more when prices are low and are discouraged from buying so much when prices are high. On the other hand, households sell their labor services and the services of the machinery and natural resources that they own in order to earn this income. Households are encouraged to supply more of their labor services and more of the services of the property they own

2. The system also is sometimes called "the price system."

when prices are high and less when prices are low. Businesses buy these services from households, using them to produce and sell products to each other and to households in the expectation that the revenue from sales will cover the costs of production and that some profit will remain. When prices of business products are high, more profit remains over and above costs of production, inducing businesses to produce more. Low prices and low profits discourage businesses from producing so much.

This system would appear to be quite chaotic. How can a society hold together if a multitude of individuals each pursue their own self-interest? How can reliance on selfish motives produce an optimum in economic welfare for society? Adam Smith, in his historic book, *The Wealth of Nations*, first published in 1776, supplied the answer by pointing to *competition* among buyers and sellers as an effective regulator.

If each business firm has a number of competitors, pursuit of self-interest by each will be channeled to provide for the social welfare. For example, a shoe manufacturer which has competitors is pressed by competition to charge the lowest price consistent with continued operation, and production will tend to conform to the most efficient methods. If one shoe manufacturer charges a higher price for shoes than that which covers all costs, competitors will find it profitable to undercut the manufacturer's price and win away customers. Since competition keeps the sales price down, a high-cost firm would suffer losses and would have to reduce its costs or go out of business. Just how the price system produces these beneficial results under the guidance of competition is the substance of this volume. We will also study how our real-world economic system sometimes fails to provide such competition for each and every buyer and seller.

II. THE EMERGENCE OF A MARKET SOCIETY

Some of the logic of market societies and some of their institutions may be better understood from the perspective provided by a short historical excursion. *Market-directed societies* are relatively new, even though elements of such societies appeared at various points in the life of *tradition-directed societies*, the kind of economic system which historically preceded the market economy. Despite the great differences in detail and institutional arrangements, the primitive societies studied by anthropologists, as well as ancient China, ancient Greece, and medieval Europe, all made their economic choices largely by tradition. A tradition-directed society is one in which economic choices are made by following patterns established by prior generations. Its technology is based on "rule of thumb," with skills passed on from father to son. Economic relationships are closely intertwined with social relationships and are subsidiary to them. Change in the social fabric, hence the economic fabric, occurs very slowly. The same is true of technology, which often remained unchanged for generations.

Much of the groundwork for market societies was laid in Western Europe in the late Middle Ages with the development of certain practices which facilitated the rapid growth of commercial activity. Long-distance trade had fallen off sharply with the end of the Roman Empire, in the fifth century A.D., and local exchange of goods and services came to be barter transactions involving the exchange of goods for goods without the use of money.[3] For several centuries, the feudal arrangements of rights and obligations dominated local economic activity in Europe. However, the gradual development of peace in the countryside and a period of rapid population growth encouraged growth of local trade and the establishment of annual fairs for the sale of exotic goods from the Near East. The Crusades provided even more contact with the Near East and more interest in its products.

These events created pressures for the *monetization of transactions*. Italian merchants were among the leaders in the long-distance trade which then experienced rather rapid expansion, and it was in the Italian city-states that several important financial practices developed. One was the emergence of banks of deposit which transferred funds within the bank from one person to another on written request—a primitive form of our check-writing practice. These banks also discovered that in normal times all depositors would not appear at once to withdraw their deposits, so it seemed safe to lend some of the deposits to people who wanted to borrow. Banks extended credit based on the holding of less gold and silver in reserve than would be necessary to cover 100 percent of the deposits. These practices facilitated the transfer of wealth from those who owned it to those enterprises which would put it to productive use. Development of this fractional reserve banking also laid the foundation for the use of bank credit as money that can expand and contract in quantity to meet the needs of the economy.

Double-entry bookkeeping is another important practice that de-

---

3. See Henri Pirenne, *Economic and Social History of Medieval Europe* (New York: Harcourt-Brace, 1937), also *The Cambridge Economic History of Europe*, Vol. II (Cambridge: Cambridge University Press, 1944).

veloped in the Italian city-states. This method of accounting for business transactions provides an accurate check on entries in business books. More important, it gives the business manager a clear picture of where the business stands whenever it is desired, regardless of the complexity of the business. As a result of this invention, business accounts became separated from the family housekeeping account of the great merchant families. As a further result, business decisions became more clearly a weighing of revenues and costs, putting the spotlight on profits.

Two more developments were necessary for the emergence of a market economy. In ancient Greece, as well as in Italian cities of the fifteenth century, money was used as a medium of exchange and products were priced in terms of money as a common denominator. One could reasonably identify markets for many products, but these nevertheless were not market-directed societies. The missing ingredient was a market for resources. Labor and land were not allocated according to prices established in a market. Instead, they were largely subject to the forces of tradition and status.

The free exchange of land for money, based on the concept of *private property,* is a fairly recent phenomenon. Although the idea of private property was known in Roman law, the feudal arrangements of tenure and proprietorship grew in importance in Western Europe in the fourth century A.D. and were the dominant forms of control into the eighteenth century. Tenure control of land—a form of control that dominated Western Europe from the ninth to the eleventh centuries—allowed those who occupied land but didn't own it to exploit the land only for their immediate needs. For example, a serf could gather only as much wood from the manor forest as was personally needed. The right of use applied to the gentry as well as to the peasants.

Proprietorship control of land involved specified and limited rights for the gentry as well as the peasants. Rights of peasants on arable land were limited to the time from planting to harvesting. After harvesting, all members of the community had the right to turn their livestock out to graze indiscriminantly on all of the arable land. Some of these specified rights had begun as obligations in the feudal system but had become abused. For example, in the early days of the manor, the lord had accepted the obligation of protecting the peasants and their crops from the depredations of wild animals. This later turned into the specified right to hunt through the fields, to the injury of the peasants' crops.

In the late Middle Ages, serfs in some areas of Western Europe had their dues-in-kind converted to money payments. This might create the impression that serfs were paying rent for land "owned" by the lords. Whereas conversion to money payments was a necessary prerequisite to the formation of a land market, the dues-in-kind had been largely a quid pro quo for protection and administration of justice by the lord of the manor. Dues-in-kind were more a tax for government than rent for land. The money payments continued to be of this same character.

In neither the tenure nor the proprietorship form of control was there exclusive possession of property. There was no freedom for private persons to transfer property as they chose. Private property as a form of control is distinguishable by this full freedom of transfer, added to the right of use and the right of abuse. Private property, encompassing such exclusive control, has been a dominant form of property control for no more than two centuries, and for a limited area of the world at that. This concept, although with some constraints, has been a basic one in the U.S. economy. Some restriction of private property rights has occurred in the United States in the twentieth century. For example, states require that owners of strip coal mines replace the overburden of dirt that they scrape aside rather than leave it, helter-skelter, in piles that subject it to leaching and to the destruction of its fertility. Federal, state, and local governments have passed laws to regulate smoke and odor emission by factories and the dumping of pollutants into streams and lakes. The Antitrust Division of the U.S. Justice Department has the power to bring suit to prevent the transfer of the property of a company through merger where the result would be to lessen competition substantially. These are some of the restrictions upon the rights of private property in the United States where the use or abuse of property adversely affects people other than the property owner.

While a property owner in the United States does not have full and exclusive rights of use, abuse, and transfer, this society can hardly be said to have returned to the proprietorship form of control. The modern prohibitions are far less limiting than the earlier specifications of rights.

A market-directed economy requires a labor market as well as a land market. In a mythical society made up entirely of single proprietors, each producing a product or service to sell to others, laborer and entrepreneur are one. Although there is no labor market, there could be a market economy. However, in a society where some people work for others, labor is allocated by prices in markets only where certain conditions exist. Labor must have a price that changes with changes in market conditions rather than a price that reflects some customary "fair" standard in the medieval or ancient tradition. Moreover, laborers must be free to move about in response to price differentials.

For example, Karl Polanyi argues that England did not have a labor market until the Poor Law Reform of 1834 eliminated parish relief.[4] Although serfs had long been emancipated, the administration of poor relief tended seriously to restrict worker mobility until that date. Unemployed workers could be assured of sustenance only in their home parish. Cities and towns were often inhospitable to new arrivals for fear that they might become public charges. While movement did occur, workers nevertheless were inhibited by the working of the poor relief system from moving freely from areas of unemployment to areas of expanding employment, or from areas of low wages to areas of high wages. To the extent that free movement was inhibited, prices failed to direct labor resources. A price system working in a pure market economy requires that all prices of resources be determined by the interaction of many buyers and many sellers in markets and that buyers and sellers are free to respond to these prices.

Today, in addition to market-directed and tradition-directed societies, we recognize the *centrally planned economy* as a third way to organize economic activity. Centrally planned economies, often referred to as command-directed societies, include countries such as Russia, mainland China, and many of the countries of Eastern Europe. A command-directed society is one in which an individual, or a limited group, makes the basic economic choices of what, how, and for whom to produce for the whole of society and then issues directives to ensure that the working of the economy reflects these choices. The decisions of the central body may be overloaded with tradition so that change occurs slowly, or the central group may operate so as to induce rapid change. The central planning group may be highly responsive to the members of the society, or weakly responsive. Modern centrally planned societies try to plan for rapid economic growth, but ancient military oligarchies combined command with strong overtones of tradition.

Details will differ among societies that fall under the same classification. Furthermore, most societies exhibit some aspect of all three forms of direction, although one form will predominate. Tradition has played a relatively small role in the making of economic choices in the United States. Command has played a role if by "command" we refer to some choices being made by authority,

---

4. See Karl Polanyi, *The Great Transformation* (Boston: Beacon Press, 1957).

rather than by tradition or markets. Government taxation and expenditure, or regulation of business and international trade, involve command direction even though they may constitute a small portion of the total number of economic decisions. Just as no economy is a pure representation of one of these three categories, so also do economies shift the proportion in which economic decisions are tradition-directed, market-directed, or command-directed. These changes are readily apparent in various national economies today, regardless of whether one accepts the convergence hypothesis that Soviet Russia is accepting more and more market price direction, while the United States simultaneously adopts a larger and larger role for government direction of economic decisions.

III.   THE LOGIC OF ECONOMIZING: SCARCITY AND CHOICE

The words *economy* or *economizing* conjure up many images, all of them restrictive or repressive in some sense. At the personal or family level, for example, an "economy kick" often means less total spending as well as reallocating some expenditures from the more frivolous to the more basic, from entertainment to meat and potatoes. In the larger social organization of community, state, or nation, economy in government again means reduction of expenditures and a shift from low-priority expenditures to those that are considered more important. Family argument and political debate quicken when calls for "economy" arise. We each have different views of what is frivolous or necessary, high priority or low. In each case in which "economy" is an issue, however, choices must be made because our limited means are insufficient to acquire all that we desire.

A. Scarcity: The Basis for Economy

Scarcity is an ever-present fact of existence for most persons and all societies. Only a few individuals and no societies have the means to achieve all of their economic objectives simultaneously. Indeed, nature is seldom so bountiful as to provide even the necessities of life in the quantity and form needed without human labor. Primitive societies constantly face destruction by starvation, by the rigors of the elements, or by the predatory activity of man and beast. Respite from these forces is the scarcest commodity in such societies. Whatever respite has been achieved has been the result of organizing society to increase the production of goods so as to alleviate hunger, exposure, and attack.

Over the centuries some societies have learned to increase production to such an extent that today we speak of an affluent society, such as the United States, rich in goods and in leisure. Yet even an affluent community constantly strives against scarcity, admittedly at a different level, but scarcity nonetheless. Using all of its accumulated knowledge, its abundant natural resources, its vast stock of productive equipment, its highly trained labor force, and its advanced technology, the United States cannot produce enough to achieve all of its goals at once. *Scarcity of the means of production relative to social goals is the first central fact of economics.*

B. Choice and the Principle of Opportunity Cost

When the means of production are scarce relative to what people want produced, choices must be made. Most of us have to pick and choose: if we choose to have some more of this, we must forgo some of that. If a family spends more on transportation services in the form of monthly payments on a new car, it must reduce its allotment of income to some other purposes. It may spend less on shoes, or on recreation, or postpone painting the house, or put less in savings for the children's education. It may cut back a bit in several kinds of spending, or reduce just one. It is obliged to choose, whether by prior planning or by struggling to adjust after buying something new on impulse. The decision is much easier if family income increases, but choice is still necessary. The cost of the new item is clearly the loss of the opportunity to spend that income for other purposes. And, in our example, the choice can only be made after comparing the value of the additional transportation with the value of the things which are being sacrificed. This is the *opportunity cost principle* applied to individual consumer behavior.

The same principle applies to societies because of the scarcity of means relative to ends. If members of a society choose to produce more complex and costly weapons systems, they must forgo building some day care centers, educating some children, rebuilding some inner cities, improving some aspects of the environment, or producing some consumer goods. At times a society may have idle resources, in which case it can increase production in many directions simultaneously until those resources are fully employed. To have idle resources at the same time that there are unfulfilled needs is, of course, wasteful, although a society may be willing to experience some amount of unemployed resources if it is a prerequisite for other goals such as freedom to quit one job to look for another, or to introduce new, more efficient equipment even though the old machinery is not worn out. But generally, the choice of one thing eliminates the opportunity to choose another because productive resources are limited relative to all of the things that the members of society would like to have.

C. Choice: What to Produce? How? For Whom?

Because of scarcity, every society, primitive or highly developed, is confronted with the choice of *what* goods and services to produce and how much for each kind; *how* to produce these goods and services; and *for whom* the production is undertaken, that is, who receives what quantities of the product. For each kind of choice, there is an enormous range of alternatives: shoes or cars, urban renewal, armaments, schools, or food; using primitive technology and large amounts of labor or new technology and heavy capital equipment; distributing to the already wealthy and well educated or to the poor, minority groups and those with fewer opportunities. Moreover, societies may organize in different ways in order to make these choices. Regardless of what economic system is adopted, all of these questions continue to exist. *The necessity to choose what to produce, how, and for whom is the second central fact of economics.*

Today the United States has a fixed amount of resources available to produce the things that its citizens may want. The population is of a particular size. The labor force is a relatively fixed proportion of that population, being determined by the age distribution and by those social mores that control how long young people remain in school, at what age old people retire, and whether women devote their time to keeping house and raising children and/or work in the labor market. The skills and abilities of the labor force cannot be changed in the short run. Further, there is only a certain amount of land in productive use and it will take time and effort to bring more into production. Similarly, the productive capability of the nation's mines is not changed quickly. To enlarge the rate of exploitation or to find and open new mines is a time-consuming enterprise. There are only a certain number of factories containing a specific quantity and kind of machinery. Thus, the quantity and quality of resources are relatively fixed in a society at a point in time.

We can, however, choose *what to produce* because resources may be shifted from what is presently produced to the production of other things. The extent of this flexibility was demonstrated dramatically in the conversion from peacetime goods to war goods at the start of World War II and the swift reconversion at the end of the war. Tens of thousands of manufacturing plants stopped producing cars, cocktail dresses, and bed sheets and started making tanks, khaki pants, and bandages. Large numbers of people stopped producing personal services and started to work in war plants. Under conditions of full employment, reallocation to produce more of certain kinds of goods always will require that less of other goods be produced. To get more of one thing entails the loss of another. Hence, scarcity requires that society determine what goods to produce, and how much of each. It forces society to make choices.[5]

How to produce is also a matter of choice. What resources should be used to produce a particular product? We have seen that resources can be shifted from the production of one thing, such as highways, to the production of another, such as missile silos. A highway can be built of gravel, concrete, or asphalt. We may use a very large number of men and few machines, or many and more complex machines with fewer men. To transport rocks to a highway site, many laborers may carry the rocks in baskets on their heads. Fewer laborers might carry the same amount of rocks by using wheelbarrows, a substitution of capital for labor. Animals drawing wagons might be substituted for the wheelbarrows and some of the remaining labor. Dump trucks powered by internal combustion engines, representing more machinery (and a change in its form), might be substituted for still additional labor in transporting rocks from quarries to roadbed.

Sometimes it appears that factors of production must be used in fixed proportions, but appearances can be deceiving. Imagine a production process which stamps out metal parts for automobiles. A quantity of parts is produced on a line of 20 punch presses, each with one operator working an eight-hour day. These men are responsible for getting their materials to the presses, removing the stamped pieces to a polishing line, and keeping the area around each machine clean. Obviously, the same output could be produced with fewer machines if more labor were applied in the form of overtime or additional shifts. Less obviously, other workers could be hired to haul the metal blanks to the presses and truck away the barrels of stamped parts. This would permit the press operators to devote more time to machine operation. In this way, the same daily output would be produced with fewer machines but more labor. Even fewer machines would be needed if janitors were hired and more intensive use made of the remaining machines. Production processes differ in the extent to which proportions among factors of production can be varied, but the possibility of variation almost always exists. Each society must develop a process of choosing how to produce.

---

5. See the appendix to chapter 5 for a more detailed treatment of the choice of what to produce.

A society must also have some institutional arrangement to answer the question: *For whom are the goods produced?* There may be different answers in different societies, with the product being distributed equally among the members in one society or distributed with varying degrees of inequality in others. Criteria for some people getting more and others less also may differ from society to society. In one society people may receive income according to their inherited status. In another, income may reflect contribution to production. In yet another, political contributions may be specially regarded. In any event, the members of every society must somehow choose how to distribute the social product.

IV.   MARKET ECONOMY: SELF-REGULATING OR SOCIALLY REGULATED?

If we put together money, prices, markets, and self-interest and then install competition as the regulator of relationships, will the economy proceed to operate satisfactorily without further social intervention? This is the first and most basic question which must be posed in both understanding and evaluating a market system. As we shall see, the levels of social intervention necessary to sustain a market system are substantially more than many realize.

Adam Smith in *The Wealth of Nations*[6] argued for a reduction of government activity in the economy because at the time that he wrote in the eighteenth century, government had often created monopoly where it need not have existed, and government regulated economic activity by law where competition could have constrained the private profit motive. Many modern advocates of the elimination of government intervention look to Adam Smith as the supposed original champion of a *laissez faire* position. Apparently few such persons have read *The Wealth of Nations*. While Smith argues for reduced government interference and greater reliance on competition that was common in the eighteenth century, he nevertheless makes a case for government intervention at many points. Most of those arguments continue to be valid today and new ones have been added. For example, he recognized that government had to provide the society with defense from foreign invasion because citizens would not, individually, produce that "product." Indeed, in today's world, defense has become an enormous enterprise, with hundreds of billions of dollars being spent by each of the great powers for development of new armaments, and the maintenance and distribu-

---

6. Modern Library ed. (New York: Random House, 1937).

tion of conventional weapons. In the United States, almost 6 percent of the nation's total output has been devoted to the military budget. Both major and minor powers direct a large proportion of their resources to the military budget.

Government also must maintain internal order—it must provide police and a system of justice for the same reason that it must provide defense. Citizens, individually, would not adequately provide for these functions. Also, if a society adopts exploration of the unknown as a major goal, government is likely to become heavily involved. Exploration had been a government-sponsored activity long before the travels of Columbus were underwritten by the king and queen of Spain. Space exploration is no exception today. In research and development, as well as actual exploration, the resource requirements are so large and the economic benefits so remote that a government is the only feasible organization for its pursuit.

The Founding Fathers of the United States recognized in the Constitution that a central government must establish and regulate a money supply. Since a market-directed economy attaches prices to all quantities, the society—through government—must establish a stable monetary unit. Similarly, it is necessary for government to establish standards of weights and measures. Further, government is required to adopt and enforce a body of commercial law to provide confidence in the contracts into which private buyers and sellers enter.

For any society, there is a category of services from which some members of the society might be excluded, but their exclusion would substantially reduce the national welfare.[7] For example, sewage disposal facilities could be provided only to a selected few. However, to enhance the public health of an entire city, these facilities must be provided to all through the power of government. Likewise, education produces both economic and noneconomic benefits to society which are not directly reflected in the incomes of the buyers of education. Consequently, if its provision were made entirely by private enterprise, too little education would be produced from society's point of view. Therefore, the government must play a role in the provision of education. In this, as in other areas, we as a nation do not accept the ethic of one dollar, one vote.

---

7. See chapter 8 for further discussion of this topic. Another volume in this series, Robert H. Haveman, *The Economics of the Public Sector,* second edition (New York: John Wiley & Sons, 1976), explores in detail the economic role of government in a market economy.

Further, there are some kinds of production which by their nature must be provided by only one seller. In these cases, the regulation provided by competition cannot come into play. Adam Smith named some of these natural monopolies and argued that they had to be regulated by government if they were not operated by government. The number of natural monopolies probably has increased over time owing to technological developments that often give great advantages in efficiency to large-scale operation. A good modern example is the provision of telephone service. We cannot conceive of the effects of a very large number of telephone firms competing with one another in a modern city. The enormous duplication of poles and lines obviously would be wasteful and a nuisance. The inability to call a subscriber of a different company (if the firms were competing rather than cooperating) would be frustrating. Although there are many telephone companies in the United States today, each company has a monopoly in the locality that it serves, granted in a franchise from the local government. Regulation provides for the interchange of calls. The reader undoubtedly can think of other cases of natural monopoly.

The accumulation of a large capital sum frequently is necessary today if a business is to reach optimum size with low costs and efficient technology. Sometimes this optimum size produces natural monopoly. Sometimes it produces few enough firms that competition is not an effective regulator in the public interest. To enable accumulation of the large capital sums which are necessary to achieve these economies, government has granted privileges to certain kinds of business organizations.

The modern corporation, for example, is a creature of the state, receiving a charter which grants its owners (shareholders) a limitation on their liability for the debts of the business. The corporate charter typically will limit shareholders' liability to the amount paid for the shares. Also, the corporate charter usually is issued for a long period, such as 99 years, or in perpetuity, so that a corporation's life is not limited to the lives of the initial owners.

A single proprietor, on the other hand, is liable for his business debts to the full extent of his personal wealth. Further, the business organization of a single proprietor dies with him. The net assets, of course, can be transferred to someone else, but creditors can claim full settlement before transfer, which can seriously interrupt the flow of business. In a similar way, partners are generally liable beyond their initial payment into the business, and partnerships are reorganized each time a partner is added or withdraws.

Government-granted privileges such as limited liability and perpetual life make possible the accumulation of a very large capital sum from a great many individuals, few of whom have the time, knowledge, or inclination to keep close enough track of the company's operations to be willing to accept unlimited liability. Furthermore, capital accumulation is encouraged because shareholders can sell their shares to other parties without interrupting the business. A legal entity created by government, the corporation is an expression of ingenuity in social organization to keep abreast of technical possibilities.

Although the achievement of large size is necessary if a firm is to take full advantage of technical possibilities in production, in other instances firms will grow to large size simply to reap the benefits of market power. Where market power exists, prices are not established by the interaction of many buyers and sellers in markets; rather, prices are set or administered by those private individuals or groups with the power to do so. To that extent, the economy and the allocation of resources are not directed by the tastes and preferences of consumers. Adam Smith considered the corporate form of organization to be inappropriate both because of the power of large size and because he believed that hired managers would not be as diligent in running the business as owner-managers. Through government, society often has decided to interfere and regulate those institutions possessing market power. Government often has attempted to regulate so as to maintain competition where the realities of technology make that possible, thereby avoiding the more detailed regulation that is found necessary in the case of natural monopolies.

There are other ways in which government may intervene in the market system. It often is assumed that, in a market system, buyers and sellers know relevant facts so that they can act rationally. Sometimes markets are viewed as institutions that find the facts. Such presumptions may be true in small, local markets. But remarkable advances in transportation and communication have established huge national and international markets.

Facts are not known unless they are explicitly gathered. Markets do not gather them, yet markets will not function smoothly unless facts are provided impartially. In the United States, for example, the government provides an extensive crop-reporting service that is valuable for agricultural markets. Similarly, government surveys of labor markets and the operation of government employment exchanges provide information to firms and households that the private economy does not provide. Labor markets may function more smoothly as more households and firms use these government services, many of which have resulted from equal employment opportunity laws and affirmative action regulations.

Today private firms or their trade associations try to forecast their sales with some precision, not only to plan their production schedules, but also to plan major, long-term investments in capital equipment. They base their forecast of particular markets on a government or private forecast of what total production, called gross national product (GNP), will be. This forecast of GNP, in turn, is based on government-collected statistics of GNP for past years. In most instances, government is the most effective organization for the impartial provision of the facts necessary for private forecasts and informed private decisions.

Most participants in a modern market-directed society are employees who produce very little for their own direct consumption. When they are unemployed, their incomes are reduced or cease, often creating serious hardships or poverty. Market systems, as they have operated, contain within themselves neither a guarantee of full employment nor the self-correction of general unemployment. Countries of the Western world have faced recurrent crises of unemployment during the nineteenth and twentieth centuries. Government has been called on to cope with widespread and persistent unemployment. Virtually all governments have taken action both to prevent general unemployment and to deal with it after the fact.

A word of caution is in order here which will need to be repeated in subsequent chapters. Neither markets nor government activity may produce perfection. Government intervention to correct market failure may not improve matters and in some cases may actually reduce public well-being relative to continued control by an imperfect market. Government intervention has been known to make a bad situation worse rather than better, as the discussion of agriculture in chapter 5 illustrates.

In summary, then, considerable social intervention may be necessary to establish the conditions for a healthy market-directed economy. Additional intervention may be called for where the economy cannot function through markets or will not function well if left to itself. Some kinds of government activity contribute to essentially noneconomic purposes, although that activity may have a substantial impact on the economy. In all of these cases, public command replaces private market-oriented activities. The existence of command modifies the market-directed character of the economy whether the command stems from democratic expression or dictatorial fiat. (Although the source of command makes no difference in the categorization presented here, it certainly makes a tremendous difference to the people of the society.)

V.   UNDERSTANDING THE MARKET SYSTEM

In this volume we shall present the theoretical structure of a simple, market-directed economy. It is so severe an abstraction from reality in the United States today that many readers will think it irrelevant. Our assumptions about business motivations may not correspond to the complexities that lie behind decisions in a modern economy where most business leaders are not owners and are somewhat insulated from the pressures typical for profit-seeking owners. Also, we may assume too much rational judgment by consumers in choosing their purchases or the sale of their services in an affluent society. How relevant is a description of a market-directed economy to a soceity in which many prices are set, not in markets, but by producers who are to some degree isolated from the pressure of competition?

It is our judgment that there are many reasons for the student to begin with the study of an idealized market system such as that presented here. One is the pedagogical reason of moving from the simple to the complex, learning about concepts, relationships, and patterns that will be useful as one moves closer to reality. For example, some current efforts to construct a new theory of the business firm make use of the theory of political process. Yet, the profit concept that our simple model is based on is included in these analyses as one measure of success and, therefore, as one element in decisions. And the decisions themselves involve the kinds of marginal changes—a bit more of this or a bit less of that—which are central to the way an economist thinks about things. Similarly, the cost and revenue concepts that we shall develop are basic notions in real-world decision making. And although costs, revenues, and profits may not be the only crucial matters considered in the actual economy, they are important and they do act as contraints on managerial freedom to make decisions based on other criteria.[8] We can read contemporary economic literature with more understanding having started from this base.

A society may have many goals associated with its economic

---

8. For an interesting example of how business firms do consider the relationship of costs and revenues—even the economist's notion of "marginal costs"—in making decisions, see "Airline Takes the Marginal Routes," *Business Week*, April 20, 1973; and reprinted in Edwin Mansfield, *Micro-Economics: Selected Readings*, 2d ed. (New York: Norton, 1975). Also see "How good are your marginal cost estimates?" *The Bankers Magazine*, Winter 1977.

activity. It may wish to have equality of economic opportunity, justice in economic relationships, economic growth so that its citizens may look toward a better life, full employment so that resources seeking employment are not idle while there are unfulfilled needs, and economic efficiency to produce the things that consumers most desire. To understand our economy and how it relates to the economies of other societies, we must consider all of these economic goals. In this volume we are especially concerned with the goal of *economic efficiency,* since a market system provides a way of allocating resources to alternative uses. The market system presented here in elementary form is applicable to any society whose primary aim is maximum satisfaction of consumer wants. It is as applicable to a socialist economy which subscribes to this goal, as to a capitalist economy,[9] although the procedures by which such allocative decisions are made will differ, as will the mechanism for the distribution of income.

We have already indicated that a market-directed economy involves prices for resources as well as for products. Resource incomes may be distributed on a different basis in a socialist economy than in a capitalist one but, in both cases, prices should reflect relative scarcity. In a capitalist society all resource prices become incomes paid to the private owners of the resources,[10] but in a socialist economy property incomes are received by the state since private ownership is limited to personal property. Although socialists consider that interest, rent, and profit incomes should not go to private individuals, these resource prices must be calculated if the resources are to be allocated efficiently to the alternative production uses.

The rent of land, for example, is a price derived from the productivity of the land, whether the land be used for growing wheat or as a downtown building site. If land is used for one purpose, its use for other purposes is foregone. The cost of its use in one way is the value of its next, slightly less preferred use. This, it will be recalled, is the *opportunity-cost principle.* Calculating of opportunity cost and its assignment as the price to the piece of property will assure that the property is used for its most preferred use, and no other. Clearly, the

---

9. See, for example, Oskar Lange and Fred M. Taylor, *On the Economic Theory of Socialism* (Minneapolis: The University of Minnesota Press, 1938), for a description of an ideal price directed socialist economy which differs from an ideal capitalist economy only in the absence of private ownership of the means of production—there is no capital market. The market system presented here also is applicable to a communist state such as the Soviet Union, as is described below in this chapter.

10. Except where taxes are a part of the price quoted.

bidding of alternative users will attract the land into its most productive use. If consumer tastes change, some other use of the land may become the preferred use. The old use will have less value and the land will be shifted to its new use. The point is that an assignment of the property which is not based on opportunity cost is less likely to produce the best allocation of the land. Moreover, the land use is even less likely to shift with changing circumstances if new demands and new costs are not reflected in prices. The price system will allocate land most efficiently (with the exceptions noted in chapter 8) in either capitalism or socialism, the difference between the two systems being who gets the rent. Similarly, interest must be calculated in a socialist economy because there are no market prices for capital. Interest must be entered into costs if scarce capital funds (and, therefore, capital goods) are to be allocated most efficiently in the provision of goods and services.

Profits provide a measure of efficiency for a production unit. Unusually high profits indicate that production of this sort should be expanded, while unusually low profits or losses indicate that such production should be contracted. High profits in one production unit relative to another producing the same thing may indicate that the prices and uses of resource inputs need to be adjusted. It may be that managerial skill is superior in the one unit and this is not reflected in the price of management. Or it may be that one location is superior to another and this is not reflected in the rent of the land. Competition for superior management or land would raise the price and, at the same time, extend the use of the superior resource relative to the inferior one.

In the middle of the 1960s, the Soviet Union made public some of its problems of production efficiency. In a prominent editorial in *Pravda*, light industries were urged to plan production "on a profit basis." The hope was that managers would be interested in producing goods of higher quality and those that met the demands of consumers, if they were given bonuses that reflected the profitability of their enterprises. A month later, *Isvestia* reported that similar incentives would be extended to heavy manufacturing industries on a trial basis. The "profits" generated by an enterprise which performed efficiently would be paid as bonuses to managers and as contributions to workers funds.

Although these changes recognized the merits of incentives designed to reward economic performance—as automatically occur in a market system—they were never implemented very effectively in the Soviet Union. The central economic planners found that these incentives had the potential of reducing their control over production decisions, and they sought to bring them under the control of the planning mechanism. As one writer stated: "[The] incentive funds and bonuses have been frequently and extensively modified in a seemingly endless process of reforming the reforms."[11] Two developments, it appears, have undermined this effort to install economic incentives. First, the rules for the establishment of the funds for the payment of bonuses became increasingly complex and intricate—numerous criteria of performance were introduced for determining how large the funds should be. Second, the rules determining who is to be paid the bonuses also became complicated and intricate. Managers had little idea concerning what sorts of economic performance would ultimately be rewarded. It is now generally acknowledged that, for numerous reasons, the basic idea to tie rewards to economic efficiency has not been well carried out in the Soviet Union and has not improved economic performance in the way its original designers envisioned.[12]

Efforts to substitute some market direction of the economy for bureaucratic direction in the People's Republic of China may be more successful. *The Economist* devoted a major section of its December 29, 1979 issue to the Chinese economy and to this particular question. While acknowledging the difficulty of overcoming opposition to change and risk which is inherent in a centralized bureaucracy, the reporters saw some hopeful signs. They pointed to the extolling of pragmatism and to signs of a new objectivity about mistakes. They also described how consumer demand has become a legitimate market force. "Angry customers have been returning locally made [television set] models, some of which, the New China News Agency tells us, 'need to be knocked constantly and give neither sound nor picture but burn and smoke.' The News Agency rejected the manufacturers' claim that the quality of the sets met the ministry's standards: 'Consumer satisfaction is the standard that manufacturers should aim at.' "[13]

The People's Republic of China began its experiment in partial self-management for some enterprises in three provinces in late 1978. The *Beijing* (Peking) *Review* reported in 1980 in an article by Lin Zili that prior to these experiments "an enterprise had to follow

11. Gertrude Schroeder, "The Soviet Economy on a Treadmill of 'Reforms'," in U.S. Congress, Joint Economic Committee, *Soviet Economy in a Time of Change* (Washington, D. C., Government Printing Office, 1979), p. 325.

12. See Alec Nove, *The Soviet Economic System* (London: George Allen and Unwin, 1977).

13. *The Economist*, Vol. 273, No. 7111, London, December 29, 1979, p. 21.

strictly the state quota in planning what, how and how much it produced. If an enterprise had bigger productive capacity than required, part of it would lie idle." In addition, "all the equipment, raw and some finished materials, fuel and power needed by an enterprise were furnished by the state. On the other hand, all the goods it produced were purchased and marketed by the state."[14] The article proceeded to describe a number of examples of expanded output, lower cost, and higher profit in manufacturing plants involved in the experiment in partial self-management. Some advertised nationally and internationally to attract direct purchases from users; some purchased raw materials through contracts with enterprises in other provinces and used part of the increased profits they were permitted to retain for bonuses, for workers benefits, or for purchase of capital goods. Some of the enterprises which achieved lower costs proceeded to lower their prices, increase sales, and increase profits.

Reliance on some competition and some guidance from the profit motive does not mean that the Soviet Union and the People's Republic of China would move toward capitalism if the experiments were more widely embraced. Capitalism involves private ownership of natural resources and capital goods. The returns of rent, interest, and profit are paid to individuals as owners who decide on the use of their resources. In China and Russia, these returns belong to the state to be used as the government sees fit.

The experiments do reflect limited use of a price system to allocate resources according to customer wants rather than allocation of resources entirely by command. Knowledge of the simple model of a price-directed economy presented in this volume will help us to understand these experiments in market economy by the Soviet Union and the People's Republic of China.

Another reason for studying the price system is to understand the stringent conditions required for a truly self-directing economy which would automatically operate in the public interest. The conditions are numerous and demanding and require, for example, competition on both sides of every market, perfect information, and perfect mobility. An understanding of the logical requirements of such a system will demonstrate that the U.S. economy does not meet the conditions, and that, in so far as it does not, there will be market failure or the exercise of private power by a few sellers or buyers. Such results have led to increased government interference

---

14. *Beijing Review*, Volume 23, Number 22, June 2, 1980, published by the People's Republic of China, pp. 16–17.

in market economies. In most Western economies, including both Britain and the United States, there has been growth in the number of economic decisions made by command of government.

It is one thing for the system to require through its working relationships that its participants behave in the public interest; it is quite another for the participants to have the power to decide whether or not to behave that way. It may be the decision of society to rely on the good will and "social responsibility" of those who have either a small or a great amount of private power. Or the society may wish to inject the pressure of government where competition does not effectively constrain private power. Before making up our minds on such policy questions, we must determine if there are "built-in" social forces other than the simple, purely competitive model presented in this volume.[15] An appraisal of the effectiveness of *all* of the significant forces must be made if the nature and extent of government intervention is to be decided on pragmatic rather than ideological grounds. The effectiveness of government intervention itself must be appraised in each particular situation to determine whether it makes matters better or worse than an imperfectly functioning market. The simple model presented in this volume is not intended to catalog all of the significant forces. Nor is it designed to be "the ideal" against which reality should be measured and to which reality should be made to conform. On the contrary, understanding this model is but a first step in understanding how our market system operates, and the public policy questions that arise from the failure or success of its operation.

VI.   CONCLUSION AND SUMMARY

While economies may be classified into tradition-directed, market-directed, or command-directed, they all face certain common economic problems. One is scarcity. Another, stemming from scarcity, is the necessity to choose what to produce, how, and for whom. This volume describes how a market-directed economy goes about dealing with these basic questions. Market direction involves response to impersonal market prices by economic participants—households and businesses. There must be markets for land and labor resources as well as for consumable products and services. While these markets organize a vast array of facts and produce an amazing number of decisions, they do not work perfectly. In addition to describing an

---

15. See Chapter 8 in this volume; also see *Case Studies in American Industry,* by Leonard W. Weiss, in this series.

idealized market system, this volume is concerned with ways in which any real market economy deviates from this ideal and the consequences for economic policy.

QUESTIONS

1. Perhaps the energy problem reflects the most pressing evidence of scarcity in the American economy today. Explain how this problem may be used to illustrate the opportunity cost principle.
2. Can you think of a production process in which the proportions of all of the factors of production are fixed so that the question of how to produce is irrelevant?
3. "The market system, as it has developed in Western civilization, has embraced the principle for income distribution of 'to each according to his contribution to production.'" Appraise this statement. Can you think of any social institutions which modify this principle of income distribution?
4. Some argue that income should be distributed equally among all in a society. Others say that even if this were done, it would not be long before those with ability would hold the wealth, and income would be distributed about as unequally as it is at present in the United States. Discuss.
5. What manner of competition must there be for the market system to function efficiently? What are the criteria of efficient functioning?
6. Scattered throughout this chapter are numerous descriptions of how the market system may fail to promote economic welfare. Such failures, it was stated, may call for some form of collective or government interference. Make a list of the types of "market failure" mentioned in this chapter. When you have finished, compare your list with the section headings of chapter 8.

2 | A Market Economy—The Model of a Simple Economic System

In this chapter and the three that follow it, we will begin to analyze the nature of a market system. In so doing, we will cut through the complexity and confusion of everyday economic events in order to see more clearly the basic underlying relationships which determine how the economy works. To do this we construct some simple and abstract models. These models will explain how a market system answers the economic questions, "What?" "How?" and "For whom?" They will illustrate both how individual households and businesses formulate decisions, and the process by which the entire system reconciles the apparently conflicting decisions of a multitude of individuals.

In this chapter we develop a simplified model of an entire free market economy. Individual sectors of this economy will be investigated in succeeding chapters.

I. SOME DEFINITIONS AND SOME ASSUMPTIONS

In our simple economy we recognize only two kinds of decision makers: households and business firms. The concept of a household is a familiar one. It includes any living unit in which decisions about what to eat, where to live, how much work to do, and how much recreation to have are made more or less jointly. The most common type of household is the family—a husband, a wife and children. However, many other types of households also exist. A group of single college students living together in an apartment form a household, an aged widow living alone forms a household, and so on. The crucial thing in defining a household is the existence of a single decision-making unit.

Business firms are also relatively familiar organizations. In defining these organizations, the process of decision making is again the crucial factor. Thus, a business firm is an organization established to make profits, in which the decisions on what to produce, how to produce it, and how to dispose of the profits are made by a single manager or group of managers. While the corner grocery store and the local manufacturing company are easily recognized as business firms, the law firm, barber shop, doctor, and newspaper delivery person are also business firms. While we often don't think of some of these organizations as businesses—perhaps because they produce services rather than goods—they indeed are.

The concept of the business firm should be distinguished from both the concept of a plant and the concept of an industry. As we have stated, the business firm contains all of the parts of an enterprise which are under one management. A plant, on the other hand, refers to a location where production takes place. One firm may have many plants. An industry is a group of firms which all produce the same product. The Ford Motor Company is a business firm; its assembly facility at Dearborn, Michigan, is a plant. All of the producers of automobiles taken together form the automobile industry.

Let us now group all of the households and all of the business firms in the model economy into two sectors—the household sector and the business sector. The household sector will be considered the consuming sector and the business sector the producing sector. Each sector operates from quite different sets of goals or motivations, just as each serves a different function in the economy. We will assume that the force that motivates behavior in the household sector is the desire to *maximize the satisfaction of wants* through consumption. Each household, it is presumed, knows best the pattern of consumption that will maximize its satisfaction. Because we are basically concerned with human welfare in this study, the center of our concern will be the way in which the working of the economy affects the household sector. In fact, we can state that our chief task is to evaluate how any economic change affects this sector and its welfare.

The business sector, we will assume, is motivated by the desire to *maximize profits*. Although real-world businesses respond to many other objectives, the central motivation for business activity is a profit.

Thus, for both households and businesses, self-interest is the driving power. As Adam Smith has said:

> It is not from the benevolence of the butcher, the brewer, or the baker that we expect our dinner but from their regard to their self-interest.

We address ourselves not to their humanity, but to their self-love, and never talk to them of our necessities, but of their advantages. [1]

For both the household and business sectors, we will assume that *private property* exists. Households can own wealth in the form of houses, paintings, land, or financial securities, and can dispose of it as they please. They also own their labor services and can sell them or fail to sell them as they please. Businesses can also own property—their plant, equipment, and inventories, for example—and can manage them in any way that will maximize profits.

Within any industry in the business sector, *pure competition* will be presumed to exist. In pure competition there are so many firms producing each industry's *standardized product* that no single firm by itself can influence the price of that commodity. There are *no barriers* of any sort to either the entry of firms into an industry or the exit of firms from the industry. (In the United States, the agriculture industry—farming—comes as close as any to meeting the requirements of pure competition. As we shall see, however, prices have not been determined by the market alone because government has interfered by providing subsidies, restricting acreage planted to certain crops, and at times prohibiting sales to foreign countries.) Pure competition as a form of business organization is only one of four types distinguished by economists. The other types, which will be discussed in chapter 7, are monopoly, oligopoly, and monopolistic competition.

The two sectors, household and business, will be engaged in various activities in the model economy in order to satisfy wants and to make profits. Most basically, both sectors exchange their commodities and services, they buy and sell, and through the exchanges attain their goals. But these exchange activities are only part of the picture. Buying and selling could not take place unless there were something to buy and sell, some goods or services to be exchanged. Besides exchange there must be production. Through production and exchange, then, the goals of both the business and household sectors are attained. Profits are earned by business and wants are satisfied by households.

For the purpose of our simple model, the economy will be assumed to exist in isolation, engaging in no trade with other nations. We will look into our economy at a moment when consumers have certain tastes for products and certain quantities of factors of production whose services they can sell. We will assume that firms have a given amount of production knowhow and facilities at their

---

1. Adam Smith, *Wealth of Nations* Modern Library ed. (New York: Random House, 1937), p. 14.

disposal. Under these circumstances, the patterns of exchange in a market economy forms a configuration well described as a *circular flow*. By describing each of the two main sectors in more detail, we will see how the circular flow works.

II.   THE HOUSEHOLD

The household sector is composed of all the independent living units in our model economy. The primary decisions made by each household revolve about the questions: "What and how much should we buy?" "What and how much should we sell?" The household must be aware of its alternatives. It must know what can be bought and what can be sold. When the household acts so as to satisfy its wants, the things it desires to buy are *consumer goods;* goods such as shoes, shirts, food, and theater tickets whose use gives the consumer satisfaction or utility. The quantities of these goods which the household can buy is limited by the income which it earns. The higher its income, the more consumer goods the household can purchase.

But where does this income come from? The answer is clear. The income of the household is obtained by selling the services of what it possesses. These services are called *factors of production* because they enter into the process of production and are transformed into output. Economists divide factors of production into three mutually exclusive categories: labor, capital, and natural resources. *Labor* does not simply mean work done with the hands or in a factory, but any effort expended by humans in producing goods or services. Carpenters, lawyers—even college professors—provide labor. For the economist, *capital* also has a special meaning. It usually refers only to real goods such as buildings, machines, tools, or inventories whose services are used in the process of production. *Natural resources* mean much the same in economic theory as they do in everyday usage. Virgin land, raw mineral deposits, even climate, all yield productive services and all qualify as natural resources. Often, what is thought to be a natural resource, say, a river, is a combination of natural resources and capital. Any man-made improvement, such as dredging a navigation channel for barge traffic, is as much a capital improvement as adding a new machine to a factory.

Sometimes economists speak of a fourth factor of production: innovation or entrepreneurial activity. This factor is the special creative ability which leads some people to organize production in new ways or to produce new things—in general, to perform creative activities that cause change and growth in the economy, often at some risk, so that the entrepreneur bears the cost of uncertainty.

This factor is distinguished from the more routine managerial activities involving supervision and direction. These are classified as labor.

The payments for the factors of production are labeled wages, interest, rent, and profits, and are discussed in more detail in chapters 1, 4, and 8. These payments accrue to households as income.

Thus, from selling the services of its factors of production, the household receives income and, with the income received, purchases consumption goods which satisfy its wants. In both buying consumer goods and selling factor services the decisions of the household are guided by its goal of maximizing the satisfaction of wants.

III.   THE BUSINESS FIRM

The other sector in the circular flow economy is the profit-maximizing sector. The business firms in this sector buy factors of production (the services of labor, natural resources, and capital) as inputs, combine these factors in the production process to produce consumer goods, and sell the consumer goods as outputs. We have seen that the payments to the factors of production are income to the household; to firms, however, these same payments are *costs of production*.

To earn revenue to cover these costs, firms sell to households the consumer goods they have produced. Profits are earned if the costs of production are less than the revenue earned by selling the output. In both buying factor services and selling consumer goods, business decisions are guided by the goal of maximum profits.

In Figure 2-1, the household and business sectors are both depicted as buying and selling. The flow of the services of the factors of production is shown as the lower line of connection between the two sectors. After buying these services from households, business

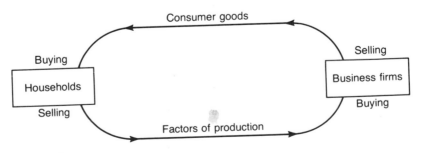

Figure 2-1

firms produce consumer goods and sell them to the households. The flow of consumer goods is depicted as the upper line of connection.

IV. PRICES AND MONEY

In our model we have not yet spoken of prices or money. Surely if our model is to depict a price system, these concepts must find their place in it. In a simple economic system such as that which we have constructed, money serves as a lubricant. Without it, all trade would be barter, in which one kind of good or service would be traded with another. With it, money is traded for goods and goods for money. Money, then, is a *medium of exchange.* As such, it is a common denominator between various goods and services, and the values of all goods and services can be expressed in so many units of money. One dress equals $10; one tie equals $1. Removing the common denominator, one dress equals ten ties.

The number of units of money attached to each unit of a good or service is the *price* of that good or service. One theater ticket, for example, has $6 attached to it; one car has $6000 attached to it. Six dollars and $6000 are prices. In a price system, when trade or exchange occurs, money invariably serves as one-half of the transaction: one hour of labor is given up for $8; one pair of socks is traded for $4. For this reason, we find the flow of real goods and services matched by an equal and opposite flow of money. This property is incorporated into a revised circular flow model shown in Figure 2-2. What we have called wages, rent, interest, profits, costs, income, and revenue are all seen as flows of money in this revised scheme.

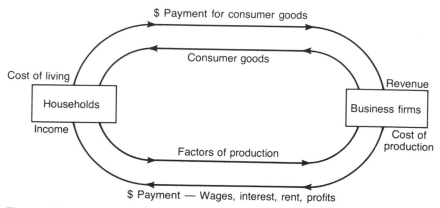

Figure 2-2

And, the flow of money is in the opposite direction to the flow of goods and services.

V. MARKETS

Having added money and prices to our model of exchange between households and businesses, we can now introduce another social device, which determines the prices of goods and the quantities of goods exchanged. This device, or institutional arrangement, is called a *market*.

A market is simply the sum of contacts between buyers and sellers of a product or service. A market may, or may not, be formally organized and geographically centered, as are the New York Stock Exchange, the Fulton Fish Market, or the Chicago Board of Trade. Neither the market for shoes nor the market for structural steel is formally organized; and neither of them can be located at some particular place on a map. Markets are simply the process through which buyers and sellers interact and by which prices and quantities are determined.

All markets have two kinds of participants: those who wish to sell and those who wish to buy. The former group of market participants we will call *suppliers* and the latter type we will refer to as *demanders*. These two groups have basically different interests. Suppliers want the goods or services exchanged on the market to be sold at the highest possible price. Demanders, on the other hand, desire the lowest possible price. It is the responsibility of the market to reconcile these conflicting interests. Let us see how this is done.

In the simple model which we have been developing, there are two primary groups of decision makers: households and business firms. Households desire consumer goods and business firms produce them. We can envision a market for consumer goods in which households are demanders and businesses are suppliers. Because there are many households and many businesses participating as demanders and suppliers, the market will be a competitive one.

As suppliers, business firms wish a high price for consumer goods; households as demanders desire a low price. How can the market reconcile these divergent interests? Suppose that when the market opens, a tentative price for consumer goods—say, $10—is posted on the board. This posted price is then taken as the going price for all consumer goods for both demanders and suppliers. Each group will respond to this initial price by demanding or supplying an amount which maximizes their own interest. Suppose that at the $10 price households desire to buy 5000 units and suppliers wish to sell 7000 units. This situation is shown in Figure 2-3.

The point labeled *A* in the figure is where the demanders place themselves. At the posted price of $10—shown on the vertical axis—they are willing to buy 5000 units—shown on the horizontal axis. The suppliers place themselves at point *B*. At the same $10 price, they wish to sell 7000 units.

Is the $10 price a stable one? Or are there forces which will lead it to change? The answer is that the price of $10 cannot be maintained in a competitive market because some market participants, unhappy with that price, will take action to change it. In our example, it is the suppliers who will be unhappy. If the $10 price is maintained, only 5000 of the 7000 units supplied will be sold. At the $10 price there is a surplus—an *excess supply*—of 2000 units.

Not wishing to leave the market without selling their goods, some suppliers will begin to bid down the price. And as the price is bid down, two things will happen. First, some suppliers will begin to drop out of the market. These suppliers were willing to supply goods at a high price of $10, but at lower prices they find it no longer worth their while. At a price of $8, for example, there may be only 6500 units of consumer goods supplied. This is shown as point *B'* in Figure 2-3. Second, demanders will increase the amount of consumer goods that they wish to buy. At the high price of $10, some

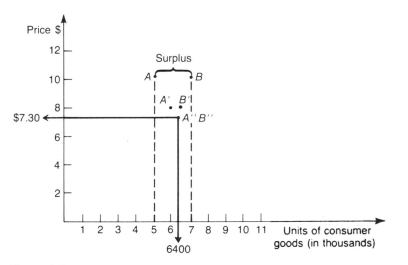

Figure 2-3

demanders were discouraged from buying. Lower prices will attract more buyers. At a price of $8, for example, demanders may be willing to purchase 6000 units of consumer goods. This is shown as point A' in Figure 2-3.

As a result of the bidding down of the price, the original excess supply of 2000 units is reduced. At a price of $8, there are only 500 units of excess supply; sellers wish to sell 6500 units at $8, but demanders will take only 6000 units at that price.

However, because there is still an excess supply of 500 units, the price of $8 is not a stable one either. Indeed, suppliers will continue to bid down the price until the excess supply is completely eliminated. In our example, this might happen when the price falls to, say, $7.30. This point is shown as A"B" in Figure 2-3.

At a price of $7.30, the amount supplied is equal to the amount demanded. No longer do suppliers have any incentive to bid down the price further. It is a stable price, and at that price an amount of say, 6400 units will be exchanged. There is no longer an excess supply and both demanders and suppliers leave the market happy. The price of $7.30 is called the *equilibrium price:* it is the price which equates the quantity supplied and the quantity demanded.

What has happened in this example illustrates how the market reconciles the interests of suppliers and demanders, and how the market process determines the price of goods and the quantity exchanged. This process is one of competitive bidding.

In chapter 5, this market process will be examined in more detail. However, our little example has suggested several characteristics of competitive markets which can, at least, be noted here. They are:

• When there is excess supply, or surplus, the market price will tend to be bid down.

• When there is excess demand, or shortage, the market price will tend to be bid up.

• A market equilibrium exists when a price is established which equates the quantity supplied and the quantity demanded.

• Suppliers are willing to sell more at higher prices than at low ones. A line drawn through B, B', and A"B" in Figure 2-3 would show this relationship. It is called a *supply curve,* even though in this case it is a straight line.

• Demanders are willing to buy less at higher prices than at low. A line drawn through A, A', and A"B" in Figure 2-3 would illustrate this relationship. It is called a *demand curve.* Again, in this case it is a straight line.

• The equilibrium price and quantity is established where the supply and demand curves intersect. This is shown in Figure 2-4.

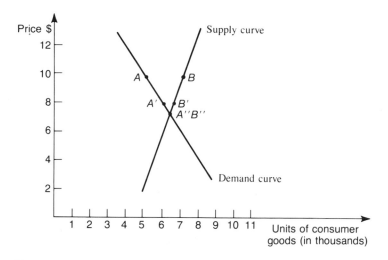

Figure 2-4

VI. THE CIRCULAR FLOW MODEL

With the economic role of markets understood, we can complete the model of the simple competitive economy. As we have seen, households and business firms participate in two kinds of transactions in this economy. They exchange consumer goods for money and they exchange factor services for money. This implies the existence of two markets: a product market and a factor market.

The two sectors play quite different roles in the two markets. In the factor market, households are suppliers and business firms are demanders. In the product market, the roles are reversed as households demand the goods which are produced and supplied by business firms.

Both of these markets can be incorporated into our simple model. Both the factor market and the product market are shown in Figure 2-5. Both of them are interposed in the process of exchange between households and business firms.

In the top half of the diagram the market for consumer goods and services—the product market—is shown. Here several things occur: (1) households as demanders interact with businesses as suppliers; (2) both the prices of goods and the quantities exchanged are determined; and (3) the flow of goods and services from businesses to households is equated in value terms with an equal flow of money from households to businesses.

In the bottom half of the diagram the market for the services of factors of production is indicated. In this market, the quantity of

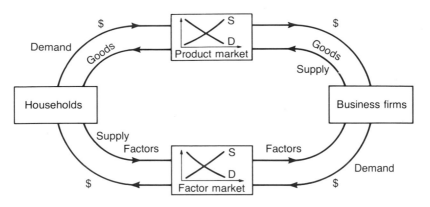

Figure 2-5

factor services supplied by households increases as the price of factor services increases. On the other side of the market, the quantity of factor services demanded by businesses *declines* as the price of factor services increases. The supply and demand curves in the factor market have characteristics similar to those in the product market, but the roles played by the participants are reversed, as are the flows of money and of services. Factor services flow from households to businesses. This flow is matched in value terms by an equal and opposite flow of money from businesses to households. Again the market forces of supply and demand determine prices and quantities exchanged.

This, then, is the simplest view possible of the operation of a market economy. Although it is a gross oversimplification of the real-world economy, it does capture a number of important features of a market economy. These deserve a brief listing.

- Producers and consumers interact in this economy, but do so with quite different motivations and objectives.
- Both parties rely on the other for both the generation of income and the flow of real goods and services.
- Exchange between the two parties involve both money and real goods and services.
- Incomes, profits, and satisfaction of wants are determined by prices which are set in impersonal markets through a process of price determination which reflects the activities of all demanders and suppliers. No external authority sets the price.
- The competitive prices also influence the composition of goods produced in the economy and the way these goods are produced.

While there are insights conveyed by the model, we should mention a few of the ways in which it fails to reflect some important features of a real market economy.

First, we have considered trading relationships only between households and firms, not between firms and firms or households and households. Moreover, we have assumed that there would be no change in the total quantity and quality of land, labor, and capital available. Because of this assumption, changes in the particular goods exchanged, changes in incomes, and changes in prices result only from changes in consumer tastes. And, because of this assumption, the size of the flow in the top half of the diagram will equal the size of the flow in the bottom half. The value of consumer goods exchanged is equal to the value of factor services exchanged.

This is clearly an artificial set of conditions. In the real world, the quantity and quality of factors of production change because of such things as population growth, technological change, or discovery of new mineral deposits. And both prices and the composition of production—the pattern of the circular flow—are altered in response to such changes. Further, not all real-world markets are competitive; many are dominated by one or a few powerful demanders or suppliers. Moreover, our simple economy has no government, nor does it engage in international trade. Both of these sectors have powerful influences on the levels of supply and demand in both the factor and product market. Indeed, government in a market economy often directly alters prices and, through taxing and spending, alters the income of households and the profits of businesses. Even though these characteristics are not captured in our simple model, the insights which it offers, as listed above, are important ones.

VII.   CONCLUSION AND SUMMARY

We have arrived at a simple model of the economy, stripped of many of the complexities of everyday activity in order to make clear the essence of a market system. Succeeding chapters will add many of the missing details. Our hope is to develop a sufficiently detailed framework to enable the reader to analyze most policy problems with some degree of accuracy and sophistication. Our simple model has highlighted the circular-flow mechanism through which incomes are earned and spent, and goods and services are purchased and consumed. The pervasive interdependence among the economic units in the system is clearly evident. Many years ago, Joseph Schumpeter stated with respect to such a system:

> *How much meat the butcher disposes of depends upon how much his customer the tailor will buy and at what price. That depends, however, upon the proceeds from the latter's business, these proceeds*

*again depend upon the needs and the purchasing power of his cus-
tomer, the shoemaker, whose purchasing power again depends upon
the needs and purchasing power of the people for whom he produces;
and so forth until we finally strike someone whose income derives
from the sale of his goods to the butcher. This concatenation and
mutual dependence of the quantities of which the economic cosmos
consists are always visible, in whichever of the possible directions
one may choose to move.* [2]

Moreover, our simple model of a free enterprise economy has
pointed up the key role played by the prices of commodities and
services. By equating quantitites supplied with quantities demanded
and clearing markets, these prices organize the economic activity in
the system. They determine incomes, organize output, and ration
consumption. In general, they provide the mechanism in a market
society for answering the basic economic questions asked of any
society: What is to be produced? How is it to be produced? For
whom is it to be produced?

QUESTIONS

1. What is meant by the word *system* when we speak of the *market system*
   or the *price system*?
2. Nearly all people serve as both "demanders" and "suppliers" during the
   course of a day. In which ways does the behavior of a person change when
   he, say, changes from a demander to a supplier? Do his basic motivations
   become altered?
3. It is often said that prices and profits guide the allocation of resources in a
   market economy. On the basis of the discussion in this chapter, can you
   perceive the basis for this statement? Describe how the allocation of
   resources would be altered in a market economy, if, say, the government
   decreed that the price of shoes would be fixed at $5 *above* the equilib-
   rium price.
4. From your observation of the U.S. economy, describe the differences in
   the retail market for groceries and the market for school teacher services.
   In each case, which sector serves as buyer? Seller? What are the characteristics of the buyers? Sellers? How many of each are there? Where is the
   market for each located? Name some extraneous forces which might
   make the equilibrium price in each market change.
5. In the text it states that ". . . the size of the flow in the top half of [Figure
   2-5] will equal the size of the flow in the bottom half." Show what the
   existence of profits has to do with this equality.

---

2. Joseph Schumpeter, *The Theory of Economic Development* (Cambridge: Harvard University
Press, 1934), p. 7.

3 | The Household—A Decision–Making Unit

The household does not exist in a vacuum but is a part of an entire economic system. Its decisions both affect and are affected by other parts of that system. The signals it receives from other parts of the system affect the decisions which it makes. Conversely, in making decisions, the household sends signals to other parts of the system. For example, if a household should decide to buy a car, the decision of what make, style, and price to choose is affected by many signals received from other parts of the economic system—the prices of smaller cars relative to larger cars, the relative effectiveness of the advertising campaigns of the various auto companies, estimates of the future prices which will be charged for gasoline, the incomes paid by the businesses which employ members of the household, the prices of all other goods, and other things. Household decisions, in turn, affect many other sectors—for example, the business firms that produce cars, the employees of these businesses, and the businesses that supply the car producers. It is this taking in and giving out of signals that is of interest in analyzing the behavior of households.

In discussing the behavior of the household we will rely upon deductive logic. We will make some basic assumptions about the household and then, on the basis of a model developed from these assumptions, deduce the behavior of the household as it makes economic choices. We will present here a basic model of household choice; a more rigorous model will be offered in an appendix to this chapter.

I. MOTIVATION AND RATIONAL CHOICE

The household as a family unit is forced to make a multitude of decisions—what food to buy, what kind of a house to rent (or buy), how much to spend on entertainment, where to work, how much to work, and the like. Because of the household's position in the circular flow of an economic system, all of these economic decisions can be placed into two groups. On the one hand, there is the choice of which and how much of the services of each of its factors of production are to be sold, and on the other, the choice of which and how much of each of the available consumption goods and services are to be purchased.

In considering these two kinds of choices, the question of motivation immediately arises. An individual choosing rationally must have some goal. With this basic objective, the decision maker can approach each decision with the question: "Which of the alternatives available will allow me to make the most progress toward my goal?" In constructing a model of consumer behavior, we shall assume, not unrealistically, that the drive which motivates the household is the desire for something called *utility* or *satisfaction* or *pleasure.* As a decision-making unit, the household chooses among available alternatives in order to maximize its satisfaction or pleasure. Consequently, when a shopper in the supermarket picks up a package of doughnuts, hesitates, and sets them down again, we conclude that he or she considers the 89¢ that would have to be spent on the doughnuts capable of giving more satisfaction if spent on other things.

II. THE DETERMINANTS OF CONSUMER CHOICE

For a household to choose rationally it must consider and weigh a number of factors. If we are to understand the behavior of the household—why it chooses as it does—we must isolate the most important factors and determine how they influence household decisions. In analyzing a household buying goods and services, the basic question is: What factors determine which commodities the household will buy, and of those it chooses, how much of each will be purchased?

The list of factors affecting a household's choice is long. At the top is something we shall call the household's set of *preferences* or its *tastes*. In calling this a determinant of choice, we assume that the decision maker has sufficient self-knowledge to be able to say, for example, "I prefer three loaves of bread to one pair of socks but I prefer one pair of socks to one theater ticket." According to one's set of preferences, the household is able to "order" or rank its alternatives. This ranking is a most important consideration in determining what alternatives the household will eventually decide upon. Clearly, a decision maker's tastes and preferences are determined by all of those forces—physiological, psychological, sociological, or religious—which influence a person's attitude toward alternative goods and services.

However, a consumer's tastes and preferences are not the only determinant of a consumption pattern. A second important determinant of consumer decisions is the *income* of the household. By observing the world around us, we can readily discern how the level of income influences consumer behavior. It is more than a difference in tastes which causes some people to live in Beverly Hills while others live in Watts. In general, an increased income will cause a household to increase the quantity purchased of those goods already chosen and, in addition, to choose a broader assortment. For example, poor people generally have fewer clothes than rich people and a much narrower range of styles. Few sharecroppers own the latest style tuxedo!

The third primary determinant of a consumer's decisions is the set of *prices* placed on the various commodities which he confronts. Again, observation of the real world demonstrates that the prices of commodities importantly influence the bundle of goods that a consumer actually chooses as well as how much of each the person stands ready to buy. Were the price of a dozen doughnuts $5 instead of $1.49, the shopper would not give them a second thought. Were the price 80¢, he or she might buy a dozen packages or maybe even two dozen.

III. THE DEMAND FUNCTION FOR A SINGLE HOUSEHOLD

Having described the major determinants of consumer choice, we can now specify more accurately the relationship between the household's demand for a good and those things that determine this demand. With respect to any of the alternative goods facing a consumer, say, good x, the quantity of x demanded(D_x) depends on the following four determinants: the price of the good (P_x), the prices of other goods (P_n), the consumer's income per unit of time (I), and the consumer's set of preferences or tastes (T). This can be written as follows:

$$D_x = f(P_x, P_n, I, T)$$

in which f signifies "a function of."

All of the variables in this *demand function* are free to change. A change in any of those on the right-hand side of the equation—the determinants—elicits a change in the variable on the left-hand side of the equation—the determined. However, our primary purpose is to understand the role of prices in a market economy, therefore, we are especially interested in one particular relationship within this equation. This is the relationship of the price of x (P_x) to the household's decision of how much x to buy—the demand for x (D_x). Assuming all things other than P_x to be constant (that is, keeping P_n, I, T unchanged), how will the quantity of the good demanded vary as its price changes? How will the number of packages of doughnuts bought by the shopper change when the price of doughnuts changes but the income of the shopper, his or her tastes, and the prices of other goods all remain unchanged? Using the Latin term *ceteris paribus* to signify "all other things held constant"—a common usage in economics—we can write this relationship as:

$$D_x = f(P_x) \text{ ceteris paribus}$$

To derive this relationship, we will, in the next section, investigate each of the determinants of demand in more detail, evaluating the influence of each on the household's decision–making process. Beginning with an analysis of the consumer's tastes and preferences (T), we will, in turn, analyze the impact of income (I) and prices (P_n, P_x) on the decisions of the consumer.

QUESTIONS

1. What do the economists mean when they speak of "rational behavior"? Is it possible to determine whether a particular individual is making rational choices? Is there a basis for asserting that any particular choice is or is not rational? If it is granted that cigarette smoking causes cancer, can one use this fact to assert that Mr. X's decision to smoke cigarettes is an irrational decision?

2. It is often noted that a person's cultural background has a good deal to do with the choices and decisions which he makes. Is this influence included in the three determinants of consumer decisions or is it in addition to them? If it is included in the three determinants, where does one find it?

3. In the demand function, the variables on the right-hand side of the equation determine the value of the variable on the left-hand side. Can the variables on the right-hand side influence each other? Can changes in the variable on the left-hand side of the equation cause changes in one or more of the variables on the right-hand side? For the equation shown on p. 39, how many separate *ceteris paribus* equations are there?

IV. CONSUMER TASTES AND PREFERENCES: MAXIMIZING UTILITY[1]

To construct a model of consumer behavior, let us assume the existence of a perfectly rational individual who maximizes his satisfaction or utility. Clearly, this is an abstraction. The behavior pattern of such an individual cannot be found in the real world. Who among us is perfectly rational in framing choices among alternatives? Who always chooses the good or service that brings him the most satisfaction per dollar? However, although people are not perfectly rational, neither are they completely irrational. By dealing with such an abstraction, we shall be able to discover, in idealized form, some very real characteristics of actual human behavior. The economist's model of human behavior is much like the model airplane of the small child. Although the model airplane makes no pretense at describing the complete reality of aerodynamics, it does clarify some of the principles of flight. The economist's abstraction, too, is not a complete explanation. However, it does clarify some principles by which humans make choices.

Let us, then, assume that this rational, utility-maximizing individual has a set of tastes and preferences—likes and dislikes—which define his or her attitude toward the myriad goods with which the person is confronted. That each person has such a unique set of tastes is indisputable. For Ms. Jones, red Thunderbirds convey enormous pleasure. For Mr. Smith, a stereo recording of a Bartok quartet conveys the same satisfaction. If we presume that satisfaction is measurable, and individual's tastes can be summarized in a set of "utility curves" of the type shown in Figure 3-1. For each good or service, the consumer will have a separate utility curve. The curve in Figure 3-1 is for the good x. On the horizontal axis, we have plotted the number of units of the good x; the total amount of utility provided by the consumption of x is shown on the vertical axis. The curve is labeled TU_x to stand for total utility derived by consuming good x. On the diagram we can see that the consumption of one unit of x (say, one glass of tomato juice) gives utility of OA. If two units are consumed, total utility increases to OB, implying that the second unit of x adds AB units of utility to the OA units of

---

1. Sections IV, V, and VI contain a basic analysis of how the determinants in the demand function affect the quantity of x demanded by a household. It is based on marginal utility analysis. A somewhat more rigorous analysis of the demand relationship and derivation of the demand curve is presented in the appendix to this chapter. It is based on indifference curve analysis. The appendix can either be used in place of sections IV, V, and VI (with no loss of continuity) or be treated as a supplement to chapter 3.

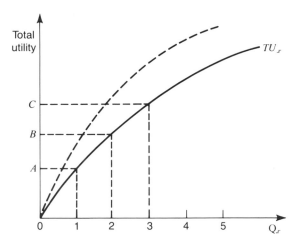

Figure 3-1

satisfaction already experienced. Similarly, if three units are consumed, total utility is *OC* with the third unit adding *BC* to the *OB*
units of satisfaction previously obtained.

Clearly, the level of the *TU*$_x$ curve describes the extent of the
consumer's enjoyment of good *x*. The higher the *TU*$_x$ curve, the
more satisfaction good *x* gives to the consumer. For example, the
dashed curve in Figure 3-1 implies a greater preference for good *x*
than does the *TU*$_x$ curve. For any number of units consumed, the
level of satisfaction on the dashed curve exceeds that for *TU*$_x$.

Similarly, the shape of the total utility curve must be noted with
care. With but few exceptions, total utility curves must possess the
general shape of *TU*$_x$ in Figure 3-1. This is so because of a most basic
characteristic of human beings. It can be described as follows. *As a
person consumes additional units of a good or service, his total
satisfaction may well increase continually. However, after some
point, the addition to total utility conveyed by each additional unit
will decrease.* Because this characteristic holds in all circumstances,
it is referred to as a law in economics—*the Law of Diminishing
Marginal Utility.* The marginal (or additional) utility obtained by
consuming one more unit of a good or service is, after some point,
smaller than the marginal utility obtained by consuming the previous unit. The third glass of tomato juice at breakfast may increase
the total utility of a person but the increase will tend to be smaller
than that provided by the second glass that morning. In Figure 3-1,
the additional utility obtained by consuming the second unit of *x*
(AB) is less than the additional utility obtained by consuming the
first unit *(OA)*; the additional utility obtained by consuming the

third unit of x *(BC)* is less than the additional utility obtained by consuming the second unit *(AB)*; and so on.

It is because of the Law of Diminishing Marginal Utility that the TU_x curve of Figure 3-1 is bowed: each additional unit consumed adds less to total utility than did the previous unit. This same property can be shown in a diagram in which the amounts of additional utility—the *marginal* utilities—are related to the number of units of the good which are consumed. Figure 3-2 plots the marginal utility curve which corresponds to TU_x in Figure 3.1. This curve, labeled MU_x, shows that the first unit of x consumed yields satisfaction of *OA*. This exceeds the addition to satisfaction gained by consuming the second unit—*OB*—which exceeds the addition to satisfaction obtained by consuming the third unit *(OC)*, and so on. Because of the Law of Diminishing Marginal Utility, the *marginal utility curve* will slope downward for virtually all commodities. This slope is reflected in MU_x of Figure 3-2.

As we have described them, both the total utility curve of Figure 3-1 (TU_x) and the marginal utility curve of Figure 3-2 (MU_x) are reflections of the same basic pattern of diminishing utility. In inspecting these two diagrams, then, note that the distance *OA* in Figure 3-2 corresponds to *OA* in Figure 3-1. Similarly *OB* and *OC* in Figure 3-2 represent the same increments to satisfaction as *AB* and *BC* in Figure 3-1.

Given the notions of total and marginal utility and the Law of Diminishing Marginal Utility, we can easily describe what is meant by "consumer tastes and preferences." Basically, consumers' preferences are defined by the complete set of total utility curves—one for each good or service which gives them satisfaction. Because each

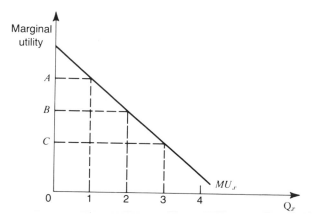

Figure 3-2

total utility curve has a marginal utility curve which can be derived from it, consumers' tastes and preferences are also defined by the whole family of marginal utility curves—one for each good or service which gives them satisfaction.

One final point about these curves should be mentioned. They can, at least in concept, be drawn for any consumer at a point in time. However, in moving from one point in time to another, these curves may change their position. For example, if a person's appreciation of small cars increases over time, his or her marginal utility curve for small cars will shift up. Similarly, any total or marginal utility curve is drawn assuming that the person's consumption of other commodities is fixed. If a person's residence changes from a home protected by trees to one which is unprotected, his marginal utility curve for the services of an air conditioner is likely to rise. In thinking about total and marginal utility curves, then, the *ceteris paribus* assumption must be employed. For any one of these curves, consumers' tastes and the level of their consumption of other goods and services is assumed to be held constant.

QUESTIONS

1. Complete the following table.

NUMBER OF PAIRS OF SHOES	TOTAL UTILITY	MARGINAL UTILITY
0	0	—
1	20	—
2	—	—
3	50	—
4	60	—
5	66	—
6	—	—
7	72	—

2. It would be a good exercise to draw the marginal utility curve which corresponds to the dashed total utility curve in Figure 3-1. How does this marginal curve relate to MU_x in Figure 3-2?

3. Draw a typical person's total utility curve for alcoholic beverages or drugs. Does either the stupor-inducing or habit-forming character of these commodities affect the general shape of the total utility curve? Draw a typical person's total utility curve for minutes of attendance at an unconscionably dull lecture. [Hint: If there is utility, there must be disutility.] Draw the marginal utility curve of each of these total utility curves.

4. Describe the implication of a total utility curve which turned down after reaching a peak. What would the corresponding marginal utility curve look like?
5. What is likely to happen to the typical person's total utility curve for cigarettes as the link between smoking and lung cancer becomes more firmly established?
6. What would happen to a typical person's total utility curve for drinking water over time if he or she were lost in a hot and arid desert? Also show what would happen to the marginal utility curve.

V. THE OTHER DETERMINANTS OF DEMAND—INCOME (I) AND PRICES (P_x, P_n)

In addition to consumer tastes, there are other determinants of how much a consumer will demand of a particular good or service. As we noted earlier, income (I) will surely be a factor. In general, we can assert that the greater a consumer's income, the more the person will demand of any good. This relationship, however, may not hold for a few, rather unique, goods. For example, it is possible that a consumer will reduce the amount of hamburger purchased as income rises. More exotic varieties and cuts of meat may be substituted for the less exquisite hamburger. Goods whose demand responds in this way to changes in income are referred to as *inferior goods*. In sum, for most goods, the relationship between the level of demand and a consumer's income is a positive one; for inferior goods the relationship is negative.

Prices are the remaining determinants of consumer demand for a good. Two types of prices are pertinent to the level of demand—the price of the good itself (P_x) and the prices of the n goods which are related to x (P_n). For example, the number of packages of doughnuts which shoppers put in their shopping baskets depends on the price of doughnuts but also on the price of related goods, say, cookies.

If the price of doughnuts rises, the shopper will be discouraged from buying as many packages of doughnuts as before and, in all likelihood, will reduce the amount of the good purchased. In general, *the relationship between the amount of a good demanded and its price is a negative one*.

The influence of the prices of goods related to doughnuts on the quantity of doughnuts demanded is slightly more complicated to discover. The difficulty here stems from the fact that some goods go well with doughnuts while others are substitutes for them. An example of a good which is *complementary* to doughnuts is milk. On the other hand, cookies are *substitutes* for doughnuts. The more doughnuts a typical consumer has, the more milk desired; the more doughnuts the consumer has, the fewer cookies desired.

What is the influence of changes in the prices of these related goods on the demand for doughnuts? Let us assume that the price of both milk and cookies goes up. As we have seen, this means that consumers will try to buy less of both of these goods. Now, let us take them one at a time and see how the change in price affects the quantity of doughnuts which a consumer demands. First, consider milk. Because the higher price of milk has caused consumers to decrease their purchases of milk, they will tend to want fewer packages of doughnuts than before. For *complementary* goods, then, the relationship of the *price* of one good and the *quantity demanded* of its complement is *negative*.

Next, let us look at the substitute good—cookies. We have seen that the higher price of cookies has led consumers to purchase fewer packages of them. With fewer cookies in hand, consumers would tend to buy more packages of doughnuts. When the price of cookies rises, consumers will tend to substitute doughnuts for cookies. For *substitute* goods, then, the relationship of the *price* of one good and the *quantity demanded* of its substitute is *positive*.

In the above paragraphs, we have explored the complex of relationships between the demand for a good x (D_x) and the determinants of that demand (P_x, P_n, I, T). In Figure 3-3, this complex of rela-

P_x ↑	$P_{comp.}$ ↑	$P_{subst.}$ ↑	I ↑	T ↑
D_x ↓ (−)	D_x ↓ (−)	D_x ↑ (+)	D_x ↑ (+)	D_x ↑ (+)

Figure 3-3

tionships is summarized. This chart can be read as follows. If the price of x rises (↑), the quantity of x demanded will fall (↓)—the relationship is a *negative* one. On the other hand, if the consumer's tastes for good x increase (↑), the quantity of good x which is purchased will also rise (↑)—the relationship is a *positive* one. While the relationships shown in Figure 3-3 hold generally, one should be careful to allow for exceptions. For example, we have seen that it is not always true that the quantity of a good demanded will increase as a consumer's income rises.

QUESTIONS

1. Describe the likely effect on the quantity of good x demanded if:
   (a) The price of a good complementary to x rises.
   (b) The price of a good which is a substitute for x falls.
   (c) The tastes of the consumer for a good complementary to x increases.
   (d) The income of the consumer falls.
2. How would you describe the relationship between two goods, x and y, if, when the price of x increases by 10 percent, the quantity demanded of y shows no change? Suggest a pair of goods which are likely to have such a relationship to each other.
3. Consider two goods, x and y. Would it be possible for the quantity demanded of x to fall by 10 percent and the quantity of y demanded to fall by 5 percent, if a 2 percent increase in the price of y was the only economic change to which the changes in quantity demanded were reacting? Discuss.
4. Which of the following items would be likely to generate an increase in the quantity of ties demanded by a man and through which of the determinants of the demand function would each of these changes work?
   (a) An increase in his taste for soup at lunch.
   (b) The death of a rich relative.
   (c) A decrease in the price of steel.
   (d) A change in fashions to wider ties with bright colors.
   (e) An increase in the price of suits.
   (f) Having a new red car.

VI. $D_x = f(P_x)$ *CETERIS PARIBUS*—THE DEMAND CURVE FOR GOOD X

In this section, we pick one particular relationship from the demand function and explore it in some depth. This is the relationship of the quantity demanded of a good (D_x) and the price of that good (P_x). From this relationship we derive the *consumer's demand curve* for a given product. Stated most basically, the demand curve relates the quantity of good X demanded (D_x) to the price of that good (P_x), when all of the other determinants of D_x (P_x, I, T) are constant.

To help us in logically deriving the demand curve, we will build a simple model. With this model, we will be able to see clearly the basis for what we will call the *Law of Demand*. First, then, let us assume a rational consumer with an income (I) of, say, \$6. This consumer can buy only two goods, x and y, and by chance, his or her *tastes* for these two goods are identical. These tastes are shown by the identical marginal utility curves $(MU_x$ and $MU_y)$ of Figure 3-4. Finally let us assume that the price of both x and y (namely, P_x and P_y) is \$1.

Given these assumptions, the first task is to determine how the consumer will allocate the $6 of income between x and y. Let us take it dollar by dollar. On which good, then, will the first dollar be spent? Because the consumer is rational, he or she will spend that dollar on the good for which the marginal utility is the greatest. In our model, however, the marginal utilities are equal. Being indifferent between spending the $1 on x or y, the consumer flips a coin and on the basis of the outcome chooses x. The utility which the consumer receives is shown by the shaded area labeled 1 on the diagram for good x.[2]

Now, on which good will the second dollar be spent? Obviously, if the consumer spends it on x, less additional utility is generated than was produced by the first dollar. This is so because of the Law of Diminishing Marginal Utility. However, because the utility from y is as yet untapped, the consumer will gain greater utility by spending the second dollar on y than by spending it on x. This additional utility is shown by the shaded area labeled on the diagram for y. By similar reasoning the consumer will spend the third dollar on x (if the flip of the coin yields the same results as the first time), the fourth dollar on y, the fifth dollar on x (again if the flip of the coin so decrees), and the sixth dollar on y. The result of this sequence is shown in Figure 3-4. With identical tastes for the two goods and with each good bearing the same price, it is not surprising that the consumer will allocate his income equally between the two goods, purchasing three units of each.

In working through this exercise, it should be emphasized that the flip of the coin is used only as a crutch. In trying to keep the discussion simple, we have assumed that the marginal utility curves for the two goods are identical. This gives us no basis for choosing one over the other in allocating the first dollar of income so as to achieve maximum utility. Hence, the introduction of the coin flipping.

This exercise has provided some notion of the nature of rational allocation. However, in order to derive a demand curve, we must observe how the quantity of a good demanded changes when *its* price changes. In working through this exercise, let us concentrate on good x. We will alter the price of x and observe how the quantity demanded changes in response to the new price. Let us assume that the price of x rises from $1 to $2, while the price of y (P_y) the consumer's income (I), and tastes (T) all remain unchanged. We will

---

2. The mathematically trained student will realize that this assumes the purchase of successive infinitesimally small units of the good up to the discrete quantity "1" shown in the diagram.

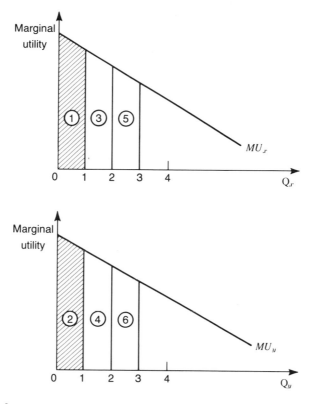

Figure 3-4

refer to the marginal utility curves in Figure 3-5 in working through this exercise. They are identical to the curves in Figure 3-4.

With this change in price, how will the consumer allocate income between x and y? Again let us assume that the dollar cannot be broken down into smaller units, such as pennies, and see how a rational consumer will allocate income. For the first dollar the consumer can buy either one-half unit of x or one unit of y. By comparing the pertinent shaded areas, it is clear that the utility from purchasing one unit of y is greater than the utility from purchasing one-half unit of x. The first dollar will go to y. The utility gained is shown by the shaded area labeled 1 in the graph for y.

Now, how will the consumer allocate the second dollar? With that dollar, either the second unit of y or the first one-half unit of x can be purchased. By the same reasoning as above, the consumer will spend the second dollar on y as well. The marginal utility from obtaining a second unit of y exceeds the marginal utility from ob-

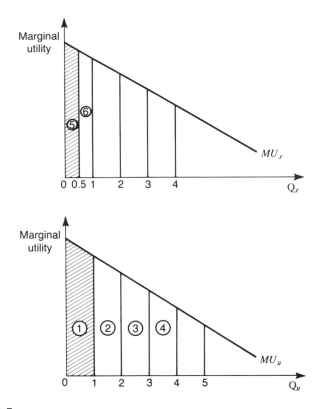

Figure 3-5

taining the first one-half unit of x. Again, by comparing areas (marginal utilities), it is seen that the third dollar and the fourth dollar will also be spent on y.

In the allocation of the fifth dollar, however, comparison of the marginal utility areas shows that the greater gain in satisfaction is obtained by purchasing the first one-half unit of x rather than the fifth unit of y. The decrease in the marginal utility of y (as more of it has been obtained) has been sufficient to compensate for the higher price of X. By the same comparison, the sixth dollar of income will be allocated to x.

The results of this allocation exercise can now be easily summarized. Four of teh $6 of income will be allocated to y, two of the dollars will be spent on x; four units of y will be purchased and only one unit of x. Because of the increase in P_x from $1 to $2 (with nothing else changed), the consumer has reallocated his income from x to y, has decreased his purchase of x from three units to one unit, and has increased his purchase of y from three units to four units.

From this logical exercise, one question rather naturally arises. If the consumer could shift income between x and y in very small amounts, where would the optimal allocation be; what characteristics would this allocation have? The answer to this question is that the consumer would allocate income between x and y so that the ratio of the marginal utility of x to the price of x would just equal the ratio of the marginal utility of y to the price of y $(MU_x/P_x = MU_y/P_y)$. Let us again use some numbers to see why this is so. Assume that the consumer found a situation in which the ratios were unequal— say, $MU_x/P_x = 20/\$2$ and $MU_y/P_y = 20/\$1$. We could write this $MU_x/P_x < MU_y/P_y$ or $20/\$2 < 20/\$1$. The consumer in this situation would find that total utility could be increased by reallocating income from one of the commodities to the other. How would this be done?

It makes sense to experiment by taking the first dollar away from the good with the lowest marginal uility-to-price ratio—in this case, x. If \$1 is taken away from x and spent on y, the consumer sacrifices 10 units of utility (by decreasing the consumption of x by one-half unit) but increases utility by 20 units (by increasing the consumption of y by one unit). On balance, 10 units of satisfaction are gained by making the shift. Clearly, it would be in the consumer's interest to continue this process as long as $MU_x/P_x < MU_y/P_y$. However, as income is reallocated, these two ratios begin to converge. Because of the Law of Diminishing Marginal Utility, the MU_y will tend to fall as more of y is consumed. For the same reason, the MU_x will tend to rise as less of x is consumed. At some point the two marginal utility ratios will become equal $(MU_x/P_x = MU_y/P_y)$. In our example this would happen when the marginal utility of x rises to 30 and the marginal utility of y falls to 15. When this adjustment occurs, the equal ratio condition will hold $(30/\$2 = 15/\$1)$. This equal ratio condition is called the *equilibrium* condition for the consumer. In equilibrium, the amount of utility experienced by the consumer is as great as it can possibly be—utility is maximized.

Now, by allowing only the price of one of the commodities to change—nothing else—we have performed precisely the kind of exercise necessary to derive the demand curve for x. It will be recalled that the demand curve of any commodity (x) relates the quantity demanded (D_x) of that good to its price (P_x), when nothing else changes. In the diagram of Figure 3-6, we have plotted the quantity of x on the horizontal axis and the price of x (P_x) on the vertical axis. In our first exercise, we found that three units of x would be demanded when the price of x (P_x) is $1. This is shown by point A in Figure 3-6. Point B was derived from the second exercise, at the $2 price of x, only one unit would be demanded. By connecting points A and B the demand curve for x $[D_x = f(P_x)$ *cet. par.*] is derived.

The shape of this curve is precisely that which our initial thoughts led us to incorporate into the table of Figure 3-3—the relationship between the quantity of a commodity demanded and its price is a negative one. This shape has become for economics what the gravity hypothesis is for physics: a stable law on which a large superstructure of further analysis has been built. This law in economics is called the *Law of Downward Sloping Demand.* It says that *because of the nature of rational consumer decision making, more of a good will be demanded when its price falls and less of a good will be demanded when its price rises.* But we must do more than simply state the law; we must also defend it.

Without question, the Law of Diminishing Marginal Utility is the basic reason for the shape of the demand curve. Because of this law, the satisfaction gained from consuming the next unit of a good is less than the utility gained from consuming the previous unit. Consequently, the consumption of each good will stop when the money spent to get one more unit of it could be used to obtain more utility by purchasing another good. It follows that if the price of a good rises, less of it and more of other goods will be consumed.

This effect is called the *substitution effect.* It states that as the price of a good falls, the consumer will tend to buy more of it and less of other goods. The consumer will tend to substitute the con-

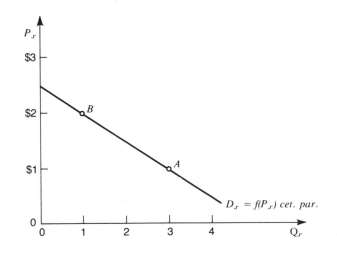

Figure 3-6

sumption of the good which has become relatively cheaper for the goods which have become relatively more expensive. (In more advanced presentations, the substitution effect requires that the utility of the consumer be held constant as one good is substituted for another in response to a price change. We have neglected this additional requirement.)

There is another effect which, in most cases, also causes the demand curve to be negatively sloped. It is called the *income effect.* It states that when the price of a good decreases, the consumer has, in effect, experienced an increase in purchasing power. Real income has been augmented. This increase in purchasing power will cause the consumer to buy more of all desired goods, including the good whose price fell. Again, the quantity of x demanded rises as its price falls. (This, of course, assumes that none of the goods which the consumer is buying are inferior goods.) The combined income and substitution effects therefore cause the inverse relationship between the price of a good and the quantity of it which is demanded—in other words, the Law of Downward Sloping Demand.

Before continuing, however, we would do well to explore briefly how changes in the other determinants of the demand for x (D_x) could be examined in terms of our simple model. In Figure 3-4, it was noted that the pair of marginal utility curves picture the consumer's tastes for the two goods. What would happen to the level of the two curves if the consumer's tastes, say, shifted away from x and toward y? How would this shift in tastes be reflected in the allocation of the consumer's income between x and y? What would happen to the demand curves of x and y? Or consider how a change in the level of consumer income would affect the consumption of x and y. If the price of x were $2 and the price of y were $1 (Figure 3-5), how much of each good would the consumer buy if his or her income rose to, say, $10? What would happen to the demand curve for good x shown in Figure 3-6? All of these questions can be answered by again working through the simple model using the same logic of allocation which we used in deriving the demand curve.

QUESTIONS

1. The marginal utility curves of a consumer for goods A, B, and C can be drawn from the table on the following page. Assume that the consumer has an income of $20 and that the prices of A, B, and C are $1, $2, and $1, respectively.

    (a) On a sheet of graph paper, draw the marginal utility curves for goods A, B, and C. (Each of these curves will be a straight line. Extend the line up to the y axis.)

QUANTITY OF A, B, OR C CONSUMED	UNITS OF MARGINAL UTILITY—A	UNITS OF MARGINAL UTILITY—B	UNITS OF MARGINAL UTILITY—C
1	50	105	25
2	45	100	20
3	40	95	15
4	35	90	10
5	30	85	5
6	25	80	0
7	20	75	0
8	15	70	0

(b) As we did in the chapter, allocate the consumer's income, dollar by dollar, among goods A, B, and C so as to maximize utility. In making this allocation, assume that each successive dollar allocated can be spent on only one good; that is, a dollar cannot be divided among two or three goods. In addition, use the rule that if equal satisfaction is obtained by allocating a dollar to either of two goods, the decision will be made in favor of A rather than B or C and B rather than C. Record on the graph where each dollar is allocated.

(c) Assume now that the price of A rises to $1.50 while the prices of B and C, the consumer's income, and his tastes remain unchanged. With these new conditions, again allocate the consumer's income, using the rules stated in (b).

(d) On a sheet of graph paper, draw the consumer's demand curve for A, using the conclusions of exercises (b) and (c).

(e) Describe (in a paragraph) what would happen to the demand curve for A if the price of B were to fall to $1 while everything else stayed the same. What would happen to the demand curve for A if the consumer's income doubled and everything else stayed the same? Why would these results occur? What would happen to the demand curve for A if the consumer's taste for A declined by 50 percent relative to that for B and C?

2. In question 1, the amount of A purchased fell as its price rose from $1 to $1.50. Can we state that that change in quantity represents a "decrease in demand?" How would you portray a "decrease in demand" in your graph of the demand curve for A?

3. In the chapter, we stated that both the income and the substitution effects would cause the demand curve to be negatively sloped. Would this be true for an inferior good? Does the demand curve for an inferior good have to be negatively sloped? What is the relationship between the income and substitution effects for a good which has a positively sloped demand curve?

4. Consider the following demands. Which ones do you think obey the Law of Downward Sloping Demand—and why?

(a) A family's demand for vacations.

   (b) A family's demand for children.
   (c) A family's demand for doctor's services.
   (d) The household's demand for funeral services.
   (e) The household's demand for passports.
   (f) A family's demand for automatic dishwashers.

5. Mr. X consumes 200 loaves of bread per year. Ms. Y consumes one loaf of bread per week. The price of bread is the same for each consumer. Which consumer has the greater demand for bread? Which consumer would have the greater demand for bread if the price of bread to Ms. Y were $1 per loaf and the price to Mr. X were $1.25 per loaf?

6. How would you respond to the person who asserted that the marginal utilities of all commodities would be equal in equilibrium?

VII. THE MARKET DEMAND CURVE FOR THE HOUSEHOLD SECTOR

Having derived the demand curve of a single household for a single good, we have taken the first step in describing the effect of price changes on the choice of goods and services by the entire household sector. To extend the analysis of a single household to the entire household sector—all households demanding goods and services— we must obtain the demand curve for each and every good from each and every household. This extension from one good to several and from one household to many is easily accomplished, however. By repeating the analysis of good x for goods $a, b, \ldots, z$ the entire set of demand curves possessed by a single household, say household I, can be derived. Similarly, by repeating this analysis for households II, III, $\ldots, N$, the set of demand curves for each of the commodities—one curve for each good from each household—can be derived. By combining these individual household demand curves for each commodity, a market demand curve for each of goods $a, b, \ldots z$ can be obtained.

Figure 3-7 shows the derivation of the market demand curve for a single commodity by combining the individual household demand curves. In Figures 3-7(a) and 3-7(b) the demand curves for good x of two independent consumers, I and II, are displayed. At a price of P_x' consumer I stands ready to purchase x_I units of the good and consumer II stands ready to take x_{II} units. Taken together, a total of x_T units $(x_I + x_{II})$ is demanded by the two households at a price of P_x' This is shown as point A in Figure 3-7(c). For example, if Ms. Jones would buy 5 dozen doughnuts a month at a price of 89¢ a dozen and if Mr. Smith would buy 2 dozen doughnuts a month at that price, the combined demand would be 7 dozen doughnuts a month at a price of 89¢. By the same summation process, a total of x_T' units $(x_I' + x_{II}')$ will be demanded at a price of P_x''. This is represented by

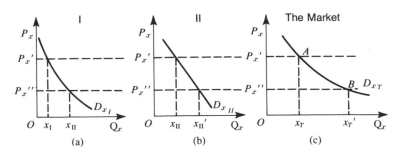

Figure 3-7

point B in Figure 3-7(c). The market demand curve, then, is produced by connecting points A and B in Figure 3-7(c), and other points derived in the same way. It shows the quantity of good x which will be demanded by all consumers in the market at all possible prices.

By *horizontally* adding each of the individual consumer demand curves, a market demand curve has been derived. This market demand curve exists for each of the commodities which the household sector stands ready to buy. As we shall see, it plays a very important role in the process by which prices are set in a market system.

VIII.   THE SUPPLY OF FACTORS OF PRODUCTION

In a price system the household sector plays a dual role. Not only does it serve as a demander of consumer goods but it also acts as a supplier of the factors of production, the services of labor, capital, and natural resources. Consequently, households not only have demand curves for consumer goods and services but they also have supply curves for factors. The household of the shopper in the supermarket not only buys doughnuts and other consumer goods but also earns the income to buy these goods by selling its services and the services of its possessions—that is, by earning wages, rent, interest, and profits. To complete the analysis of the household sector, we must discuss the household's willingness to supply factors of production. By way of illustration, let us consider the labor factor.

To derive the consumer's demand curve for a good or service, we worked with a pair of marginal utility curves showing the household's set of preferences between two desirable goods. We called them good x and good y. To analyze the behavior of the household in supplying the factors of production, we must again deal with the household's tastes and preferences. Again, choice must be made between alternatives. In the case of the labor factor, the household must choose between leisure, which a supplier of labor possesses in the amount of 24 hours per day when no hours of work are supplied, and money income which is earned by supplying hours of labor—working for wages. (For most people, other than misers, money income represents an array of consumable goods and services for which it may be exchanged.) A worker is able to substitute income for leisure in the same way that a consumer may substitute cookies for doughnuts. A person must decide how to allocate time between earning income (work) and leisure. The question we must answer is: How many hours of labor does a possessor of lesiure, a household, supply at different wage rates? From the answer to this question, we shall obtain the supply curve for labor, a curve showing the quantity of labor supplied by the household at all possible wage rates. The reasoning will run in terms of a person which can be translated into household by adjusting for the number of persons in the household.

To derive the labor supply curve, we will proceed in the same way that we did to obtain the consumer demand curve. We will isolate the determinants that affect a household's willingness to supply labor and then single out one of them, the price of labor, or the wage rate, for special consideration.

What are the determinants of how much labor a person will supply? They appear to fall into four categories. First, the preference for leisure, its marginal utility schedule (Z), will obviously have something to do with the amount of labor time a person is willing to offer. The quantity of leisure retained is equal to 24 hours minus the quantity of labor supplied. In accordance with the principle of diminishing marginal utility, it appears reasonable to say that the greater the amount of leisure possessed, the more of it a person is willing to give up in the form of labor.

Second, the wage rate or the price offered for hours of labor (W) will also affect how much leisure a person would be willing to give up or how much labor would be offered in the labor market. A person will be willing to devote different amounts of time to work depending upon how much can be earned per hour.

Third, because the choice here is between income and leisure, the household's tastes and preferences for consumable goods and services (T) which can be purchased with income will also be a determining factor.

Finally, the role of income depends not only upon tastes but upon the prices of consumable goods and services (P_n). The supply of labor by the household, then, depends upon the preferences for leisure of the members of the household, the wage rate, the household's tastes for consumer goods, and the prices of these goods. This can be written as

$$S_l = f(Z, W, T, P_n)$$

As we did for the demand function in the preceding section, let us set up a table summarizing the expected relationships between the determinants (Z, W, T, P_n) and the determined (S_l) for the labor supply function. This is done in Figure 3-8.

Z ↑	T ↑	P_n ↑	W ↑
S_l ↓ (−)	S_l ↑ (+)	S_l ↑ (+)	S_l ↑ (+) or ↓ (−)

Figure 3-8

Consider the tradeoff between income and the preference for leisure. If a person begins to value leisure hours more, fewer hours of labor will be offered, other things being equal. Conversely, valuing leisure less at each possible number of leisure hours will result in offering a larger number of hours of labor in the market. An example of such a change in preference for leisure relative to work would be the individual who, after learning the details—the ins and outs—of the job discovers a good deal less discomfort from spending time at work than he or she did while still learning the job. The disutility of work decreases; the individual's tastes and preferences shift toward work and away from leisure. One would anticipate that such a person would be willing to increase the supply of working hours (decrease leisure hours) even though tastes for consumer goods, consumer prices and wage rate showed no change. The relationship is inverse.

Should the person's tastes for consumer goods and services increase while wage rates, consumer prices and preferences for leisure remain the same, we would expect the person to be willing to work more hours to earn greater income—the quantity of labor supplied would increase. This relationship can be stated as $S_l = f(T)$ ceteris paribus, with the function expressing a positive relationship. When (T) increases, the quantity of labor supplied will increase.

Next let us consider the relationship between consumer prices (P_n), and the quantity of labor supplied (S_l). If consumer prices were to rise, the individual would be likely to work more hours to earn more income to purchase consumer goods, assuming the same wage rates, tastes for consumer goods, and schedule of preferences for leisure as existed before the change in consumer prices. (It should be noted, however, that this positive relationship, while likely, need not always hold. Higher consumer prices may lead to less consumer goods purchased and, hence, a constant or reduced need for income).

Finally, let us deal with the relationship between the quantity of labor supplied (S_l), and the price paid for labor—the wage rate (W). It is this relationship which describes the supply curve for labor $[S_l = f(W)$ *ceteris paribus*]. To analyze it, let us assume that the wage rate for a worker rises from $8 per hour to $10 per hour. Will this lead to a change in the number of hours of work which the laborer will supply and, if so, will S_l increase or decrease? In answering this question, we have to be concerned with two effects which we encountered before—the income effect and the substitution effect. Let us take them one at a time.

First, the *income effect*. If the worker was working 40 hours per week when the wage rate was $8 per hour, his or her weekly pay would be $320. When the wage rate rises to $10 per hour, weekly pay increases to $400, if the number of hours worked is not altered. What would one expect the influence of this increased income to be on the worker's allocation of leisure time? As we learned in analyzing the consumer's demand curve, an increase in income tends to be allocated among all of the items which convey utility to the decision maker—food, travel, theater tickets, and so on. Perhaps the worker can enjoy *both* more income *and* more relaxation time because of the increase in W. This can be done if the number of hours worked is reduced, assuming businesses permit this flexibility. For example, if the worker decides to reduce working time from 40 to 35 hours a week as W rises from $8 to $10 per hour, both an increase in money income (from $320 per week to $35 \times $10 = $350 per week) and an increase in relaxation time (five hours per week) are experienced. Indeed, because of this reasoning, it is generally accepted that the income effect usually leads to a *negative* relationship between W and S—as W rises, the additional income which it affords causes the amount of labor supplied S_l, to fall.

The *substitution effect* leads to an opposite relationship. When the worker was supplying 40 hours of labor per week, enjoyable hours of relaxation were being sacrificed for unenjoyable hours of work. The worker was willing to do this because he or she was being "paid off" for making this substitution at the rate of $8 an hour. If now the wage rate rises to $10 an hour, there is an added incentive to shift even more hours from relaxation to work. If this incentive works like other incentives in the real world, the worker will respond to the higher wage rate by supplying more hours of work—a *positive* relationship between W and S_l.

On balance, what can we expect concerning the relative sizes of the income and substitution effects? Will the income effect (generating a negative relationship between W and S_l) override the substitution effect (generating a positive relationship) or will it not? In truth this question cannot be answered definitively. However, most economists tend to feel that usually the substitution effect is the more powerful of the two. On this basis the supply curve of labor is often drawn with a positive slope as we have shown it in Figure 3–9.

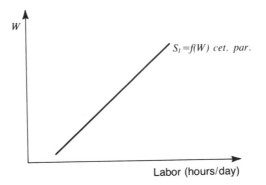

Figure 3-9

It must be emphasized, however, that there is no Law of Upward Sloping Labor Supply which we can call on, as we could in the case of the downward sloping demand for consumer goods. Indeed, it makes some intuitive sense to draw a labor supply curve with both positive and negative slopes—a supply curve which bends back on itself. We have pictured this curve in Figure 3–10. The reasoning for such a curve goes like this. When the wage rate (W) is low, the worker's income tends to be low. Consequently, an increase in the wage rate (W) is likely to induce additional hours of work from the laborer. The substitution effect will be dominant, and the supply curve will have a positive slope. However, when the wage rate is rather high, the worker's income will also tend to be high. In this case, an increase in the wage rate is likely to raise his income high enough that he or she would be willing to sacrifice some potential income in order to obtain additional nonwork time. The income effect will be dominant. If at the higher income less labor is supplied when W rises, a negatively sloped supply curve for labor will result.

Indeed, when the supply of labor curve of a household of two or more workers is contemplated, the possibility of a backward bending curve seems even more likely. At a low wage, other members of the family are likely to supplement the income of the primary income earner by working at least part-time. When the wage of the primary earner is high, other members of the household are likely to turn to pursuits other than paid employment.

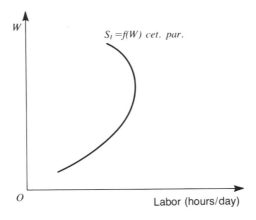

$S_l = f(W)$ *cet. par.*

W

O

Labor (hours/day)

Figure 3-10

Because such a backward-bending supply curve would substantially affect our further analysis only under the most extreme circumstances, we will use a supply curve of factors of production which bears a positive slope—one which slopes upward and to the right as in Figure 3-9. The higher the factor price, the greater will be the quantity supplied.

In our discussion, we have focused on the labor factor to illustrate the concept of the supply curve for factors of production. The derivation just as easily could have used either of the other factors— natural resources or capital. The supply curves for these factors would also be seen to have peculiar characteristics.

Consider for a moment the supply curve for natural resources. Households have title to parcels of land, and—like labor—the services of these parcels is made available to buyers for a price. However, the quantity of arable land is fixed at any moment of time. Therefore, above some price the quantity supplied would not expand in response to higher prices—the supply curve would become a vertical straight line. Much the same can be said for building sites in large urban areas.

The supply curve of capital—factory buildings, blast furnaces, turret lathes, and so on—has peculiarities of its own. Capital goods are produced in the same sense that consumer goods are produced. They differ from most consumer goods because they are usually long-lived and because they enter into the production process. Because they are long-lived, the amount of them which society decides to supply is affected by society's view of the future. The more uncertain the future appears, the less valuable any long-lived factory or piece of machinery will appear and the less of it that will likely be supplied. The price of producing capital goods in a fully employed economy is the value of the consumer goods which must be given up today in order to secure the production of the capital goods. Because more capital means more consumption goods in the future, a decision to produce more capital goods is, in effect, a decision to sacrifice present consumption in favor of future consumption. Again, society's view of the future—the cost which it places on waiting for consumption—determines the amount of capital supplied. This notion of the view of the future is just another way of describing the taste component of the determinants of supply. It is to the supply of capital what tastes toward leisure and income are to the supply of labor. For these reasons—uncertainty and the cost of waiting for consumption—the supply curve of capital has its own peculiar characteristics.

For natural resources and capital, as well as labor, these peculiarities will only rarely cause the supply curves to deviate enough from positively sloped curves to alter our analysis. The supply curves of natural resources and capital will also be drawn with a positive slope, as in Figure 3-9.

As in the discussion of demand, our analysis would be incomplete if we stopped here. At this point we have derived the supply curve for only a single factor for a single household. Again, we must extend the analysis from a single household to all. But, as before, the task is not conceptually difficult. We must simply add horizontally the resulting curves for each of the factors. In so doing, we shall obtain the market supply curves for labor, capital, and natural resources. These curves represent the factor-supply reaction of the entire household sector to changes in the price of the respective factors. This is the concept we were after when we began the analysis—the quantity of the factors supplied by the household sector at all possible prices.

QUESTIONS

1. Consider the following things, each of which is likely to influence how much labor a worker would be willing to supply. Through which of the determinants of the supply of labor (W, Z, T, P_n) would each of these effects influence the supply?
    (a) A heat wave drives the thermometer to 105° for a week.
    (b) The bus fare for commuting to work rises from 75¢ to $1.
    (c) A husband and wife agree to share the housework and child rearing.
    (d) A rapid transit system is constructed enabling the person to cut commuting time in half.

(c) The payment for overtime work rises from "time and one-half" to "double time."

(f) A grouchy, unpleasant person is hired to work at the next desk.

2. In the chapter, we asserted that the income effect tends to cause the relationship between S_l and W to be a negative one. Does this imply that leisure (for which the worker has a demand curve) is a normal or an inferior good?

3. It is often asserted that: "The higher the hourly wage rate, the higher the worker's income." Is this necessarily true? Why or why not?

IX. HOUSEHOLD DEMAND AND SUPPLY CURVES: SOME APPLICATIONS

This chapter has focused on the household as a decision-making unit. The analyses we have presented emphasize two of the major types of decisions which households make, the allocation of income among various goods and services and the allocation of available time between leisure and work. From these analyses, two important behavioral relationships were derived: the demand curve for a good or service and the supply curve of factors of production.

As we will see, these relationships are very important ones for understanding how a market system functions. However, they are also important relationships in their own right. Both demand and supply curves of households are central concepts employed by economists in approaching a broad range of business and public policy issues. A few examples will make this clear.

Consider first a retail clothing firm which is considering opening a branch in a new shopping center. To make a rational decision, the managers of the firm need to have a good idea of the demand which will exist in the area in which the new store is to be located. In contemplating this issue, the firm may well undertake a study of the determinants of the demand for clothing in that area: the income of the residents of the area, their tastes and preferences, the presence of other stores which would supply substitute goods, the extent to which the quantity of clothing demanded will change when the price goes up or down, and so on. Such a study of demand conditions would rely on the theory of household choice which this chapter has presented.

Or consider a public policy issue related to the energy crisis. As we all now realize, because of the Middle East oil suppliers' cartel—OPEC—the source of a large proportion of U.S. oil consumption has become very uncertain. Due to unpredictable political reasons involving either the producing states or confrontations among the super powers, the foreign supply of oil to the United States can be suddenly cut off. Indeed, the 1973 embargo did just that. To reduce its dependence on foreign source of supply, the federal government is attempting to reduce the consumption of oil by U.S. citizens, thereby reducing the need for imports from the Middle East. One important proposal designed to accomplish this is a tax on gasoline. This proposal, it will be recalled, was an issue in the 1980 presidential campaign. If a gas tax were implemented, the price of gas would be increased, and because of the negatively sloped demand curve for gasoline, less gasoline would be demanded. To evaluate the effectiveness of the tax, however, one has to know how much the quantity of gasoline demanded would decrease in response to various levels of the tax. In effect, the demand curve for gasoline has to be estimated. Only then could a sound judgment be made on the effectiveness of a gasoline tax in reducing the consumption of gasoline, relative to the merits of other alternative measures. The gasoline tax had not been adopted because, among other reasons, the estimation of the demand for gasoline by economists suggested that, at least in the short run, the demand curve was very steep. As a consequence, it was judged that only a relatively small reduction in gasoline consumption would result from imposing such a tax, until consumers had time to change the nature of their automobiles and their commuting patterns.

As a final example, consider the classic case of a large factory which is the major employer in a small community. The wage rate which the factory pays determines the prevailing wage rate in the community. Assume now that the firm needs to expand its output and to do so it must hire more workers. If there is no unemployment in the community, it must raise the wage rate to attract additional workers—housewives who otherwise would stay home, workers from neighboring towns, and so on. However, to set a higher wage is a very costly thing for a business to do; it must then pay that higher wage to all of its existing employees in addition to any new ones which it hires. The firm would reduce its profit if it raised the wage higher than necessary to attract the required employees. To determine the correct wage increase, the firm needs to have a reliable estimate of the supply curve of labor in that community—a measure of how the quantity of labor supplied would respond to various wage rates.

In the following brief sections, two slightly more detailed examples of the importance of household demand and supply concepts in public policy decisions are presented.

A. Measuring the Demand Curve for Outdoor Recreation

The U.S. government is the largest supplier of outdoor recreation services in the economy. The National Park Service supplies the services of unique facilities scattered around the country; the National Forest Service supplies the services of forest preserves; and the Corps of Engineers, by damming rivers and creating lakes, supplies, fishing, boating, and swimming services.

Consider, as an example, the question of whether a lake should be created in a particular area. This is an important economic question because the creation of a lake requires resources which have an opportunity cost. The lake should be created only if the demand for the recreation services is large enough to yield benefits which are greater than these costs.

To assist in evaluating the economic worth of proposals for new recreation facilities, then, the potential demand for these services must be estimated. The estimation of demand curves generally is a difficult task; it is especially difficult in the case of outdoor recreation services. The reason for this is that these services are not typically sold; there are no prevailing prices which can be relied upon to measure the strength of people's tastes for outdoor recreation services.

Economists have spent substantial time and effort to devise means of estimating the demand curve for proposed new recreation sites.[1] To find the relationship between quantity demanded—number of visitor days, in this case—and the value which people attach to visiting the site, an ingenious method has been developed. It has been observed that as the distance from a recreation site is increased, there are fewer visitors to the site per 1000 population. Hence, if one draws a set of concentric circles on a map with the park at the center, there is a decrease in the number of visitors per 1000 people in each ring, going from rings close to the center to rings further away. In Figure 3–11, for example, the number of visitors to the park per 1000 population would be smaller from the area represented by ring D than from the area represented by ring A. In effect, the time and cost of traveling to the park works just like a price: the greater the time and cost of traveling, the fewer the people who visit the park. It was discovered then that if the relationship between

---

1. See Marion Clawson and Jack Knetsch, *Economics of Outdoor Recreation* (Baltimore: Johns Hopkins Press for Resources for the Future, 1966).

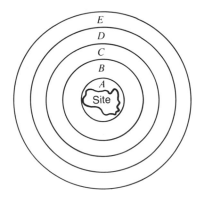

Figure 3-11

distance from the recreation site (and the time and cost of traveling this distance) and the annual number of visitors to the site per 1000 population could be determined, this information could be used to draw the demand curve for the recreation services offered by the park or lake. The demand curve, in turn, enables the benefits of these recreation services to be measured—and to be compared with the costs of creating the facility.

This procedure is being increasingly followed in evaluating major proposed developments by those government agencies responsible for developing and managing outdoor recreation facilities. While this procedure has some drawbacks, it is the best technique available for measuring the value or demand which households assign to outdoor recreation services, relative to the other goods and services on which they spend their income.

Indeed, this same procedure was used by a group of economists to measure the value which citizens placed on the privilege of attending another sort of event—the 1969 March on Washington to protest the Vietnam War.[2] They observed that attendance at the demonstration per 1000 population was greater for states close to Washington than for states farther away. Again, the time and cost of travel was serving as a price. They used this information to estimate the demand curve for participating in this event and, from the demand curve, the value to the participants of having the opportunity to demonstrate in this way was estimated. The estimate derived was about $17 million, or over $50 per marcher. The basic concepts

---

2. Charles Cicchetti, Myrick Freeman, Robert Haveman, and Jack Knetsch, "On the Economics of Mass Demonstrations: A Case Study of the November 1969 March on Washington," *American Economic Review* LXI (September, 1971).

analyzed in the theory of household demand were central to developing these estimates.

B. Measuring the Supply Curve of Low-Wage Labor

One of the chief proposals for reducing the level of poverty in the United States is the negative income tax. This scheme was first proposed in the early 1960s by the Nobel Prize-winning economist, Milton Friedman. If it were passed into law, a floor would be placed under each family's income: if the family had zero earnings, it would receive a grant from the government equal to this floor.[3] However, as the family's earnings rise, the amount of the grant is reduced, and at some earnings level, the subsidy disappears altogether. This level is called the break-even level, and if earnings rise above it the family would pay positive income taxes. A commonly proposed level for the income floor is $4000 for a family of four. The breakeven level of earnings would be about $8000.

While this sort of plan has many merits which are widely recognized, it has not been adopted. One of the reasons for its failure in the Congress is the fear that such a scheme would reduce the amount of work done by recipients of the income supplement. Indeed, a negative income tax has two effects which make one suspect just this sort of reduction in labor supply. One is an income effect, the other is a substitution effect.

Consider first the *income effect*. If a negative income tax were established, families with low earnings would receive a grant to supplement their other income. And, as we observed in discussing household labor supply, an addition to income is, *ceteris paribus*, likely to induce the family to choose more total leisure—that is, to supply less labor. The grant would allow the family to enjoy both more income and more relaxation time.

The *substitution effect* would also tend to result in a reduced supply of labor. One of the characteristics of a negative income tax is that the size of the grant is reduced as the earnings of the family rise. This has particular significance to workers in the family: an increase in earnings from, say, working more hours is partially offset by a reduction in the grant. As a result, the *net* pay-off to working more hours is less than it would be otherwise and workers would be less likely to choose to increase their working time. In effect, the negative income tax would appear to a worker as a reduction in the wage rate which is paid for working additional hours, and there would be an incentive to substitute hours of leisure for hours of work. Again,

---

3. See Robert H. Haveman, *The Economics of the Public Sector*, 2d ed., in this series.

the quantity of labor supplied would tend to be less than it would without such a plan.

Because of both the expected substitution and income effects of the scheme, a reduction in work effort was feared. Clearly, however, the extent of the reduction which would actually take place would depend upon the strength of these effects. They could be very powerful or they could be nonexistent. To frame a judgment on this aspect of the proposal, an estimate of the labor supply curve and its component income and substitution effects was required.

To obtain such measurements, the government sponsored a large experiment—the first real social science experiment. Thirteen hundred low-income families living in cities in New Jersey and Pennsylvania were chosen at random. About one-half of the families were placed on a negative income tax scheme in which benefits were actually paid out depending on the family's earnings; the other one-half served as a control group and were simply observed. The purpose of the experiment was to measure the labor supply effect of a negative income tax—to see how much less those families in the experimental group worked relative to those families in the control group.[4]

Using detailed data obtained from interviewing the families over the three years of the experiment, researchers concluded that such a plan would have some adverse labor supply effect, but that it would not be large. The husbands in these families had a strong attachment to the labor force and the data indicated that a negative income tax would cause a very small reduction in the hours that they worked—no more than about 5 percent. Wives showed less attachment to the labor force and the percentage reduction in the hours they would work was somewhat more. For families considered as a whole, the total reduction in hours worked from a negative income tax would be no more than 10 percent.[5]

As a result of this measurement of the components of the labor supply curve, one of the concerns regarding this sort of antipoverty policy has been substantially reduced. The income and substitution effects exist, but they are not strong. As a consequence of this effort to measure labor supply, any future judgment on the desirability of

---

4. This experiment was initiated in 1968, and lasted for three years. It was undertaken by the Institute for Research on Poverty at the University of Wisconsin, Madison, in conjunction with Mathematica, Inc., a private research firm.

5. More detail on the experiment and its results can be found in a symposium in *Journal of Human Resources* IX, No. 2 (Spring, 1974); and Joseph Pechman and Michael Timpane, eds., *Work Incentives and Income Guarantees* (Washington, D.C.: The Brookings Institution, 1975).

such a policy will be more informed and less likely to be based on unfounded suspicions. Again, the basic concepts developed in our theory of household choice served as the basis for this research.

X. CONCLUSION AND SUMMARY

The road has been long and perhaps hard to follow. Having finished our analysis, we would do well to retrace our steps briefly. This will enable us not only to determine just where we are in the analysis of the entire price system but also how we got there.

In this chapter, we postulated some rather well–known and largely accepted elementary human motivations and, then, logically deduced the behavior or choice patterns which a rational person with such motivations would display. We considered the household sector both as buyer of consumer goods and also as seller of the services of factors of production. We first isolated those factors that determine "the choice of which and how much of each of the available consumption goods are to be bought" and "the choice of which and how much of each of its factors of production are to be sold." We saw how subjective phenomena—preferences—and objective phenomena—prices and income—interact to determine the nature of demands and supplies. On the basis of these factors, we derived the demand and the supply curves presented by the household sector to the marketplace. We secured firm relationships between the prices of consumer goods and the quantities of them which households demand. We also explored the relationship between the prices of factors and the quantities which households are willing to supply.

Finally, we emphasized the importance of these relationships in both understanding the workings of the market system and in providing the basis for rational decisions on both business and public policy issues. The need for the measurement and estimation of household demand and supply curves was illustrated in two areas—the provision by government of outdoor recreation services and the development of income support programs for the poor.

Appendix: The Indifference Curve Model and the Demand Curve

In sections IV, V, and VI of chapter 3, we presented a simple model from which the household demand curve for a particular good—good x—was derived. Basic to that model was the notion of marginal utility and the Law of Diminishing Marginal Utility. Implicit in both the concept and the law is the assumption that this thing called "utility" is measurable. However, no one has yet found a meter which can measure levels of satisfaction. As economists became more concerned with the need to apply empirical tests to theory, the marginal utility approach came under growing criticism. Economists have searched for a means of deriving the consumer demand curve and demonstrating the Law of Downward Sloping Demand without having to rely on the notion of measurable satisfactions. The model which was developed and is presented below is called the indifference curve model.[1]

A. Consumer Tastes and Preferences

To obtain a concept of consumer tastes and preferences appropriate for the indifference curve model, let us conduct an experiment. We will ask a typical rational consumer to choose between a series of *combinations* of two goods which we will call "staples" and "luxuries." On the basis of that person's choices, we will develop a picture of that person's tastes and preferences.

---

1. The analysis in this appendix accomplishes much the same task as the marginal utility model in the text. It derives the consumer demand curve for a rational consumer using the $D_x = f(P_x, P_n, I, T)$ demand relationship presented in the chapter. As such it can be used to substitute for sections IV, V, and VI in the text or to supplement them.

Being rational, the consumer is able to rank the desirability of any series of combinations of staples and luxuries. For example, the consumer is able to state that the combination of 50 units of staples and 20 units of luxuries is preferable to less of both goods, for instance, 25 units of staples and 10 units of luxuries. Such statements enable us to derive a basic *Principle of Rational Behavior* applicable to most people in the modern world, namely, *more of both goods is preferred to less*.

In beginning the experiment let us draw a set of axes, as in Figure 3A-1, plotting the quantity of luxuries on the vertical (or y) axis, and the quantity of staples on the horizontal (or x) axis. (Later in the analysis we will use the letters x and y instead of staples and luxuries.) Next we will give our subject a certain quantity of both staples and luxuries, say 50 units of staples and 20 units of luxuries. We record this combination in Figure 3A-1 as point A. Then, we will give the person a large number of other combinations of these two goods, each time asking how the new combination compares with A. We allow only one of three answers to be given to each combination presented. The person may state that (1) the new combination is preferred to A, (2) it is not preferred to A, or (3) he or she is indifferent between them.

In the first combination which we present to the subject, combination B, we double both the amount of staples and the amount of

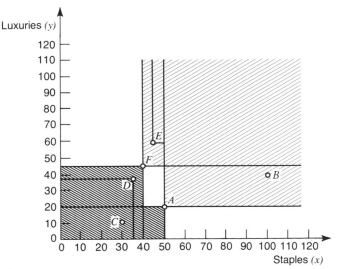

Figure 3A-1

luxuries; we give 100 units of staples and 40 units of luxuries. We ask the subject, "Which combination do you prefer, *A* or *B*?" The subject states: "I prefer *B* to *A*. As a rational decision maker, I clearly prefer more of both goods to less." Because of this principle, any combination containing more of both staples and luxuries than combination *A* will be preferred to *A*. Therefore, if Figure 3A-1 is viewed as a map, any combination in the light-shaded area to the north and the east of point *A* will be preferred to combination *A*. By the same principle, combination *A* is preferred to any combination composed of less of both commodities than it. Thus, combination *C*, containing 30 units of staples and 10 units of luxuries, is less desirable than *A*, as are all of the combinations in the dark shaded area to the south and the west of *A*.

We tell the subject to consider combination *D*. "Is it preferable to *A*?" He or she replies: "No, given my set of preferences, I would choose *A*." Because of the Principle of Rational Behavior, we immediately shade in heavily the rectangle south and west of *D*, since all points in it are less desirable than *A*. If *A* is preferred to *D*, it is surely preferable to combinations less desired than *D*.

Now combination *E*. "Combination *E*," the subject replies, "is preferred to combination *A*." Again, because more of both goods is preferred to less, we shade in lightly the quadrant north and east of *E*. Because *E* is preferred to *A*, all combinations preferred to *E* will be preferred to *A*.

Next, combination *F* is presented. It contains less of both commodities than combination *E* but more of both than combination *D*. The answer is, "I am indifferent between *A* and *F*." For the same reasons as above, we now shade in heavily the quadrant below and to the left of *F* because all of these combinations are preferred to *A*. In combination *F*, and this is the significant point, we have a point which lies on the borderline, or boundary, between those combinations that are more desired than *A* and those that are less desired. Combination *F* is the second point in Figure 3A-1 at which the dark shaded area meets the light shaded area. By continuing this kind of experiment, clearly all of the points on the borderline can be found.

In Figure 3A-2, we have pictured just such a borderline along with some familiar points. The outstanding characteristic of this curve is that at every point on it the consumer is receiving the same amount of satisfaction. The consumer is *indifferent* between any two points on the curve. Because of the Principle of Rational Behavior, every combination above the curve—in the light shaded area—is preferred to any combination on the curve. Every combination below the

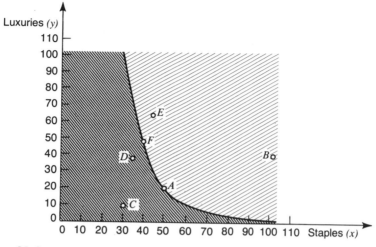

Figure 3A-2

curve—in the dark shaded area—is less desirable than any point on the curve. This curve is called an *indifference curve.*

Now, beginning with any point not on the original indifference curve, we can, by repeating the experiment, derive another indifference curve. In fact, an *infinite* number of indifference curves can be found. In Figure 3A-3, a few of these are pictured along with some familiar points. This family of curves—this *indifference map*—is a picture of the consumer's tastes and preferences (T). Clearly, higher indifference curves represent greater satisfaction than do lower curves. That is reading $<$ as "is less preferred than," we can say $U_1 < U_2 < U_3 < U_4, \ldots, < U_n$. Being a rational maximizer of utility, the consumer will strive to reach the highest indifference curve possible.

Before we observe the consumer scrambling up the indifference map, let us look at three outstanding characteristics of the map itself. First, all of the indifference curves slope downward and to the right throughout their entire length. They have a negative slope. Second, no indifference curve intersects any other. Finally, all of the curves are drawn convex to the origin. They bow in toward point zero. Let us consider each of these characteristics in turn.

Consider first the need for indifference curves to slope downward and to the right. From studying Figure 3A-1 it is seen that if an indifference curve should slope upward and to the right, the Principle of Rational Behavior would be violated. A consumer who pos-

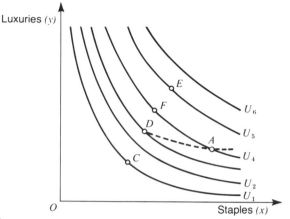

Figure 3A-3

sessed such a positively sloped curve would be indifferent between two combinations of staples and luxuries, one of which contains more of both commodities than the other. Because more of both goods is always preferred to less, indifference would not be rational by common definition. Therefore, indifference curves must be negatively sloped.

By much the same sort of "negative proof," we can demonstrate that indifference curves cannot intersect. Imagine that the dotted line in Figure 3A-3 is an indifference curve passing through both D and A. The following inconsistency results. A is indifferent to both D and F because it lies on indifference curves passing through both of these points. F is preferred to D because it contains more of both goods than does D. Because F and A are of equal utility and because F is preferred to D, A must also be preferred to D. Consequently, the impossible situation of A being both indifferent to D and preferred to D results. Hence, the indifference curves of a rationally consistent consumer cannot intersect.

To justify the convex shape of indifference curves, we need to be introspective about our own tastes. Consider the single indifference curve displayed in Figure 3A-4. We have drawn it convex to the origin or bowed in. As the consumer moves from A toward B along this curve, it becomes less and less steep, like a ski slope. Because the *slope* of a curve is defined as $\Delta y/\Delta x$ (read as the change in the value on the y axis over the change in value on the x axis, ignoring the sign), we can say that the slope of the curve decreases as the consumer moves from A toward B. This phenomenon of decreasing

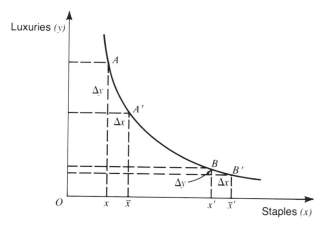

Figure 3A-4

slope is known as the *Diminishing Marginal Rate of Substitution of x for y* (MRS_{xy}); as such, it describes the convex nature of the curve. The question now is: Why is there a Diminishing Marginal Rate of Substitution?

At point A on the indifference curve in Figure 3A-4, the consumer possesses a relatively large amount of luxuries and a small amount of staples. The opposite situation prevails at point B where the consumer possesses a large amount of staples and a small amount of luxuries. Now, let us assume that the consumer performs two mental experiments. First, assume that the subject begins at point A and moves to Point A', giving up some luxuries (Δy) and gaining some staples (Δx). Second, assume that the subject makes the same sort of trade but begins at B and moves to B'. Beginning at points A and B, then, the consumer gains, say, a *single unit* of staples (Δx) and gives up just enough luxuries (Δy) to keep on the same indifference curve. In both cases, satisfaction is unchanged.

The significance of the convex shape now becomes clear: when the consumer has an abundance of luxuries but only a few staples, there is a willingness to give up a rather large amount of luxuries to get an additional unit of staples, the movement from A to A'. When one is well stocked with staples one is willing to give up only very few luxuries to get another unit, the movement from B to B'. Thus, while in each of these movements, from A to A' and from B to B', the value of Δx is the same, the value of Δy is substantially larger when a small amount of x is possessed than when x is held in abundance. Hence, as one moves down the indifference curve, the slope of the curve $(\Delta y/\Delta x)$ falls. For this reason, indifference curves are drawn convex to the origin and we speak of the Diminishing Marginal Rate of Substitution of x for y $(MRS_{xy} = \Delta y/\Delta x)$.

With this discussion of the indifference map we have taken the first step in constructing our model of consumer choice. For a consumer choosing between two commodities, this map is an accurate picture of the variable in the demand function which we called consumer tastes and preferences (T). Let us complete our model by analyzing the remaining determinants in the demand function—the consumer's income (I) and the structure of prices $(P_n$ and $P_x)$.

B. Consumer Income and the Structure of Prices: The Budget Constraint

Considering only one's tastes and preferences, a rational consumer will attempt to reach the highest possible indifference curve. However, in making the climb up an indifference map in the real world, the consumer is constrained or limited by other forces. Several of these are summarized in the consumer's budget. Thus, the shopper in the supermarket fails to buy the dozen doughnuts because of a limited budget. Or the accountant with last year's Ford fails to make a trade this year because he is constrained by his budget. The *budget constraint* must also be incorporated into the model.

The budget of a consumer is based on his or her income and the prices of the goods that are purchased. At the same prices, a person with a higher income is less constrained than a person with a lower income, although both are constrained to some extent. Or, of two people with the same income, the one buying in a market with higher prices is more constrained than the one buying in a market with lower prices. Indeed, it is conceivable that a person with a high income in a situation with very high prices could be more constrained than one with a lower income in a situation with very low prices.

Consider a single consumer with an income of $6000. Assume that he or she spends this income on only two goods, good x and good y, whose prices are $100 and $60, respectively. By confronting the consumer with both a fixed income and a set of prices, we are limiting the range of choice in a realistic fashion. Before we established an income level or the prices of the goods purchased, the consumer could conceive of choosing any point above and to the right of the two axes in Figure 3A-5. However, with the imposition of the price and income constraints, this wide range of choice is cut back. Let us define more precisely the range of choice which re-

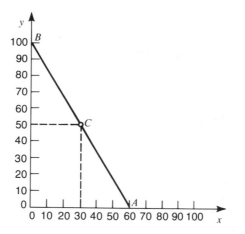

Figure 3A-5

mains open to the consumer after the constraints of a budget have been imposed.

Assume, first, that the consumer spends his or her entire income on good x. Given the price of x, the most that could be purchased with this income would be 60 units ($6000/$100), show as point A in Figure 3A-5. If 60 units of x can be purchased, surely any amount less than 60 units can be purchased. Next assume that the consumer spends the entire income on good y. In this case, the maximum that could be purchased with $6000 would be 100 units, represented by point B on the diagram ($6000/$60). If point B is attainable, any amount of y less than B can also be obtained. Finally, let us assume that the consumer divides the income equally between the two goods, spending $3000 on both x and y.

Given the prices of these goods, 30 units of x ($3000/$100) and 50 units of y ($3000/$60) can be purchased. This combination is represented by point C on the diagram. Not surprisingly, point C lies on a straight line connecting points A and B. In fact, if the consumer divides the income between the two goods in all possible ways— $6000 on good x, nothing on good y; $5999 on good x, $1 on good y, and so on—all of the combinations will lie on that straight line. By experimenting with a number of alternative ways of dividing up the income, the reader can easily demonstrate this.

To see this still more clearly, consider the equation

$$I = P_x(x) + P_y(y)$$

which is known as the budget constraint. Of the five symbols in this equation, three represent determinants in the demand function: I, P_x, P_y. By working with this equation, it can be seen that, given values for I, P_x, and P_y, any combination of two numbers for x and y which maintains the equality will fall on the line. We call this line the *line of attainable combinations* or, alternatively, *the budget line*.

From this example, we can derive the *slope* of the line of attainable combinations—a number which will have significance shortly. Because the slope of a line is given by the ratio $\Delta x/\Delta y$ (ignoring the sign), it follows that the slope of the line of attainable combinations in the example just discussed (Figure 3A−5) is $100/60 = 1\ 2/3$. The value of 100 is taken from the y axis and the value of 60 is from the x axis. The value of the slope can also be stated in symbols as $(I/P_y)/(I/P_x)$, which reduces to $P_x/P_y = \$100/\$60$ or $1\ 2/3$.

Quite legitimately, this line can be considered a boundary line between two distinct sets of combinations of x and y. It separates all combinations which the consumer can obtain with his or her income—all points on the line or below it—from all combinations which are out of reach—all points above the line.

We have now incorporated all of the determinants of D_x into the indifference map (T) and the line of attainable combination (I, P_x, P_y). What remains in order to complete the model is to put all of the determinants together and to analyze the impact of each determinant on the decision-making behavior of the consumer.

C. $D_x = f(P_x, P_y, I, T)$—A Model of Consumer Behavior

To analyze a consumer's behavior in deciding the quantity of good x to purchase, let us first introduce his or her indifference map. It is pictured in Figure 3A-6. By itself, it depicts the tastes and preferences (T) of an individual consumer faced with a choice between good x and good y. As a second step, let us provide the consumer with an income (I), the price of good x (P_x) and the price of good y (P_y). In other words, let us provide a line of attainable combinations. By determining the value I/P_x, the maximum amount of x attainable is found. This is shown as point A in Figure 3A-6. In the same way, I/P_y locates point B, the maximum amount of good y attainable. By connecting these two points, we obtain the line of attainable combinations, AB. (In this discussion, we assume that y is the only other good besides x. Hence n becomes y and P_n becomes P_y.)

We are now prepared to investigate the process of rational decision making, the process of rational consumer choice. Let us again pose the basic question: "Facing a set of alternatives, any one of which is available, how will the household choose?" In answering

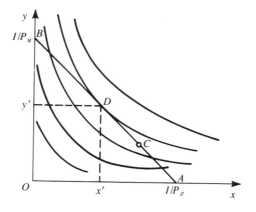

Figure 3A-6

this question, we must first isolate the "set of alternatives" open to the consumer. This set includes all of the combinations of good x and good y on or below the line of attainable combinations (AB), namely, all of the points in the triangle OAB. How will the consumer choose among these possibilities? The answer is easily obtained. Because he or she maximizes utility, the consumer will choose that combination of x and y which gives the greatest amount of satisfaction; that combination which is on the highest possible indifference curve.

For example, in considering *only* the combinations A, B, and C in Figure 3A-6, a rational consumer would discover C to be the most preferred of the three and choose it. It lies on a higher indifference curve than the other two. Combination C gives greater satisfaction than either A or B.

Now let us open up the consumer's range of choice to the entire triangle OAB. With this broader set of options, even C is replaced as the most preferred point. By moving along the budget line from C toward B—by exchanging x for y—the consumer attains higher and higher levels of satisfaction.

Until point D, each exchange leaves the consumer better off than before. Continuously higher indifference curves are attained with each exchange. However, beyond point D, the reverse occurs; now additional substitutions of x and y give successively lower levels of satisfaction. Each exchange places the consumer on a lower indifference curve. At D, the consumer is unable to move to any other combination which yields a greater utility. Combination D produces the highest indifference curve attainable given the budget constraint. A rational maximizer will choose this combination from among all the others.

Two important characteristics of this choice immediately appear. First, point D is located *on* the line of attainable combinations, not below it. Indeed, any point below the budget line would not maximize satisfaction. Second, combination D is located at the only point where an indifference curve is *tangent* to the line of attainable combinations. Because it is the only point on the diagram from which the consumer feels no desire to move, this point defines the equilibrium. At this point, the slope of the indifference curve (MRS_{xy} or $\Delta y/\Delta x$) is equal to the slope of the line of attainable combinations, or P_x/P_y. Thus, if the consumer is on the line of attainable combinations, we can locate the equilibrium (or utility maximizing) point where

$$MRS_{xy} = \Delta y/\Delta x = P_x/P_y$$

This conclusion can be summarized as follows. When each determinant of the quantity of x demanded (D_x) is given (P_x, P_y, I, T), the consumer finds the most desirable yet attainable choice to be that combination which both exhausts the budget and maximizes utility. With reference to Figure 3A-6, the consumer will obtain the most utility from his or her income if x' units of good x and y' units of good y are purchased. For the assumed income, prices, and tastes, the value of the dependent variable—the demand for good x—is x' units.

The two *equilibrium conditions* of the consumer can be found from this discussion. First, in equilibrium, the consumer is on the line of attainable combinations—the amount which is paid for the goods exhausts his or her income.

$$I = P_x(x) + P_y(y)$$

Second, in the equilibrium, the rate at which the consumer is willing to substitute the goods is equal to the inverse of the ratio of their prices,

$$MRS_{xy} = \Delta y/\Delta x = P_x/P_y$$

These two properties are the equilibrium conditions in the model of consumer choice.

D. $D_x = f(P_x)$ *Ceteris Paribus*—The Derivation of the Demand Curve

Our analysis of the demand function is not yet complete. Determining D_x for a particular set of P_x, P_y, I, and T is but a first step. We must also analyze how the quantity demanded of a good (D_x) changes in response to changes in its price (P_x), when all of the other variables remain constant. That is, we must derive the consumer's demand curve for a given product.

To derive this relationship, let us return to the consumer equilibrium shown in Figure 3A-6. This same equilibrium is redrawn in Figure 3A-7. From the equilibrium represented by combination D, one point on the demand curve for x is observed; at a price of P_x, the consumer chooses x' units. We can plot this choice on a set of axes on which are measured the price of x (P_x) and the number of units of x demanded. Thus, in Figure 3A-8, point D depicts one point on the demand curve for good x, the choice corresponding to point D in Figure 3A-7. At a price of P_x, x' units are demanded.

Given our definition of the demand curve, we must now determine how the consumer will change the amount of x demanded when the price of x changes. We must find a second point on the demand curve which can be plotted in Figure 3A-8. By definition, this new quantity demanded can be found only when the price of x—and nothing but P_x—has changed.

To observe how a price change will affect the quantity of x demanded, let us refer to Figure 3A-7. By lowering the price of x from say, P_x to P_x', something in the diagram is going to change. Surely the indifference curves will not change. They represent the tastes of the consumer and these are independent of the price of the goods. Thus, it is the line of attainable combinations, the consumer's budget, which must adjust to allow for the decrease in the price of x. But just how will the line of attainable combinations be modified to take account of the price change?

The budget line AB in Figure 3A-7 is drawn for a particular income (I) and for a particular set of prices (P_x and P_y). In fact, the slope of the line is equal to the ratio of the prices P_x/P_y. Thus, if the price of x decreases the line will surely change its position. Point B, however, will not change when P_x changes. Its location is determined by the ratio of I and P_y (I/P_y), both of which remain constant. Because both the slope of the budget line, P_x/P_y, and the location of point A depend on the price at which x sells, both will be modified. If P_x decreases to P_x', the slope of the budget line will decrease as the constant P_y is now divided into a smaller number. Likewise, the location of point A will move further out the x axis as the constant I is placed over P_x', which is lower than P_x. Thus, with the lower price of x, we derive a new line of attainable combinations for the consumer, a line which again begins at point B but which now bears a smaller slope than line AB. This line is pictured as line $A'B$ in Figure 3A-7.

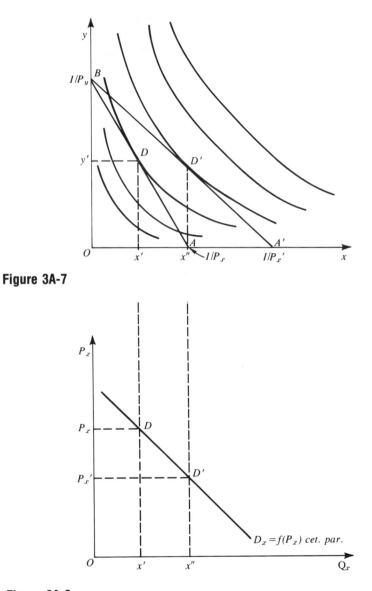

Figure 3A-7

Figure 3A-8

One very important thing to notice with respect to the line $A'B$ in Figure 3A-7 is that, because of the decrease in the price of x, the number of attainable combinations—the range of choice—has increased for the consumer. Thus, such a decrease in price is looked upon most favorably by a consumer. It will allow a higher indifference curve to be attained. Although money income has not changed, the consumer's real income has increased.

With the decrease in the price of x and the new line of attainable combinations, the consumer is back in the business of making decisions. Being thrown from the old equilibrium (point D) by the price change, one must now reallocate the budget so as to again maximize utility. By choosing that combination of x and y depicted by the tangency of an indifference curve with the new budget line, point D', the consumer again chooses rationally and maximizes satisfaction. Again an equilibrium position is achieved and the two equilibrium conditions hold; $I = P_x(x) + P_y(y)$ and $MRS_{xy} = P_x/P_y$.

The information supplied by this new equilibrium is precisely what is necessary to derive the demand curve for x. By changing only the price of x while holding all of the other determinants I, T, P_y) constant, we observe how the quantity of x demanded (D_x) responds to a change in the price of x. Because of the change in P_x, the consumer has had to reallocate income and adjust the pattern of purchases. The consumer has moved from D to D' in Figure 3A-7, representing an increase in the quantity of x purchased from x' to x''. This new equilibrium is shown in Figure 3A-8 as point D'. By definition, it forms a second point on the demand curve for x. Connecting this point with D and all of the other points derived from assuming different prices of x, we find the consumer's demand curve for good x. It is labeled $D_x = f(P_x)$ cet. par., in Figure 3A-8.

The demand curve which we have derived is, in concept, identical to that derived in the main body of the chapter. Only the method of derivation is changed. We have substituted the indifference map for the marignal utility curves and the Diminishing Marginal Rate of Substitution for the Law of Decreasing Marginal Utility. In the appendix, it should be noted, we did not have to presume that utility was measurable; all the consumer had to do was to rank the various alternatives.

QUESTIONS

1. What would an indifference curve between, say, cigarettes and automobiles look like if smoking made you sick?
2. "An indifference curve embodies the assertion that a consumer can substitute one good for another with no loss of utility." "By its very shape, an indifference curve implies that a consumer will not spend all of his income on one good." "If combination A (of two goods) is preferred to combination B, it can lie to the northeast, the northwest, or the southeast of B on an indifference map." Draw an indifference map and illustrate each of these assertions in terms of it.

3. What would the budget line look like if the more you purchased of a good the higher its price became?
4. How would you show a shift in tastes from good x toward good y on an indifference map for goods x and y?
5. Draw a set of indifference curves for right shoes and left shoes.
6. Show on an indifference map how the equilibrium would change when a consumer's income increases. Will both the old and the new equilibrium fall on a straight line, passing through the origin?
7. Can you relate the notion of the substitution effect which was discussed in the chapter to the change in the quantity of x demanded due to a change in the price of x which was discussed in the appendix? (*Hint*: The substitution effect showed how the amount of x demanded changed when its price changed, holding real income constant.)

4 | The Competitive Business Firm—A Decision-Making Unit

The second basic sector in a market system is the business sector. While the household sector is known primarily for its role as a consumer of goods and services, the business sector plays the primary role in producing and distributing these outputs. In analyzing the household sector, we focused on the behavior of individual household units. Now we will focus on the individual business units in the business sector. These units are business firms. As we noted previously, firms are clearly distinguishable from other kinds of business units such as plants and industries. General Motors, for example, is a firm. It produces automobiles in many plants. Together with Ford Motor Company, the Chrysler Corporation, and others, it forms the automobile industry.

Because of their position in the circular flow, business firms perform certain specific functions: they purchase factors of production from the household sector as inputs, they transform these inputs into a useful and desired output, and then they sell the output back to the household sector. In performing these functions, firms make two basic types of choices. They must first decide how much to produce and offer for sale and then they must determine how much to buy of the available factors of production. The manufacturer of shoes, for example, must decide not only how many pairs of shoes to produce but also how much labor and how many machines to employ in producing the output.

I. MOTIVATION, RATIONAL CHOICE, AND THE PROFIT CONCEPT

As in the case of the household, we immediately confront the basic question: What motivates the behavior of firms? Why do they buy, produce, and sell? What do they get out of it? What is their goal? In order to answer the question of motivation, we must determine what the firm is and who (or what) makes its decisions.

Basically, the firm is a production process, absorbing inputs (the services of land, labor, and natural resources) and producing an output. It operates under a single management. In our model economy, management, whether a single individual or a collectivity, serves as the firm's decision maker. In building our model of the firm, we will assume that management operates the enterprise so that it will earn the greatest return possible. Because in economics this return is known as profit, we are claiming that the firm is operated to maximize profits; that the criterion of profitability is the firm's sole guide, its sole motivation, in framing decisions.

In a "corner grocery store" type business, the owner and the manager are the same person. The goal of maximum profits seems sensible in this case because the interests of both owner and operator are identical. In the case of the modern corporation, however, the owners and the managers are different people. The stockholders legally own the firm, but they seldom manage it. Instead managers are hired by the stockholders to run the firm so as to make the most profit for the stockholders. For example, the stockholders of General Motors hire managers to operate the company so as to maximize the firm's profits and thus the returns to the owners. Even though the decision-making function in a corporation is one step removed from the ownership, the use of hired managers as *agents* of the stockholders implies that the profit maximization model which we shall develop also applies in this case.

A. Profit

Before constructing our profit maximization model explaining how rational firms behave, let us digress a bit to understand more fully the economist's definition of the term *profit. Profit,* as the economist uses the term, is not a simple concept to comprehend. This is largely the case because its popular meaning is different from the meaning the economist finds useful. As commonly used by accountants, profit is defined as the income which a business has left after meeting its expenses and paying taxes. The economist, however, seeks a definition of profit which will help explain business behavior. This concept might have little to do with business reports or legal practices.

For both the accountant and the economist, profit is a residual. Moreover, for both, profit is the difference between the total cost and the total revenue of a firm.

$$Profit = TR - TC$$

The difference in the way the two define profit, then, stems from differences in the way total revenue and total costs are defined.

To the accountant total revenue *(TR)* is the income received from sale of the firm's product. It is calculated by multiplying the price of the product by the quantity sold.

$$TR = P \times Q$$

For example, the total revenue of the hairdresser who has given 40 haircuts at $6 per cut is $240. The economist calls this income the *explicit revenue* of the firm. In some cases, a firm might receive special allowances or might exchange its product for some other product or service. For example, a firm may provide some of its output to the local professional football team in exchange for some season passes. In such cases, the firm is not receiving an explicit revenue, but it is receiving something, the value of which could be measured in dollars. The economist refers to this kind of income as *implicit revenue*, and insists that it be counted along with explicit revenue in defining total revenue.

The economist and the accountant also differ on the definition of total cost *(TC)*. To the accountant, costs arise when the firm makes payments to individuals or other firms for labor, materials, and capital. To the economist, however, this definition is too restrictive. It includes only *explicit costs* and fails to consider *implicit costs*. The definition of the accountant considers costs to be only payments for inputs made to outside suppliers of the firm. It ignores the firm's use of valuable resources for which it does not pay. For example, the concept of costs does not include the contribution of unpaid labor typically provided the firm by an owner-manager. Thus, the economist would claim that the drugstore owner-operator who arrived at costs by toting up those payments to "outsiders" was underestimating costs. Because the economic definition seeks to measure the *value of all the resources used* in production, the value of the labor, land, or capital supplied to the firm by the druggist—the implicit costs—are included in the cost calculation.

The measurement of both implicit revenues and implicit costs is not as straightforward as measuring explicit values. The concept used by the economist for determining these implicit values is the concept of *opportunity costs*. As we have seen, the opportunity cost of choosing something is the value forgone by giving up the chance to choose its alternative. Thus, in our drugstore example, the druggist should have included in the costs the opportunity costs of his or her labor, capital, or natural resource services as determined by the amount of wages, interest, and rent that they could have earned if they had been sold to someone else. Given these distinctions, the economist states that the firm gains a profit whenever it receives a total revenue *(TR)* which exceeds the sum of its explicit and implicit costs *(TC)*.

Perhaps the following example will clarify the economist's definition of these cost, revenue, and profit concepts and their relationship to each other. Consider a two-chair hairdressers shop in which one of the hairdressers is the owner. Assume that during a week the two of them give 140 haircuts at $6 per haircut, earning a total revenue of $840. The owner of the shop has to pay the other hairdresser a salary of $250—an explicit wage cost. Because the owner gives as many haircuts as the employee, the owner of the shop charges up a cost of $250 even though it is not paid as salary. This is an implicit wage cost. Indeed $250 is as much as the owner could have earned in any other occupation and is thus the opportunity cost. The rent cost totals another $125. The depreciation on the capital equipment—hairdressers chairs, clippers, etc.—plus a competitive return on capital (also an implicit cost) totals another $80—depreciation plus interest. The total cost, then, including both explicit and implicit payments to the factors, is $705 ($250 + $250 + $125 + $80). This leaves the owner a profit—a residue—of $135.

But is profit defined in this way merely a residue, a leftover? Is it unrelated to what decisions the firm makes? If profits accrued to firms willy-nilly with no relation to their performance, profits would be of importance only as a residue or a leftover. Although it is sometimes true that profits stem from events over which the firm's decision maker has no control, this is not the way the market economy usually works. In general, profit results from change—change in consumer tastes, change in methods of production, change in the markets served or the products sold, or change in a million and one other variables. All of these affect the firm's cost and revenue situation. Over some of these changes the firm's decision maker has control, over others there is none. When management carries on routine activity it earns a wage or salary income, which is income to labor as a factor of production. When management is creative in introducing or reacting to change, when it faces risk and uncertainty in the market, it earns profit, which is a return to entrepreneurship. We will call profit, then, the *return to entrepreneurship*. Indeed, it is the firm's decision maker, displaying creativity and entrepreneurship by seeking to maximize this elusive profit in competition with others, who makes an economy dynamic and responsive.

II. RATIONAL CHOICE AND ITS DETERMINANTS

Given these definitions, let us now investigate how firms choose rationally to maximize their profits. By citing the nature of "rational choice" as the object of our analysis, we again step into the world of theory—the world of abstraction. In taking this step, we do not claim that our theory—based as it is on profit maximization—completely describes the real-world behavior of businesses. We do not claim that maximum profit exists as the sole objective of firms or, even if it did, that they would pursue this goal with perfect rationality. What we are claiming is that among the many objectives of the real-world firm, profit is the dominant goal. Thus, when the National Biscuit Company builds a new plant in the Midwest, we conclude that the action was approved primarily because the increased revenue from the plant is expected to exceed the cost of building and running it. In substantiating this claim, we need cite only the fact that firms, in making decisions, do measure, weigh, and compare alternatives in an effort to choose the "most profitable" among them. Conscious attempts to choose with this goal in mind are much in evidence.

In constructing a model of behavior of the firm, let us first treat the business sector in its role as supplier of goods and services and, then, in its role as demander of the factors of production. In considering the business sector as seller, we will assume for purposes of simplicity that *each firm produces only one homogeneous commodity*. Moreover, to simplify our analysis further, we shall assume that *each product is produced by a large number of independent firms*. By grouping together all of the firms producing a single product, we have an industry. Because each industry comprises a large number of independent single–product firms, the structure of each industry is *competitive*.

To break into this sector, let us pick at random a single industry, producing a single homogeneous product, say product x. Then let us pick at random a single firm in this industry. By prying into the workings of this firm, let us attempt to evolve some basic principles of rational decision making. These principles will deal with the firm's decisions in producing and supplying its product to the market.

The primary question which we ask this firm's entrepreneur is: *Given your goal of maximum profits, how do you determine how much output to supply in any period of time?* Clearly, the list of factors considered by the entrepreneur is long. We can, however, identify the most important ones. Because we have defined maximum profits to be the sole goal of the firm, the factors that are able to modify its profit position clearly affect the firm's behavior. Moreover, because profit equals total revenue minus total cost, the factors that affect either total cost or total revenue also affect profit. Let us attempt to isolate the primary factors which influence the level of total cost and total revenue.

A. Product Price

First, the price of the firm's product (P_x) will have a strong, perhaps dominant, influence on the amount of the product (x) which the firm will produce and supply to the market. This relationship between price and quantity supplied holds because the price directly affects total revenue *(TR)* which, in turn, directly influences profits. *The price of the product times the quantity sold equals the firm's total revenue;* and total revenue, together with total cost, determines profitability. In addition to this theoretical linkage between price and profitability, there is substantial real-world evidence of the existence of the relationship of product price to the firm's profits. The briefest encounter with business leaders convinces us of their ultimate concern with the price of their product. When the president of the United States questioned the advisability of an increase in the price of steel on a notable occasion in the 1960s, the ire of the entire industry fell on his shoulders. The battle over aluminum prices and the price of structural steel in more recent years has brought on much the same reaction.

Because we are primarily concerned here with how prices are set in an enterprise economy, we will center our anlaysis on this determinant of the economic behavior of the firm.

B. Input-Output Relationship

The second determinant of the quantity of output supplied by a firm is somewhat trickier to grasp. We have argued that the firm maximizes the difference between its total revenue and total costs—the firm's profit. Ignoring the prices of both inputs and outputs of the firm, the greater the output obtained from a given amount of factor inputs, the greater will be the firm's profits. Likewise, the smaller the amount of inputs required to produce a given output, the greater will be the firm's profits. Thus, the technological relationship between the quantity of inputs and the output—the input-output relationship $(I\text{-}O)$—will affect the profitability of the firm. Like the price of the product (P_x), the input-output relationship $(I\text{-}O)$ will have an important impact on the firm's economic behavior. Put simply, because the input-output relationship determines the profits of a firm by affecting its total revenue relative to total costs (or vice versa), this technological relationship influences how much of its product a firm will choose to sell. If, for example, a new production technique permits a farmer to increase his yield of wheat by 10 bushels per acre, the quantity of wheat he will supply to the market will clearly increase.

C. Factor Prices

The final factor which determines how much of its output the firm will supply follows almost directly on the heels of the two already mentioned. Both the price attached to the output (P_x) and the prices attached to the factor inputs (P_F)—the wage rate, the interest rate, and the rent—are needed to transform the relationship of inputs and outputs into the relationship of total cost and total revenue. In the same way as the price of the product (P_x) transforms physical output into total revenue *(TR)*, the prices of the inputs transform physical factor inputs into total costs *(TC)*. Hence, just as the price of the firm's product (P_x) and the input-output relationship $(I\text{-}O)$ serve as determinants of its economic behavior, so do the prices of the inputs (P_F). Because factor prices directly affect the firm's costs and therefore its profits, they also form an important determinant of the quantity of output which the firm will produce and supply to the market.

III.   THE SUPPLY FUNCTION FOR A SINGLE FIRM

We have seen that there is a functional relationship between the quantity of x supplied (S_x) and the determinants of this quantity— the price of x (P_x), the input-output relationship $(I\text{-}O)$ and the prices of the factors (P_F). This relationship may be written

$$S_x = f(P_x, \text{I-O}, P_F)$$

In this functional relationship S_x is the dependent variable and P_x, $I\text{-}O$, and P_F are the independent variables. From this general function we will isolate and investigate in great detail the relationship between the price of the good (P_x) and the quantity of output a firm desires to supply (S_x). By holding the other independent variables constant, we can write this relationship as

$$S_x = f(P_x) \text{ ceteris paribus}$$

With this general function as a basis for our model of the firm, let us analyze each of the independent variables asking how changes in them influence the willingness of the firm to supply its product. We will then be able to explain the behavior of the firm in supplying its product to the market. First, we will discuss the input–output relationship $(I\text{-}O)$ and then the prices of the factors (P_F) and the price of the product (P_x).

QUESTIONS

1. Consider a small business owned and operated by Ms. A, who is a horse fancier. In her business Ms. A breeds horses and races them. In fact, she has a stable of over 20 horses. Ms. A oversees the business, serving as manager, accountant, veterinarian, breeder, trainer, horse trailer puller, and general manager. Ms. A is a trained accountant who could earn $20,000 per year in that activity if she devoted full time to it. Having obtained her veterinarian degree, she could also set up a full-time practice and earn about $30,000 per year. Rather than pursue either of these occupations, she prefers her present business. Her husband also spends all of his time working at the stables. In addition, Ms. A has two hired hands who assist her in the operation. The income to Ms. A's business derives from the success of her horses on the race track and the winning purses which they bring home. The costs of the business are, among other things, the wages paid to the hired hands, the feed costs, the rent paid on the stable, and so on. The 1979 income statement for Ms. A's business is shown in the following table.

Income Statement—Ms. A's Stables

Horse Race Winnings (*Income*)		$120,000
Outlays		
Depreciation expense	$12,000	
Wages paid to two hired hands	30,000	
Stable and track rent	5,000	
Transportation costs	16,000	
Feed costs	10,000	
Equipment costs	5,000	
Medicine and veterinarian supplies	8,000	
Miscellaneous expenses	10,000	
Total		96,000
Profits		$ 24,000

(a) The accounting statement shows that, in an accounting sense, Ms. A's stables have been a profitable venture—after expenses were subtracted from income, there was $24,000 left over. Do you think that the income statement gives an accurate picture of how profitable—in an economic sense—Ms. A's stables were? Why or why not?

(b) If you answered No to the above question, you probably think that there are some items which should be added to the cost concept to give a better estimate of economic profit. From the description of the inputs to Ms. A's business, what items would you add? How would you find values for these items so that you could include them in the *economic* accounting statement? How would you define the concept which would give you a basis for valuing these cost items?

(c) In the text, the discrepancy between accounting profits and real economic profits is, in part, attributed to implicit costs which the accountant does not place in the income statement. The discrepancy may also be due to implicit revenue or income. In the case of Ms. A's stables, can you imagine any implicit revenues or incomes which should be taken into account in calculating the economic profit of the enterprise? How would you define these items? How would you value them? Is there any principle which would guide you in valuing them?

(d) Ms. A often tells the story of how some of her friends were kidding her about running the stable. They said, "Ms. A, running the stable is child's play for you. Why, you get as much satisfaction out of running that stable as we do out of playing bridge." "I admitted it," said Ms. A. "I told them that I get as much fun out of running that stable each year as I would get out of having a no-strings attached bundle of $50,000 to spend as I please." Does this give you any assistance in answering question (c)? How?

(e) On the basis of the information given in the description of Ms. A's business and in question (d), do you think that Ms. A's stables are yielding an *economic profit*? Defend your answer.

(f) In the text, the determinants of a firm's supply were discussed. How would you define the output of Ms. A's stables? How would you measure the supply of output? Discuss the meaning of the input-output relationship in the case of Ms. A's stables. Make a list of the prices of the inputs and outputs which would influence the willingness of Ms. A to supply output. Describe some technological change which might alter the input-output relationship of Ms. A's stables.

2. Costs, we have stated, refer to the value of opportunities which have been forgone. For each of the following decisions which a firm might make, describe the possible nature of the "costs" involved and discuss how you would value each cost.

(a) The decision of a grocery store owner to fire a stock clerk.

(b) The decision of a grocery store owner *not* to advertise this week in a local newspaper.

(c) The decision of a grocery store owner to advertise this week in a local newspaper.

(d) The decision of a grocery store owner to renovate the interior of the store.

IV. THE INPUT-OUTPUT RELATIONSHIP OF THE FIRM

The second important determinant of the output or supply of a firm is the relationship between the quantity of inputs and the quantity of output. It should be emphasized that this relationship between inputs and outputs ties together physical units. So many units of labor plus so many units of capital produces so many units of output. It follows, then, that this input-output relationship is a *technological* relationship and not an economic relationship.

How does this relationship fit into the decision-making framework of the firm? Consider a simple model of a firm that produces one kind of output, x. Assume that this firm produces its product by using two kinds of inputs, *l* and *c* (standing for labor and capital). Figure 4-1 presents a simplified picture of the *firm* and its "fit" into the circular economic process. The firm buys factor services (inputs) from the household sector and, after transforming them into product, sells its output to the household sector. This input-output relationship is often referred to as the *production function* of the firm. It can be written as

$$x = f(l,c)$$

which is read: output is a function of (depends upon) the inputs, labor and capital.

In analyzing the relationship between inputs and output, we will concentrate on a period of time that economists call the *short run*. This is a period which is insufficient for the firm to vary all of its inputs. Stated another way, we will assume that the input-output relationship refers to a period of time in which at least one input must remain fixed or constant in amount. In our model, we will assume that the firm can vary the amount of input *l*, while the amount of input *c* remains fixed. This assumption is a reasonable

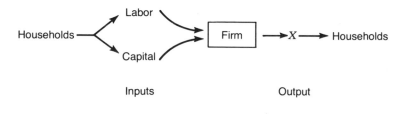

Figure 4-1

one. Indeed, real-world firms produce under just such conditions. Within short periods of time (say, up to a year), firms are forced to produce with physical facilities, plants, and equipment that are fixed in amount. It is only in the long run that such inputs to the production process can be varied.

If, for example, the demand for steel should fall by 50 percent next month, the U.S. Steel Corporation could not and would not dispose of some of its furnaces, mills, or other capital facilities. The same situation occurs in a small business like a barber shop. It too has inputs which are fixed in the short run. If business were to increase by a third next month, the owner of the shop could not immediately add to his building in order to create room for an additional chair.

On the basis of this assumption, two important propositions hold true. First, even if the firm were to produce zero units of output (x), the input of capital would remain unchanged and would be greater than zero. That is, the firm's plant and equipment would stay in place and not be affected. Second, this assumption means that increases in the output of x result only from the application of additional amounts of the variable input, labor. Let us, then, investigate this relationship between the quantity of inputs—one variable (l) and one fixed (c)—and the quantity of output (x).

A. The Total Product Curve

The uniquely shaped curve in Figure 4-2 displays this input-output relationship for our model firm. It is called a *total product curve* and

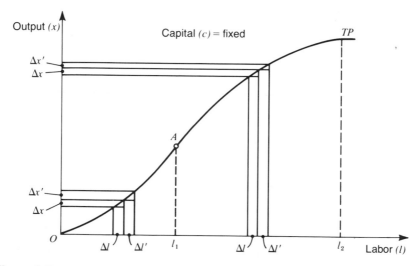

Figure 4-2

is basic in understanding the economic behavior of a firm. The total product curve relates the total output produced (x) to the quantity of inputs entering into production—input l being variable and input c fixed.

From the total product curve of Figure 4-2, it is clear that some amount of both labor (l) and capital (c) is necessary for production to take place at all. There would be no haircuts given in a shop having no barber but only barber chairs. This property appears in the diagram at the origin; with a zero amount of labor input, even though capital is on hand, nothing is produced. The amount of capital used, it should be noted, is specified in the diagram.

A secondary property of the input-output relationship is also seen in Figure 4-2. From the total product curve, it is clear that the more labor that is employed, the higher will be the total output of x. Note that the total product curve slopes upward and to the right throughout. It should, perhaps, be added that at some point additions of input l will lead to decreases in output, rather than increases. When this occurs, the curve will turn down. However, because this phenomenon will not influence the remainder of our analysis, we will ignore it here.

Finally, the curve as drawn possesses a peculiar _____ shape. For any amount of labor input from O to l_1, each additional unit of labor (Δl) yields an increase in output (Δx) *greater* than the increase generated by the preceding unit of labor; for any amount of labor from l_1 to l_2, each additional unit of labor (Δl) yields an increase in output (Δx) *smaller* than the increase induced by the preceding unit.

Each of these three properties of the input-output relationship forms an essential element in our analysis of the behavior of the firm. Consequently, we would do well to pause briefly to gain a clearer understanding of them. The first two are intuitively obvious. Taken together, they claim that (1) the input-output relationship—the total product curve—begins at the origin and (2) it slopes upward and to the right. The third property is substantially more difficult to understand. More importantly, it rests on a basic economic law whose meaning we must comprehend. This law determines the peculiar _____ shape of the total product curve. It is known by economists as the *Law of Diminishing Marginal Returns*.

B. The Law of Diminishing Marginal Returns

First hinted at by Thomas R. Malthus in his *Essay on Population* in 1798, this law was formulated by other famous economists, among them David Ricardo (1817), Nassau Senior (1836), and Alfred Marshall (1890). None other than John Stuart Mill pronounced it to be "the most important proposition in political economy." Marshall went so far as to claim it as "the cause of Abraham's parting from Lot," citing Genesis 13:6, which reads, "The land was not able to bear them, that they might dwell together." In verbiage characteristic of his era and profession, Senior stated the law as follows:

> *Additional labor employed on the land within a given district produces in general a less proportionate return, or in other words, that though, with every increase in labor bestowed, the aggregate return is increased, the increase of the return is not in proportion to the increase of the labor.*

Senior was referring to a situation similar to ours—a situation in which additional units of a variable input (labor) are added to a fixed input (land). The law which he presented described an inexorable and unavoidable relationship between inputs (one of which is fixed) and output. Although Senior made his point, perhaps we can restate the law somewhat more precisely. *If equal additional increments of a variable input, say, labor, are added to a fixed input, say, capital, the resulting additional increments to output (Δx) will, after some point, decrease.*

In Figure 4-2, this point is shown as A. This proposition is true even though the additional units of the variable input generate *increasing* additional increments to output before A is reached.

For a better grasp of the meaning of this law, consider the following example. A small shoe manufacturing business possesses a plant, an appropriate set of shoe-making equipment, and a stock of leather and other materials. The plant, equipment, and material form the fixed input necessary for production to occur. However, with this fixed input alone, there will be no production: shoes will not be produced if no one runs the machines. Labor must be added if there is to be output. Labor becomes both the variable input and the input essential for production. Recall characteristics 1 and 2 of the total product curve on p. 94.

Let us now assume that the business executive begins adding equal additional units of labor to the fixed input, and observes the rate of output after each addition. The result is recorded in Table 4-1 and pictured in Figure 4-3. In Figure 4-3, the shaded rectangles represent the marginal or additional output.

As Table 4-1 shows, nothing is produced with zero units of variable input. Total output is zero. However, if one unit of labor is added to the fixed factor, 20 pairs of shoes are turned out. The addition to output (Δx) or the marginal return is 20 pairs of shoes. With two units of labor, the total output rises to 50. Total output is

Table 4-1

PLANT, EQUIPMENT AND MATERIALS	UNITS OF LABOR	TOTAL OUTPUT	MARGINAL OUTPUT
Fixed	0	0	20
Fixed	1	20	30
Fixed	2	50	15
Fixed	3	65	13
Fixed	4	78	10
Fixed	5	88	7
Fixed	6	95	5
Fixed	7	100	

increased by 30 pairs of shoes owing to the additional unit of variable input. This represents an increased marginal return; one man no longer has to run *all* of the machines. However, as still more units of the variable input are added to the fixed input, the additional, or marginal, increments to output begin to decrease—from 30 to 15 to 13 to 10, and so on. Indeed, if enough laborers become added to the fixed plant, the marginal returns would not only diminish but would even become negative. After some point, additional laborers would simply find themselves in one another's way.

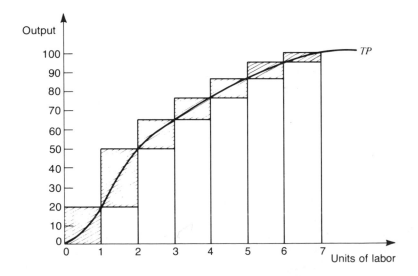

Figure 4-3

This example, then, illustrates the Law of Diminishing Marginal Returns. As equal additional increments of a variable factor are added to a fixed factor, a point is reached where the *additions* to output decrease. As with the law of gravity, there are many who would defy the law but none who have succeeded. Indeed, if the law could be defied, enough wheat to feed the world could be grown in a football stadium, simply by adding labor, seed, and fertilizer.

V. THE PRICES OF INPUTS AND THE COST OF OUTPUT

As we have seen, the firm's total cost of production results from multiplying the quantity of factor inputs by their prices (P_F). Total cost, together with total revenue, determines profit. Because profit is the firm's primary motivation, the total cost of production is an important variable in analyzing the firm's behavior.

A. The Total Cost Curve

In deriving this total cost concept, let us begin by attaching prices to both the variable input (l) and the fixed input (c). In so doing we derive a relationship called the *total cost curve*. The total cost curve is the relationship between the output of a firm and the total cost of producing that output. In drawing the curve, we place output on one axis of the graph and the costs of production on the other. Because costs are simply physical inputs measured in dollar terms, the shape of the total cost curve will be similar to the shape of the total product curve. To clarify the relationship between these two curves, we will redraw the total product curve in a slightly different way. From this, we will construct the total cost curve.

Figure 4-4 is the redrawn version of the total product curve. It will be noticed that although the relation of inputs to output in Figure 4-4 is identical to the one in Figure 4-2, we have reversed the axes on the diagram. Now, instead of having output (x) on the vertical axis and labor input (l) on the horizontal axis, we have plotted output (x) horizontally and labor input (l) vertically.

As we have seen, the total product curve combines information about two kinds of physical inputs—fixed (c) and variable (l)—and relates this information to the physical volume of the resulting output. By extending the distinction between fixed and variable inputs, we can distinguish two kinds of costs to the firm. We will call these fixed and variable costs.

Fixed costs are those expenses borne by the firm to pay for fixed inputs (c). These costs include depreciation expense on plant and

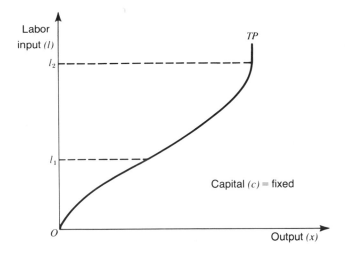

Figure 4-4

equipment, interest payments, rental payments on the land used, and taxes. A prime characteristic of fixed costs is that they do not change when output changes. They neither rise when output rises nor fall when output falls: they are fixed. Even if output should fall to zero, the firm would, in the short run, incur these costs. Total fixed cost *(TFC)* can be thought of as the sum of the products of the fixed inputs and their prices. That is,

$$TFC = P_{c_1}c_1 + P_{c_2}c_2 + \ldots + P_{cn}\,c_n$$

Since our model contains only one fixed input, capital fixed cost is equal to the product of the number of units of capital and the price per unit. If both the price of the fixed inputs and its quantity are fixed regardless of the level of output, total fixed costs always remains constant. The total fixed cost curve, therefore, appears as a straight, horizontal line in Figure 4-5.

To derive the curve, which describes *variable cost,* we proceed in much the same manner. In the case of fixed costs, we have seen that neither the quantity nor the price of the input changes as output changes. This is not so with variable costs. As the total product curve in Figures 4-2 and 4-4 shows, the quantity of the variable input is directly related to the output. As one increases, so does the other. Only the price of the input remains constant. The variability in quantity, however, is not a substantial complication because the total product curve defines precisely how output and variable input

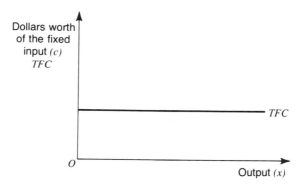

Figure 4-5

relate to each other. By measuring the amount of the variable input (l) in value terms instead of in terms of physical units, the total product curve is transformed into a total *variable* cost curve. This is accomplished by changing the vertical axis of Figure 4-4 from physical units of labor to dollars worth of labor. Figure 4-6 pictures this change.

The total variable cost curve has the same shape as the total product curve pictured in Figure 4-4. At first, total variable costs increase slowly as output increases. Then, after the production of *OA* units of output, the Law of Diminishing Marginal Returns begins to apply. Costs now increase much more rapidly as output increases. Whereas the Law of Diminishing Marginal Returns causes *diminishing* increments to output after some level of input (observed in the total product curve), it causes *increasing* incre-

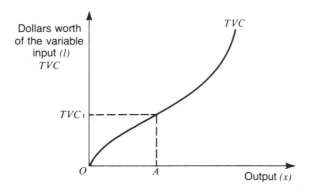

Figure 4-6

ments in cost after some level of output (observed in the total variable cost curve). This follows logically. In the one case we add labor unit by unit and find that increments to ouput diminish. In the other case we add output unit by unit and find that increasing amounts of labor are required for each additional unit of output. Costs are increasing. Decreasing returns transformed into value terms imply increasing costs.

In Figures 4-5 and 4-6, we see the two kinds of cost-output relationships which confront the firm—the total fixed cost curve and the total variable cost curve. By combining these curves, we derive a still more important cost-output relationship—one between the firm's total cost and its output. To derive this relationship, let us ask: What is the total cost required to produce each of all possible outputs; that is, what is the relationship between total cost and output?

The answer is easily obtained. The total cost of producing any level of output (TC) is equal to the sum of the total variable costs at that output (TVC) and the total fixed cost (TFC). This may be written as

$$TC = TVC + TFC$$

Figure 4-7 reproduces the total fixed cost relationship of Figure 4-5 and the total variable cost relationship of Figure 4-6—the two dotted lines. Following the definition of total cost, we add these two curves *at each output* to form the total cost curve. This is shown as the heavy curve in Figure 4-7. As can be seen, the *vertical* distance between TC and TVC is a constant amount equal to TFC. To see how variable and fixed costs are added to obtain total costs, consider the costs of producing output x_4. At output x_4, distance ab represents TFC and the vertical distance ac represents TVC; added together they equal the vertical distance ad which represents TC at output x_4.

The total cost curve is of great importance in analyzing the behavior of the firm. It will be recalled that the total cost of production is one of the two determinants of the volume of profits, the primary motivation of the firm. By combining the input-output relationship $(I\text{-}O)$ with the prices of the inputs $(P_l$ and $P_c)$, then, we have obtained one of the two primary determinants of the willingness of a firm to supply its product to the market. However, before introducing the price of the output (P_x) and hence total revenue, which is the other determinant of firm behavior, let us place the cost concept in a form which will be more helpful to our analysis.

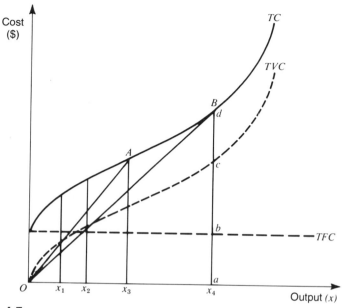

Figure 4-7

B. Marginal and Average Cost

Marginal and average costs are derived directly from the total cost concept. In order to derive these concepts graphically, we must fully understand both their meaning and their relationship to the total cost concept. First, we will define them. Then, we will illustrate the definitions by means of an arithmetic example. Finally, we will derive average and marginal cost curves from the total curve.

How do we define average cost and marginal cost? First let us take *average cost*, which is the firm's per unit cost of producing the output. If, for example, a firm were to produce 100 units of output at a total cost of $200, the average cost—the cost per unit—would be $2. In our previous example, when the hairdresser gave 140 haircuts and incurred a total explicit and implicit cost of $705, the cost per haircut—the average cost—was about $5.36; that is $705 divided by 140 haircuts. In symbols, the average cost is the ratio of total cost (*TC*) to level of output (*x*):

$$AC = TC/x$$

With this definition, average cost can be computed if the total cost of producing any given output level is known.

Marginal cost is a basically different, and ultimately more important, concept. Rather than referring to costs at a particular level of output—as in the case of average cost—marginal cost deals with the relationship of the *change* in total cost to the *change* in output. Whereas the average cost concept answers the question: "What is the cost per unit of producing x units?" the marginal cost concept answers the question: "Given that we are producing so many units of output (x), what is the *additional* cost of producing an *additional* unit?" Indeed, just as the marginal product referred to changes in the amount of output relative to changes in the amount of input, the marginal cost concept refers to changes in total cost relative to changes in output. If the total cost to the hairdresser of producing 140 haircuts is $705 and the total cost of producing 141 haircuts is $710.89, the marginal cost of producing the last haircut is $5.89. Marginal cost then, is the additional cost incurred by increasing output one unit:

$$MC = \Delta TC/\Delta x$$

In the hairdresser example,

$$MC = (\$710.89 - \$705)/(141 - 140) = (\$5.89/1) = \$5.89$$

Both the marginal cost and average cost concepts are closely related to the total cost curve of Figure 4-7. By selecting any output level, say x_4, average cost can be computed by dividing total cost *(ad)* by the number of units of output *(Ox_4)*. Marginal cost is obtained by observing movements along the curve. By definition, marginal cost equals the *slope* of the total cost curve in the output range under consideration. As we have seen, the slope of a curve is the change in the magnitude plotted on the vertical axis divided by the change in the magnitude plotted on the horizontal axis—$\Delta y/\Delta x$. Because total cost is plotted on the Y axis and output (or units of x) is plotted on the X axis of Figure 4-7, the slope of that curve is $\Delta TC/\Delta x$, which is precisely the definition of marginal cost.

C. The Marginal-Average Relationship

Although the average and marginal cost concepts relate to different characteristics of the total cost curve, they are not unrelated to each other. Indeed, the relationship between them is intimate and fixed. This relationship is described as follows: Whenever the marginal value lies *above* the average value, the average is *rising*; whenever the marginal value lies *below* the average value, the average is *falling*. Thus, the marginal concept can be thought of as pulling the average along with it. If it is above the average, it pulls the average up; if it is below the average, it pulls the average down. This relationship can be seen clearly by considering the season record of a basketball player, shown in Table 4-2.

The source of all of the numbers in the table is clear and the format is a familiar one. Indeed, if the first two columns of Table 4-2 were changed to "course hours" and "total grade points," the table is precisely the kind needed to compute your cumulative college grade-point average. In this analysis, we are interested in the relationship between columns 4 and 5—marginal points and average points. Both of these columns are derived from the total season point concept in column 3.

From columns 1 and 2, we see that the basketball player started the season with a great first game—22 points. However, in succeeding games, his performance failed to live up to this first game's record. In the second game he scored 20 points, in the third he scored 15 points, and in the fourth he was held to 3 points. This deteriorating performance is reflected in his average point record, which decreased from 22 at the end of the first game to 15 at the end of the fourth game. Indeed, not until the end of the season was he able to reverse the downward trend in his average.

It was clearly his game-by-game performance which caused this movement in the player's average point record. More precisely, his average point record was determined by the number of points he added to his season total in each additional game—his marginal point record. Whenever the additional or marginal points scored in a game were the same as his previous average, the average remained constant (game 5). Whenever the marginal points scored in a game exceeded his previous point record, the average rose (games 6 and 7).

Table 4-2

GAMES (1)	POINTS (2)	TOTAL SEASON POINTS (3)	MARGINAL POINTS (4)	AVERAGE POINTS PER GAME COLUMN 3 ÷ COLUMN 1 (5)
0	0	0		0
1	22	22	22	22
2	20	42	20	21
3	15	57	15	19
4	3	60	3	15
5	15	75	15	15
6	21	96	21	16
7	23	119	23	17

With this understanding of the "marginal" and "average" concepts, how can they be related to the total cost curve pictured in Figure 4-7? As was mentioned earlier, the marginal cost concept is represented in Figure 4-7 by the *slope* of the total cost curve. As we can see by looking at the curve, the slope—marginal cost—first falls as output rises. However, after a certain point, as output continues to rise, the slope reverses its course and begins to rise. The point at which the slope changes from "decreasing" to "increasing" is called the *inflection point* and is represented by A in Figure 4-7. Stated alternatively, the slope of the total cost curve switches from decreasing to increasing as output increases beyond x_3.

The marginal cost relationship is shown in Figure 4-8 as curve MC. It has been derived from the total cost curve of Figure 4-7. That diagram shows marginal cost decreasing up to output x_3, where it reaches its minimum point. Beyond x_3 it increases.

Derivation of the average cost curve from the total cost curve is not as easily accomplished. However, by introducing a crutch, this relationship can also be obtained. As we have seen, average cost is found at any level of output by dividing the total cost by the quantity of output. $AC = TC/x$. Therefore, in Figure 4-7, the average cost as output x_3 is equal to the distance x_3A (total cost) divided by OX_3 (the output of x). This ratio, it is important to note, is equal to the *slope* of the straight line OA which connects the origin (O) with point A. The average cost at any output level is derived by drawing a line from the level of total cost at that output to the origin and then

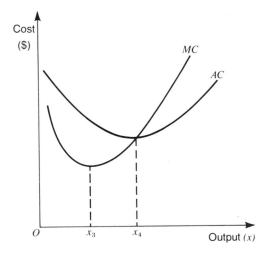

Figure 4-8

measuring the line's slope. Following this process for successive amounts of total cost, we can obtain the average cost curve.

From inspecting the diagram it is clear that the straight line from the origin to the curve is very steep at low levels of output; average cost is high. As output increases, the slope of the line (and average cost) falls until a minimum is reached. Then average cost rises again. Clearly, the output at which the slope of the straight line from the origin is least steep represents minimum average cost. In Figure 4-7, this occurs at output level x_4. At this output level the straight line from the origin (in this case OB) is as flat as is possible. At x_4, both the slope of the straight line and average cost are at a minimum.

By combining this information with our understanding of the relationship between marginal and average concepts, the average cost curve can be drawn (Figure 4-8). Thus (1) at output x_4, AC is a minimum and (2) whenever the MC lies below AC, AC is falling; whenever MC lies above AC, AC is rising; whenever $MC = AC$, AC is constant or horizontal. The marginal cost curve, therefore, intersects the average cost curve at its minimum point.

This last characteristic follows logically. At point B in Figure 4-7, it will be noticed that the slope of the total cost curve (marginal cost) is equal to the slope of the straight line from the origin to that point (average cost). This is so because the straight line is tangent to the total cost curve at point B.

D. The Nature of Average Costs

Before proceeding to develop the model of firm behavior, let us look somewhat closer at the shape of the average cost curve. Must average cost curves always be U-shaped and, if so, why? In the short run, as long as some inputs (and therefore costs) are fixed, the relationship between average cost and output will be U-shaped. There are two reasons for this.

First, the downward portion of the curve occurs because of the influence of *fixed costs*. As Figure 4-7 demonstrated, total cost is the sum of the total fixed costs and the total variable costs. By definition, total fixed costs are constant even though the firm's level of output changes. It follows from this fact that the share of the fixed costs borne by each unit of output (average fixed costs) becomes smaller as the output of the firm increases. For example, if the fixed costs of a hairdresser are, say, $125, the *average fixed cost* is $5, if the shop turns out only 25 haircuts. Average fixed costs, however, decrease to $1.25 if the shop turns out 100 haircuts. As output increases, the fixed costs are spread over an increasing number of units of output, thereby decreasing the fixed cost absorbed by each unit. Decreasing average fixed costs tend to pull down average total cost as output increases. Falling average fixed costs, therefore, contribute to the downward sloping portion of the average cost curve.

A second factor explains the upward portion of the average cost curve. This factor is one already encountered: the Law of Diminishing Marginal Returns. As will be recalled, this law states that, if there is a fixed input, additional equal increments of a variable input will yield decreasing additional increments of output beyond some level of production. The law may be restated to say that if there is a fixed input, additional equal increments of output will require increments of a variable input of successively larger amounts. By measuring the inputs in dollars so that we can speak of costs, it is clear that when more units of a variable input are required to produce one more unit of output, variable costs per unit of output will rise. Eventually, rising variable costs per unit of output will more than offset falling fixed costs per unit of output. At that point the cost of another unit of output—marginal cost—will rise. We know that increasing marginal costs will pull average costs up as well.

For these two reasons, the average cost curve is, as we have drawn it, U-shaped. It slopes downward because of the existence of fixed costs and slopes upward because of the effect of the Law of Diminishing Marginal Returns.

With this derivation of the marginal and average cost curves, the second determinant of supply—the prices of the factor inputs (P_F)—has been incorporated into our model. What remains is to introduce the final determinant, the price of the output (P_x).

VI. $S_x = f(P_x)$ CETERIS PARIBUS—THE PRICE OF THE OUTPUT AND THE SUPPLY CURVE OF THE FIRM

Given the average and marginal cost curves, it is relatively easy to determine the quantity of product that the firm wishes to supply (S_x). It has been accepted that the force motivating firm behavior is the desire to maximize profits—the difference betweeen total cost (as the economist defines it) and total revenue. Consequently, in deciding how much of his product to supply to the market, the rational businessman will choose that output which yields him the greatest profit.

Figure 4-9 reproduces the average and marginal cost relationships derived in Figure 4-8. Before introducing the price of the product

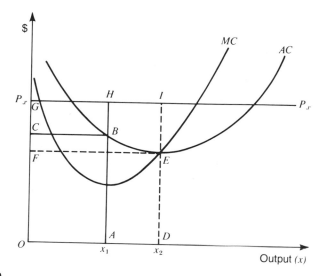

Figure 4-9

into our model, we should notice that the *total* cost of producing any output can be represented on this diagram. At any output, total cost is equal to the average cost *(AC)* times the level of output *(x)*.

$$TC = AC \times x$$

In Figure 4-9, the total cost of producing x_1 units is represented by the rectangle *OABC*—the average cost of producing x_1 units *(AB)* times the number of units produced *(OA)*. Similarly, for output x_2 the total cost is represented by the rectangle *ODEF*—the average cost *(DE)* times the number of units *(OD)*.

Total revenue can be represented in much the same manner, and here the price of the product (P_x) enters the analysis. The total revenue of a firm is found by multiplying its output (x) by the price of the output (P_x).

$$TR = P_x \times x$$

Referring to Figure 4-9, if the price of a firm's product equals *OG* and if the firm sells x_1 units *(OA)*, the total sales revenue will be *OG* × *OA* or the area of the rectangle *OAHG*.

If total cost and total revenue can be determined graphically, so too can the size of the firm's profit. Because profit is defined as total revenue minus total cost (profit = *TR* − *TC*), the profit accruing to the firm from producing x_1 units is equal to the rectangle *CBHG*.

This is the amount by which total revenue (*OAHG*) exceeds total cost (*OABC*). By the same reasoning, if the price remains at *OG* but x_2 units of output are produced and sold, the profit retained by the firm is *FEIG*. This is equal to total revenue *(ODIG)* minus total cost *(ODEF)*. Clearly, if these two outputs—x_1 and x_2—were the only alternatives open to the firm, it would, without question, choose output x_2. Total profit at x_2 exceeds total profit at output x_1 (*FEIG* > *CBHG*).

Now the crucial question can be put: How much output will the firm produce and supply at all possible prices? Stated another way, given the input-output relationship *(I−O)* and the prices of the factors of production *(P_F)*, what is the relationship between the price of the firm's output *(P_x)* and the quantity it will decide to supply *(S_x)*?

To help in answering this question, the firm's cost curves are again reproduced in Figure 4-10. It should once more be emphasized that these average and marginal cost curves embody the input-output relationship *(I−O)* and the prices of the inputs *(P_f)*. Let us assume that the market price confronting the firm is, say, P_x. This price is also shown in Figure 4-10. At that price, the firm can sell as much of its output as it desires. The question then is: How much output will the firm decide to produce if it can sell any quantity at price P_x? Immediately, we can exclude some outputs from consideration. For example, any level of output which is either less than x_1 or greater than x_5 leads to a total cost for the firm which exceeds the

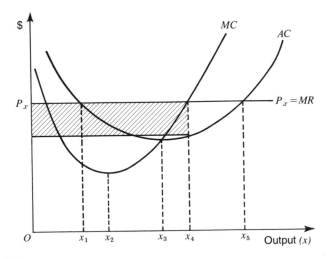

Figure 4-10

total revenue, and can therefore be excluded. This is seen by comparing the cost per unit (average cost) and the revenue per unit (price) for any output level above x_5 or below x_1. For each and every output level in these ranges, cost per unit exceeds revenue per unit. This means a negative profit, an inability to cover costs, a loss.

On the other hand any output between x_1 and x_5 appears to be fair game. For any output in this range, total revenue exceeds total cost and the firm receives a profit. However, some outputs are clearly superior to others. Which output between x_1 and x_5, then, is optimum; which output level will lead to maximum profit?

As will be recalled, the marginal cost *(MC)* curve is a curve which relates "the cost of producing one more unit" to the level of output. For example, at output x_1 the cost of producing the next unit is seen to be less than the cost of producing the previous unit—the *MC* curve is decreasing. Similarly, the curve representing the going market price can be called the *marginal revenue (MR) curve*. If each unit is sold at price P_x, the revenue obtained from selling one more unit—the marginal revenue—is P_x. With the two concepts of marginal revenue and marginal cost in mind, we can determine the optimum output.

Let us experiment. The firm's entrepreneur is asked: "If you are producing and selling x_1 units, would it be worth your while to produce and sell one more unit of output?" After checking the cost and revenue situation, the manager answers, "Yes." His reasoning is not hard to follow. It is based on the *marginal principle,* a basic concept in economics. Because $MR > MC$ at ouput x_1, the firm will add more to its total revenue than it will add to its total cost by producing one more unit. And, if total revenue rises more than total cost, the profit of the firm grows. A rational firm would produce the additional unit. "If you were producing x_2 units," the manager is asked, "would it again be worth your while to produce and sell one more unit?" He again checks his cost and revenue situation and again, proceeding on the marginal principle, answers affirmatively. Again $MR > MC$. Indeed, the manager will answer "Yes" to the question at any output lower than x_4, for in each case $MR > MC$. Beyond output x_4, however, the situation changes. For any output greater than x_4, the next unit of output will cost more to produce than the additional revenue it will bring in—$MC > MR$. Thus, profits will fall if an additional unit is produced. Consequently, at any output beyond x_4, a rational firm would *not* produce any additional units. In fact, if the firm is producing at a rate greater than x_4, it would pay the firm to cut production back toward X_4.

The principles of firm behavior thus become clear. At any output level at which $MR > MC$, it would be in the firm's interest to increase its output. At any output level at which $MR < MC$, it would be in the firm's interest to reduce output. At output x_4, there is no motivation to change. The *optimum level of output* for the firm is the unique output at which $MC = MR$. At that level of output the profits of the firm are maximized.

Note that the profit-maximizing output for the firm is *not* where average cost is the lowest and profit per unit of output is maximized, that is, at x_3. The firm is interested im maximum *total* profits and not maximum profit per unit. Maximum total profit occurs only at x_4—where $MC = MR$.

The application of this marginal principle to the firm with the cost curves of Figure 4-10 is a simple matter. Given the going price, P_x, the quantity that the firm will supply is x_4. At that output, $MC = MR$ and the profits of the firm are maximized. At any output level below x_4, the firm has incentive to increase its output; at any output level above x_4, it has incentive to decrease it. In Figure 4-10, the shaded rectangle describes the profits which the firm receives by producing and selling x_4 units. It is the maximum-sized profit rectangle which it is possible to drawn in the diagram given the price of x (P_x). The equation $MC = MR$ is consequently the *equilibrium condition* which rational firms seek. $MC = MR$ *is the most basic maximizing condition in all of economics.* And, because in perfect competition the price of the output P_x is equal to marginal revenue MR, we can write this equilibrium: $P_x = MC$.

A. The Firm Supply Curve

In the analysis of the preceding section, the equilibrium quantity supplied at a particular price of x was derived. This same analysis can now be extended, with little trouble, to other prices of x. Because the horizontal line drawn at the price of the output, P_x, is the marginal revenue curve at that price and because the firm, as a rational profit maximizer, will choose to produce where $MC = MR$, the equilibrium output of the firm will depend on the marginal cost (MC) curve. This is easily verified by drawing a horizontal line at several different possible prices in Fugre 4-10. In each case the point ay which $MC = MR$ lies on the MC curve. In effect, *the marginal cost curve becomes the supply curve of the firm.* Thus, in Figure 4-11, at a price of P_x', The firm will supply x_1; at a price of P_x', the firm will supply x_1; at a price of P_x'', the firm will supply x_2 and so on.

The supply curve of the firm can be given a somewhat more precise definition—one which excludes some parts of the marginal

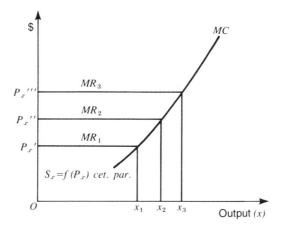

Figure 4-11

cost curve from serving as part of the supply curve. Thus, it would be more accurate to say that the *positively sloped portion of the marginal cost curve* is the firm's supply curve, and still more accurate to state that the positively sloped portion of the marginal cost curve *above average variable costs* is the supply curve of the firm. The first of these modifications arises because the negatively sloped portion of the *MC* curve presents an unstable equilibrium with the *MR* curve. An additional unit of output at such an intersection causes *MR* to exceed *MC* and output would move away from the "equilibrium" instead of toward it. The second modification arises because the firm would not even be able to cover all of its variable costs, to say nothing of meeting its fixed costs, if the price of the output falls below average variable cost. By producing *zero* in this situation the firm can avoid all variable costs and therefore absorb a loss of only fixed costs—a better situation for the firm although still not a good one.

This supply curve is what we have sought from the very beginning of our analysis of firm behavior. It signifies the relationship between the quantity of output which the firm is willing to supply *(Sₓ)* and the price at which the firm can sell the output *(Pₓ)*. The important thing to notice about this relationship is its general form—upward sloping to the right. This shape explains a most basic behavioral pattern of the individual, competitive firm. Because of the technological and economic forces under which such firms operate, they are willingly to supply more output at high prices than at low prices. This is a natural and not unexpected result. Indeed, in the case of the competitive business firm, this behavior can be described as the *Law of Upward Sloping Supply*. Moreover, the basic root of this relationship is not difficult to find. We have run into it before— the Law of Diminishing Marginal Returns. If additional units of input yield diminishing increments to output, it seems only reasonable to expect the firm to require a higher price per unit in order to produce and supply additional units. Or, to put it the other way around, a higher price will induce the firm to supply more output because it will compensate the firm for the higher additional costs which it will incur as output is increased.

B. The Market Supply Curve

Having come this far, we have almost—but not quite—completed the analysis. Just as we had to derive the market demand curve from the individual household demand curves, so must we go from the parts to the whole in deriving the market supply curve. The question we must ask is: How will the *total* supply of good x respond to changes in the price of x? Again the process is one of *horizontally* summing the curves of each of the individual units.

In the household sector each individual unit demanded a multitude of goods and services. We had to ferret out the individual demand curves for good x from each household before we could add them together. In the business sector, however, each firm supplies but one commodity. Each firm presents only one supply curve to the market. Because all of the firms producing the same product form an industry, we are deriving the *industry* supply curve for that product.

By horizontally adding the supply curves (marginal cost curves) of each member of industry x in the same way as we added demand curves in the last chapter, we obtain the market or industry supply curve for good x. This curve relates the various quantities of a particular good which suppliers are willing to offer for sale at a series of possible prices. By repeating the analysis for each of commodities a, . . ., z, we can determine the industry (market) supply curve for each commodity produced in the economy. Because the individual firm supply curves are upward sloping, it follows that *the market or industry curve will slope upward*.

QUESTIONS

1. Consider the table on p. 115 showing short-run production data for a firm producing standardized power lawnmowers. Assume that the plant and equipment possessed by the firm cannot be altered in the short run. Only labor and materials are variable. These latter inputs are used in a con-

VARIABLE INPUTS PER YEAR	CAPITAL GOODS	OUTPUT OF LAWNMOWERS PER YEAR
0 bundles	Fixed	0
1 bundles	Fixed	20
2 bundles	Fixed	50
3 bundles	Fixed	100
4 bundles	Fixed	140
5 bundles	Fixed	170
6 bundles	Fixed	185
7 bundles	Fixed	195
8 bundles	Fixed	200
9 bundles	Fixed	203
10 bundles	Fixed	204
11 bundles	Fixed	204

stant relationship to each other—1 man-year of labor to 200 units of material. We will call each of these combinations a "bundle" of variable inputs.

(a) Plot the relationship of inputs to output on a sheet of graph paper. If all of the points are connected by straight lines, at what input level does the point of inflection appear to occur?

(b) Construct a table in which you display the marginal and average output data. From these data, plot the average and marginal product curves on another diagram. (A question often arises as to where to plot the marginal output and cost data. Because the marginal concept refers to a change in some variable, it cannot be tied to any one point on the scale. As a convention, plot the marginal numbers at the *midpoint* of the interval to which they refer.)

(c) Does this input-output relationship satisfy the Law of Diminishing Marginal Returns? Explain.

(d) What pieces of information do you need in order to derive the total cost curve?

(e) Assume that each bundle of labor and materials costs $7000 and that the annual cost for capital is $10,000. Form a table showing (1) marginal and average fixed costs for each output level shown in the table, (2) marginal and average variable costs for each output level, and (3) total marginal and average costs for each output level. Plot all six of these cost relationships on a new diagram. For each pair of curves demonstrate that the average-marginal relationship described in the text holds.

(f) Which of the six curves plotted in question (e) would you inspect to determine the output level at which the Law of Diminishing Marginal Returns begins to take hold? Does this output level have any relationship to the output level at which the inflection point occurred?

(g) Using the curves plotted in question (e), defend the proposition that fixed costs contribute to the downward sloping portion of the average cost curve.

(h) Using the curves plotted in question (e), explain why the text stated that "the positively sloped portion of the marginal cost curve above average variable costs is the supply curve of the firm."

(i) What level of output will the firm produce if the market price of lawnmowers is $280? Why? For what reason would the firm not produce one more lawnmower? or one less?

(j) What is the total profit earned by the firm when it is in equilibrium? Demonstrate that the equilibrium output level is superior to the output level at which average costs are at a minimum.

(k) What would happen to the supply curve of the firm if the annual cost for capital rises to $15,000? If the cost of each bundle of labor and materials rises to $8000? If the level of output for each of the input levels shown in the above table rises by 10 percent? What would be the equilibrium output in each of these cases if the price of lawnmowers is $280?

2. "The Law of Diminishing Marginal Returns implies a Law of Increasing Costs." Discuss.

3. "Marginal costs help the firm to decide how much to produce; average costs help the firm to decide whether or not to produce the good at all." Discuss.

4. Why is the marginal revenue curve for the *competitive* firm a horizontal straight line drawn at the level of the price? Where is the average revenue curve?

5. Consider the following expenses of a firm. Classify them as fixed or variable and state why you so classified them.

(a) Maintenance expense on a large computer which the firm owns.

(b) Rental expense on a large computer.

(c) Rental payments on a building which the firm occupies on five-year lease.

(d) Electric utility costs.

(e) Depreciation expense on machinery.

(f) Gasoline for delivery trucks.

(g) Insurance on factory and machines.

(h) Costs for security after hours.

(i) Costs for cardboard boxes in which output is shipped.

VII. $D_F = f(P_F, I-O, P_x)$—A MODEL OF BEHAVIOR FOR THE COMPETITIVE FACTOR DEMANDER

At the beginning of this chapter, we stated that there are two dimensions of firm behavior which are particularly relevant for analyzing how a market system works. We have explained the process of rational choice for the firm as a supplier of output. Now we must observe the firm in its role as a buyer or demander of inputs. We must analyze how the firm decides which and how much of the available inputs it will purchase. Again we will isolate the factors that determine firm behavior and then single out one of them, the price of the inputs (P_F), for particular scrutiny.

What, then, are the forces that determine firm behavior as it purchases factors of production? Surprisingly (although perhaps, on second thought, not so surprisingly), these forces are the same as those that interact to determine the firm's supply decisions. For example, it can hardly be questioned that the input-output relationship $(I-O)$ is a relevant consideration. Without doubt a change in this relationship would lead to a change in the quantity of inputs demanded to produce any given output. Similarly, because the price of the firm's product (P_x) is a prime determinant of the level of its output, this variable product price must also influence the quantity of inputs demanded. If a higher P_x elicits an increased output (as the upward sloping supply curve indicates) it will also elicit changes in the demand for inputs. Finally, few would deny the influence of the price of the factor itself (P_F) as a determinant of the amount of it which the firm will demand.

Given these determinants of factor demand we can write the following demand function:

$$D_F = f(P_F, I\text{-}O, P_x)$$

Because we are again primarily interested in the impact of one of these forces on the demand for a factor—namely, its price (P_F)—we can hold the other determinants constant and isolate the influence of price alone. The function then becomes

$$D_F = f(P_F) \text{ ceteris paribus}$$

While each firm has a demand curve for each of the inputs which it uses, we will concentrate on only one factor—labor. In so doing, we can modify the functional relationship to refer to this one factor. Because the price of labor is the wage rate (W), we can write

$$D_l = f(W) \text{ ceteris paribus}$$

In analyzing the demand for labor, we will assume a firm that produces one kind of output (x) by combining two inputs, labor (l)

and capital (*c*). Again consider capital (*c*) to be fixed and labor (*l*) to be variable. This, it will be recalled, is the same simplified model analyzed in deriving the supply curve for the product. With these assumptions, the input-output relationship (*I-O*) pictured in Figure 4-2 will again serve us in dealing with the demand for factor inputs. It is reproduced in Figure 4-12. As before, this total product (*TP*) curve increases throughout, with a section displaying increasing marginal returns (*OA*) and a section displaying diminishing marginal returns (*AB*).

A. The Total Revenue Product Curve

We can now incorporate into this *I-O* relationship a second determinant of the firm's demand for factors, the price of the output (P_x). By multiplying each output level on the total product curve in Figure 4-12 by the price of the output, the relationship between input of labor and total revenue is obtained. This multiplication transforms the physical relationship between the quantity of labor (*l*) and the quantity of output (*x*) into a relationship between the quantity of *l* and the *value* of the output of *x*. For example, if the hairdresser turns out 15 haircuts with 10 hours of labor, a physical relationship, and if the price of haircuts is $6, we can say that the 10 hours of labor produces $90 worth of haircuts, a relationship of physical input to value of output. Because total revenue is defined as the quantity of output which the firm sells *(x)* multiplied by the price at which it is sold (P_x), we will call this transformed total product curve the *total revenue product (TRP)* curve. It is shown in Figure 4-13. In deriving the total revenue product curve, the price of *x* (P_x) is held constant, as is the input-output relationship *(I-O)*. They will continue unchanged throughout the analysis.

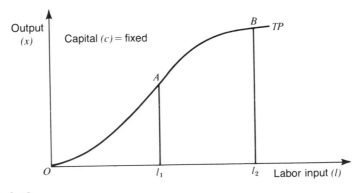

Figure 4-12

As seen in Figure 4-13, the *TRP* curve has the same general shape as the total product curve in Figure 4-12. Indeed, by multiplying each output level by a constant number of dollars—the price of *x* (P_x)—the only thing that changes on the diagram is the concept plotted on the vertical axis. Instead of plotting output in physical units on ther vertical axis as in Figure 4-12, we now have the value of the output measured in dollars—the total revenue product.

Embodied in this total revenue product curve *(TRP)* are two of the three determinants of the demand for the input labor, namely, P_x and *I-O*. Only the final (and primary) independent variable—the wage rate *(W)*—remains to be incorporated.

B. The Marginal Revenue Product Curve

In order to simplify introduction of the wage rate into the model, we must make a familiar kind of adjustment in the total revenue product curve *(TRP)*. In much the same way as we secured the marginal cost *(MC)* curve from the total cost *(TC)* curve, we will now derive the *marginal revenue product (MRP)* curve from the total revenue product *(TRP)* curve. This is done to show the relationship between the number of units of labor employed and the *addition* to the firm's revenue resulting from employing one more unit. For example, if the hairdresser produces 15 haircuts with 10 hours of labor and earns $90, and if by employing one more hour of labor it could turn out two additional haircuts and earn a total of $102, the marginal revenue product at that level of labor use would be $12. In mathematical symbols:

$$MRP = \Delta TRP/\Delta l$$

As was emphasized in our discussion of the marginal cost-total cost relationship, the marginal curve is equal to the *slope* of the total curve. Therefore, when *TRP* slopes upward at an *increasing rate* (from *O* to *A*), the *MRP* will be *increasing*. Where *TRP* slopes upward at a *decreasing rate* (from *A* to *B*, the *MRP* will be *decreasing*. Figure 4-14 shows the *MRP* curve as derived from the *TRP* curve of Figure 4-13. Up to l_1 units of labor input, *MRP* increases. From l_1 to l_2 units of labor input, the *MRP* decreases. With this adjustment, we can incorporate the price of labor—the wage rate *(W)*—into the model. It is the final step in deriving the firm's demand for labor.

In Figure 4-14, let us assume that the going market wage rate is W_1—that the firm must incur a cost of W_1 for each additional unit of labor it hires. Given the input-output relationship *(I-O)*, the price of the firm's product (P_x), and the price of labor *(W)*, how much labor will the firm decide to hire? How many labor hours will the firm

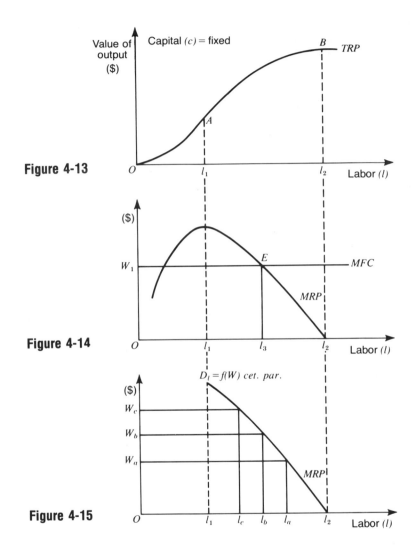

Figure 4-13

Figure 4-14

Figure 4-15

demand? Again using the principle of marginal comparisons, the firm is able to answer the question and easily explain its decision. At a wage of W_1, the firm will hire l_3 units of labor, for at this level of labor input profits are maximized. Let us examine this decision as well as the marginal principle underlying it.

Why does the firm choose to demand l_3 units of labor at a wage rate of W_1? Why is point E in Figure 4-14 an *equilibrium* position for the firm? We can best answer this question by demonstrating why no amount of labor other than l_3 could be considered optimum.

Take, for example, a quantity less than l_3, say l_1. At l_1, the wage rate (W_1) is substantially less than the marginal revenue product of labor *(MRP)*. Therefore, by hiring an additional unit of labor, the firm earns additional revenue (from selling the additional output which is produced) which exceeds the additional cost of hiring the extra unit of labor. The marginal revenue product exceeds the *marginal factor cost (MFC)* or the wage rate *(W)*. Because $MRP > MFC$, the addition to the firm's total revenue exceeds the addition to total cost and, consequently, profits are increased by the hiring of the additional unit of labor. Therefore input l_1—and, indeed, any amount of labor less than l_3—is less than optimum. The firm can increase its profits by hiring additional amounts of the factor at any input level below l_3.

The reverse situation occurs for any level of labor input greater than l_3. In this range, the marginal factor cost *(MFC)* or the wage rate *(W)* exceeds the revenue from selling the extra product *(MRP)*. Thus, for amounts of labor in excess of l_3, the firm would decrease its profits if it hired an additional unit of the input. More important, total profits could be increased if fewer units of labor were hired. By decreasing the use of labor, total revenue would decrease more slowly than total cost and profits would rise.

By exploring levels of labor input which are both less than and greater than l_3, we have concluded that, at a wage rate of W_1, the firm would increase its use of labor up to l_3, but not beyond. At l_3 there is no tendency to change. An equilibrium results as profits are maximized. *For the competitive firm in the factor market, the equilibrium condition is MRP = MFC.* And, because the wage rate W is equal to the marginal factor cost *(MFC)* for a competitive firm, we can also write this equilibrium: $W = MRP$.

C. The Demand Curve for Factors

By extending this analysis, we can derive the firm's demand curve for labor. Given that the firm maximizes profits where $MRP = MFC$ and given that the price of labor *(W)* to the competitive firm equals *MFC, the firm will equate the wage rate with the marginal revenue product no matter what the wage rate.* Thus, as pictured in Figure 4-15, the negatively sloped portion of the *MRP* curve becomes the firm's demand curve for labor. Just as the negatively sloped portion of the *MC* curve formed an unstable equilibrium with the price of the output and thus could not be a part of the supply curve for the firm, so too the *positively* sloped portion of the *MRP* curve is disqualified from being part of the firm's demand curve for a factor. This segment of the *MRP* curve relates the quantity of labor demanded (D_l) at all possible wage rates (W), holding the other determinants of demand constant. This is the basic concept which we set out to derive.

As we have derived it, the firm's demand curve for factors of production slopes downward to the right. This is the same general shape as the household's demand curve for goods and services. Althouth the reasons lying behind the shape are substantially different in each of the two sectors, the result is the same: more is demanded at lower prices and less is demanded at higher prices. Again, we call this the *Law of Downward Sloping Demand*. It is worth noting that the demand for factors is often referred to as a "derived demand." Firms demand inputs only because they can sell the output produced from the inputs, that is, because there exists a demand for their output. Therefore, the firm's demand for inputs is *derived from* the demand for the firm's product.

To complete our analysis, we must go from the single firm's demand for a single factor to the market demand for all three factors. The process of getting there is the same as before. By repeating this analysis of the labor demand curve for natural resources and capital for this firm and every other factor demander, and horizontally summing the individual firm demand curves for each of the factors, the market demand curve for each factor can be obtained. Because the firm demand curves slope downward to the right, the market demand curve for each of the factors will also show a negative slope. These market curves describe the behavior of the business sector in demanding factor inputs. They yield the relationships which we need to analyze the market system—the relationships between the price of factors (P_F) and the quantity demanded by business firms (D_F), holding all other determinants constant. At higher factor prices, the business sector demands fewer units of any factor than at lower prices.

Questions

1. Consider the table in question 1 of the previous set of questions (p. 115) and the information in part (e) of that question. Assume that lawnmowers are selling for $280 each.
   (a) Construct a table showing the total, marginal, and average revenue product for each level of variable inputs.
   (b) Plot the total and marginal revenue product curves. (Again, plot the marginal variables at the midpoint of the interval over which they are measured.)
   (c) At what level of variable inputs does the Law of Diminishing Marginal Returns take effect?

(d) How many bundles of variable inputs will the firm purchase?

(e) Show *graphically* the effect on the quantity of variable inputs demanded of a $20 increase in the price of lawnmowers. Of a $500 increase in the price of a bundle of variable inputs. Of a 10 percent increase in the level of output at each input level. Of an increase of $1000 in the cost for capital.

2. Assume that you are operating a factory and discover that some input used is generating *increasing* marginal revenue product. What would you do? Why?

3. "If a producer uses his or her inputs efficiently an increase in the price of one of them will alter the amount of it which is used." What force causes this change? A central planning agency memo? Pressure from some government agency?

4. "The basis for the Law of Downward Sloping Demand for factors of production is identical to that for the Law of Upward Sloping Supply of output." Do you believe this? If so, why? If not, why not?

5. It has been noted that a competitive business firm operates between two horizontal lines—one on the demand for inputs side and one on the supply of outputs side. Identify the two lines and explain why the firm is so constrained.

6. In all of our discussion in this chapter, we have failed to introduce the notion of "input substitutability." In the text we assumed that there was only one variable factor—labor. In the questions dealing with the lawnmower factory, we did so by assuming that the *two* variable inputs—labor and materials—had to be used in a fixed relationship. Obviously, however, firms can substitute inputs for each other. In nearly all production processes, machines can be substituted for some workers with no change in the level of output, or vice versa. For example, as motor vehicles become cheaper relative to horses, milk companies substituted trucks for horses on home delivery routes. Clearly it is the relative prices of the inputs which determines how factors will be substituted for each other. In this question we shall use some of the concepts developed in the appendix to chapter 3 to illustrate "input substitutability." A glance ahead at the Appendix to chapter 5 might help here as well.

(a) On a piece of graph paper, draw a diagram like that of Figure 3A−6. Instead of plotting goods on the axes, plot inputs, say, labor on the *x* axis and machines on the *y* axis.

(b) Whereas on the indifference map each of the curves represents a constant amount of satisfaction, in this diagram each of the curves represents a constant level of output. If you choose, you can label the curves 100 units, 200 units, and so on. Because we are dealing with output quantities, let us call these curves *isoquants*. By definition, each curve shows the combinations of inputs which can be used to produce any quantity of output. By referring to the discussion in the appendixes to chapters 3 and 5, explain why the isoquants slope downward and to the right. Why do they not intersect? Why are they bowed in toward the origin?

(c) Draw a straight line on your diagram tangent to one of the isoquants like the line of obtainable combinations *AB* in Figure 3A–6. This line is called an *isocost* (or equal cost) line. Why? Why should it be a straight line? Just as the line of attainable combinations in Figure 3A–6 depends on a certain number of dollars (total income) and two prices, so too does the isocost curve. What is the dollar value on which any isocost line depends? What are the two prices on which it depends? How is the slope of any isocost curve defined? What values would you have to know in order to calculate the slope?

(d) The tangency of any isocost and isoquant curve is called an *equilibrium*. Describe what any such tangency or equilibrium tells you. Why should a point of tangency be an equilibrium?

(e) On your diagram, show what will happen to the isocost line and the equilibrium inputs and outputs if you double the level of total cost.

(f) Is the result of doubling the price of labor consistent with the Law of Downward Sloping Factor Demand? Discuss.

VIII.   SUPPLY AND COST CURVES: THREE APPLICATIONS

As in chapter 3, this chapter has derived two important relationships: the supply curve of output for the competitive business firm and the firm's demand for inputs. The former of these relationships describes the behavior of the firm in deciding how much to produce; the latter describes the firm's choice regarding how to produce.

Both of these relationships are important in understanding the functioning of the market system, as we will show in chapters 5 and 6. However, these relationships by themselves have importance in dealing with practical economic problems confronted by both business firms and government. In this section, we will present three examples of how the concepts of costs and firm supply have been applied to real-world problems.

A. The Price of Oil and Reducing Oil Imports

In chapter 3, we referred to a proposal for dealing with the political uncertainties of the foreign oil producers' cartel: the use of a gasoline tax to reduce the quantity of gasoline demanded and, thereby to reduce the dependence of the United States on oil imports. An estimate of the demand curve was required to evaluate that proposal. The question was: How much would the quantity of gasoline demanded decrease if the price of gasoline was raised because of the imposition of a tax on its use? It was noted that some people believe that the demand curve of gasoline is steep in the short run, and conclude that this policy would not substantially reduce the quantity demanded. Others, however, believe that a higher price of oil and gasoline would lead to substantial economizing over the longer run.

Other policies to reduce the dependence of the United States on Middle East oil have also been proposed. One of these—indeed, one supported by the Ford and Carter administrations and the major oil companies—would seek to increase the supply of oil produced by oil companies in the United States. By increasing domestic supply, so the argument goes, the nation could decrease its reliance on foreign oil. And the policy instrument proposed to increase the domestic supply is price. The policy is to remove the controls on the price of oil produced in the United States, allowing the domestic price of oil produced in the United States to rise toward the world price set by the cartel. It is believed by advocates of the proposal that the increased price would stimulate both additional production of oil and additional activities to discover more oil in the United States.

As in the case of the gasoline tax, evaluation of this proposal requires information on how decision makers—in this case, oil companies—would respond to the incentive of a higher domestic price for oil. This response is precisely the one depicted by the supply curve of domestic oil. However, the amount by which output would respond to a rise in price depends on many things. Perhaps oil companies are already operating their wells at capacity. Perhaps there is little more oil to be discovered in the United States. In these cases, the supply curves will be very steeply sloped and the increase in the price of oil will not result in a substantial increase in the amount supplied. The policy in this case would be an ineffective means of achieving independence from foreign suppliers. On the other hand, the supply curve may indicate that the supply of domestic oil is highly responsive to its price. If existing wells have excess capacity, or if more intensive drilling would result in the discovery of major new fields, and if the higher price would stimulate such activity, a large supply response would occur. In this case, the proposal would be an effective means of promoting independence.

The importance of the supply curve for evaluating this proposal is shown in Figure 4–16. Two possible supply curves for oil are shown: S_1 which indicates a good deal of responsiveness. Assume that today the price of oil is P_1, implying that Q_1 units of oil are being supplied by U.S. oil companies. Assume also that the price would rise to P_2 if existing controls on the price of oil were relaxed. From the diagram, it is now clear why the shape of the supply curve is crucial to the success of this policy. If S_1 is the true supply curve,

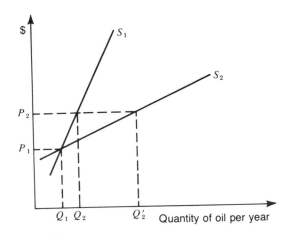

Figure 4-16

allowing the price to rise will have little effect on the quantity of oil brought to the market—the quantity supplied by U.S. companies will increase only from Q_1 to Q_2, and the United States will remain dependent on foreign producers. However, if S_2 is the true supply curve, output forthcoming from domestic suppliers will more than double from Q_1 to Q_2, and the dependence of the United States on foreign suppliers would be greatly reduced.

At the present time there is no agreement on the shape of the supply curve for domestic oil. The oil compaines argue that the quantity of oil supplied would respond rather quickly and substantially to higher prices and profits. Those who oppose this policy strategy have a quite different view of responsiveness. Many of these opponents believe that there are a number of reasons why higher oil prices will not bring forth a large increase in the quantity of oil supplied. Some argue that the oil industry is not a competitive industry, and therefore oil companies will simply divert the higher profits to other activities. As a result, little additional production and exploration will take place unless higher profits attract new firms into the industry. A more sophisticated argument is that oil companies will be able to find more profitable outlets for their increased revenues than drilling for more oil. As rational decision makers, the oil companies will use their revenues to diversify their outputs, thus developing lines of production other than oil. And, again, the quantity of oil supplied will not increase very much. A third point made by critics is that oil prices and oil company profits are already high enough to make additional production and exploration worthwhile. Those holding this view—including the Carter administration and ultimately the Congress—have prevailed and have imposed a "windfall profits tax" to capture some of the increased profits accompanying the higher price of oil.

The issue here is again an empirical one: what does the supply curve for domestic oil look like? Economists have been working to develop reliable estimates of this supply relationship, but so far no generally accepted measurements are available. Indeed, the problem of accurately estimating the supply response is a more complex one than this discussion suggests. The reason for this is that the supply of oil can be increased not only by pumping it out of the ground, but also by producing it from shale, which is found in abundance in the western United States, obtaining it from tar sands which are plenteous in western Canada, and converting it from coal through a process called gasification. The domestic supply curve of oil depends on the cost of recovery from all of these sources. Of course, the price of oil might rise along the supply curve to a point high enough to attract expanded production of substitutes for oil whose supply curves are also relevant to the problem. Knowledge of the supply curves for coal, solar energy, gasahol, nuclear energy and hydroelectric energy would help us to identify the price levels at which they each might be substituted for oil in various uses. Although difficult, obtaining reliable estimates of the supply relationship is of crucial importance in framing a rational energy policy.

B. Costs and the Optimal Amount of Pollution

The issue of costs and supply is also central to making rational policy in the area of air and water pollution. To secure a cleaner environment requires some combination of changes in production and consumption processes, changes in the sorts of products consumed by people, and the construction and operation of plants to treat wastes. All of these activities have costs, and because of these costs, it makes sense to think about the supply curve for environmental quality.

The upward sloping curve in Figure 4–17 depicts the total cost curve for improving environmental quality. It is drawn with an increasing slope because of the difficulty of removing additional residuals from the flows of wastes to the environment after the easiest ones have already been removed. In effect, the curve reflects the Law of Decreasing Marginal Returns which results in the Law of Upward Sloping Supply. In the same way that the total cost curve of the competitive firm yields a marginal cost—or supply—curve of the

firm, this total cost curve can be transformed into a supply curve of
environmental quality. Just such a supply curve is shown in Figure
4–18. It will be recalled from the discussion earlier in this chapter
that the marginal cost curve is the slope of the total cost curve.
Hence, the shape of the supply curve of environmental quality (Figure 4–18) depends on the *slope* of the total cost curve for achieving
different levels of environmental quality (Figure 4–17).

Considering this supply curve—or marginal cost curve—one can
now ask the question: How much environmental quality should we
as a nation choose? Stated in terms of Figure 4–18: How far along
the x axis, the environmental quality axis, should we move? As
shown in Figure 4–17, we could have a completely pure environment if we were willing to pay enormous costs. That would mean
sacrificing large amounts of other aspects of our economic well-
being: cars, concerts, housing, education, and so on. Because of the
rapidly rising costs of improving the environment, after a certain
level has been reached, society would maximize its well-being by

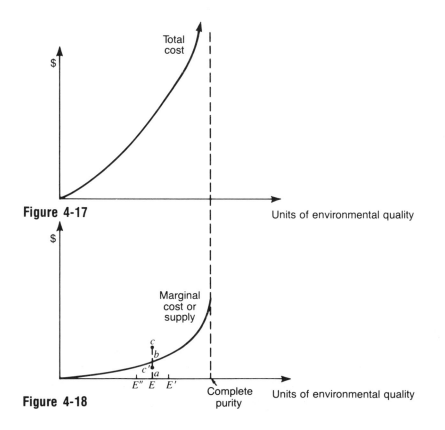

Figure 4-17   Units of environmental quality

Figure 4-18

not choosing a completely pure environment. However, a smaller amount of pollution than is experienced in many places in the United States might well be chosen. Ultimately, the choice will depend on a balancing of the costs of supplying an improved environment with the benefits which this improvement yields.[1]

The choice of this optimal level of environmental quality—or, looked at from the other side, the choice of the optimal amount of pollution—depends on a comparison of the measured costs of achieving environmental improvement (depicted in Figures 4–17 and 4–18) with the measured costs or damages which result from environmental pollution. For example, if the current level of environmental quality was shown by E in Figure 4–18, the marginal cost of achieving one unit of improvements would be ab. If the measured benefit—or, conversely, the *reduced* pollution damages—of achieving this unit of improvement were ac, it would be in the society's interest to move to a higher level of environmental quality, say, E'. On the other hand, if the reduction in pollution damages (i.e., marginal benefits) were only ac' it would be in society's interest to choose an even lower level of environmental quality than E—say, E''. By comparing these two kinds of costs through altering the level of environmental quality, the optimal level of pollution can be found.

Much work is underway to estimate both of these sets of costs, all of this work rests on the theoretical principles underlying the cost and supply curves developed in this chapter. Again, the formation of efficient policy requires estimates of these cost and supply relationships.[2]

C. Determining the Size of Public Facilities

In all developed countries, some level of government is responsible for constructing and operating large facilities: parks, libraries, hospitals, highways, post offices, dams and so on. In nearly all of these situations, decisions must be made regarding the scale of the facilities to be built. Clearly, this is an economic question of substantial importance, especially if the per unit costs of a facility are related to its size. If such a relationship does exist, either too large or

---

1. For a more complete analysis of this choice, see Myrick Freeman, Robert Haveman, and Allen Kneese, *The Economics of Environmental Policy* (New York, John Wiley — Sons, 1973).

2. Rough estimates of both the costs of improving environmental quality and the costs of pollution can be found in The President's Council on Environmental Quality, *Environmental Quality—1979* (Washington, D.C., 1980). See also Henry Peskin and Eugene Seskin, eds., *Cost Benefit Analysis and Water Pollution Policy* (Washington, D.C.: The Urban Institute, 1975).

too small a facility could result in costs which are higher than they need be, and economic inefficiency and waste would result.

Because most of these activities of government occur in sectors in which the market fails to operate—indeed, the services of some of these facilities are provided free of charge to users, for example, city streets—there are no observed prices to signal preferences and opportunity costs to decision makers. In cases such as these, explicit studies of cost curves must be made if government is to make sound choices regarding efficient sizes of facilities to be constructed.

A particularly interesting example of this problem is in the National Health Service in Great Britain. In Britain, responsibility for constructing hospital facilities is lodged in a division of the health service, which must not only decide when and where hospital facilities are to be built, but also which size to build. While there are some reasons to believe that small hospitals have lower average costs than large hospitals (they may be located closer to patients, for example), there are other reasons which suggest that larger hospitals are more efficient than small ones (they can have equipment which can not be justified by smaller hospitals and they can achieve organizational efficiencies which are not attainable in small facilities). Moreover, it seems likely that above some size, the difficulties of managing an enterprise would make its average costs rise. The accuracy of these speculations cannot be determined, however, without an explicit measurement of the relationship of average costs to size.

A few years ago, just such a study was undertaken for Great Britain by an economist, Martin Feldstein.[3] Using data from 177 hospitals ranging in size from 72 beds to 1064 beds, he estimated the relationship between size and average costs. His conclusion is stated as follows:

> The average cost function ... is a shallow U-shaped curve with a minimum at the current average size (300 beds). Costs rise beyond this size but level off after 600 beds at about 10 percent above minimum cost. [Hence], the medium size hospital (300 to 500 beds) is ... at least as efficient ... as larger hospitals.[4]

While Feldstein never drew the average cost relationship, his results indicate that it could be depicted as in Figure 4–19. Average costs decrease to about a size of 300 beds and then gradually increase to about 600 beds. This measurement effort was based on the concept

---

3. Martin Feldstein, *Economic Analysis for Health Service Efficiency* (Amsterdam: North-Holland Publishing Co., 1967).

4. Ibid., pp. 86 and 297.

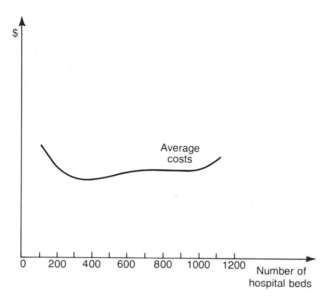

Figure 4-19

of average costs developed in this chapter, and again it yields important information on which to make rational choices.

IX.   CONCLUSION AND SUMMARY

By following much the same type of logical analysis as we developed in the chapter on the household sector, we have come to an understanding of the nature of decision making in the business firm. Whereas in the household sector, utility maximization served as the primary motivating force, the goal of maximum profits has been taken to be the prime mover of the firm. In this chapter we have sought the logical implications of this objective in both the product (or supplying) market and the factor (or buying) market. We first isolated the relevant determining factors in each case and then, putting these factors together in a model, logically derived both a *product supply curve* and a *factor demand curve* for the firm. In each case the variable quantity (the quantity supplied or demanded) was related to a price and, in each, the impact of the price on the quantity was stated as a functional relationship. Through this approach, we were able to explain rational firm behavior in both the sale of its output and the purchase of inputs.

In the following chapter, we will extend this understanding of decision making in both the household and business sectors by permitting these two key economic sectors to interact in the marketplace. In so doing, our goal will be to understand how a market *system*, through the interactions of independent buyers and sellers, establishes prices, determines income, rations consumption, and organizes output—that is, how a market system answers the basic economic questions of what, how, and for whom.

5 | Organization and Functioning of Competitive Markets

The household and the business sectors are the principal elements of the economy. In chapters 3 and 4 we dissected and studied these elements in an attempt to understand their internal operation. We analyzed how these sectors confront certain basic data, incorporate them into their decision-making framework, and make decisions which satisfy certain objectives.

Now our task changes. Rather than observe individual parts of the economy in isolation, we will create a model of how these functioning members of the economy interact. The task is now one of amalgamation. To achieve this, we will first establish a mechanism through which these constituent parts of the economy can interact. We call this mechanism a "market." It is an arena in which the household sector meets the business sector, where demanders meet suppliers, where goods are exchanged for money where prices are made. We will analyze both the structure of markets and their functioning, emphasizing the mechanics of their operation.

I.   THE STRUCTURE OF A COMPETITIVE MARKET

A market is a collection of individual decision-making units, some of which desire to buy (demand) and some of which desire to sell (supply) a particular good or service.

In our model of a competitive economy, there is a market for shoes, a market for tomatoes, a labor market and, indeed, a market for every good and service which is bought or sold. In the words of one economist, a market in a money economy has the function of "bring[ing] together buyers and sellers who wish to exchange goods and money . . .; individuals who together play the primary role in determining prices and quantities." This statement puts the spotlight on the prime characteristic of a market; some people give up money and get goods or services while other people give up goods and services and get money. The demanders (buyers) exchange money for commodities, and the suppliers (sellers) exchange commodities for money.

Although markets are often found in a single location as, for example, the New York Stock Exchange, they need not be so restricted. We can talk about the market for haircuts in South St. Louis, the market for steel on the West Coast, or the market for automobiles in the United States. Nor is it necessary for the buyers and sellers to confront one another face-to-face in the marketplace. For example, if we were to decide to buy 15 shares of Fruehauf Trailer Co. stock on the New York Stock Exchange, the transaction would be handled by specialized intermediaries known as brokers. We would have no idea from whom we bought the stock, and the person who sold the stock would have no knowledge of the purchaser. As long as buyers can make their desires known *in some way* to sellers (and sellers to buyers) a market can exist.

In analyzing the structure and functioning of markets, we will deal with a special kind of theoretical market model. It is a market that is both *perfect* and *competitive*. In discussing theory, we should again point out that we are not presenting a description of the real world. Rather, we are attempting to understand a few aspects of real-world behavior by examining some fundamental cause-and-effect relationships which exist in the world. Our aim is to explain some elemental facets of economic behavior in the real world through the use of logical concepts and relationships. The function of economic theory is to enable us to understand what goes on in real-world markets without having to completely describe them and without having to know each of the buyers and sellers. By understanding the nature of some strategic economic relationships we can construct models to predict market outcomes.

A. A Perfect Market

What, then, is meant by a *perfect* market? Basically, we refer to an attribute of the participants in the market. We assume that both the buyers and the sellers have *complete knowledge* of market conditions; that any change in market conditions will be immediately known and acted on. When, for example, the price of cola goes from 15¢ to 20¢ and the price of all other sodas remains unchanged, we assume that all consumers learn of it immediately and are free to react as they please. Such perfect knowledge possessed by buyers and sellers causes the market itself to be perfect. Because the participants are aware of each change in market conditions and can react to these changes without delay, the market itself adjusts instantaneously to any disturbance. Unlike real-world markets in which ignorance of market conditions is widespread, there is no adjustment lag in perfect markets. In an economy with perfect markets, there is no need for advertising or other supplemental market information services.

B. A Competitive Market

The concept of a *competitive* market, like that of a perfect market, is' an abstraction. Like other concepts which we have discussed, competition means something quite different to the economist than it does to the businessman. Whereas the businessman tends to equate competition with the idea of personal rivalry ("Football is a competitive sport."), the economist speaks of competition as a situation in which there is no rivalry.

A competitive market possesses *a multitude of participants* with each participant so small relative to the entire market that he has *no significant influence* on the market or on the other competitors. Instead of a kind of hand-to-hand combat situation, competition in economics is an impersonal phenomenon. To the economist, then, the maket for, say, corn is substantially more competitive than the market for steel. Several hundred thousand farmers enter the corn market as sellers, whereas there are but a dozen or two sellers of steel. Ironically, while no corn farmer considers another farmer to be a competitor, each steel firm considers itself in hard competition with its rivals.

The most important characteristic of a competitive market is that no single participant has the power to affect the market outcome in any significant way. The quantity of corn which an individual seller puts on the market, even when it is the seller's entire harvested crop, is so insignificant an amount compared to the total quantity of corn supplied to the market that one seller's entire harvested crop is so insignificant an amount compared to the total quantity of corn supplied to the market that one seller's supply has no effect upon price. The seller's entire output can be sold at one time at the going market price without depressing it. If one seller withholds the entire farm's crop, once again it is so small a quantity compared to the total that the price of corn will not be affected. Only if a very large number of sellers increase (or decrease) the quantity of corn supplies will there be a noticeable enough change in the market supply to affect price. Because of the impersonal character of the market, none of the participants in a competitive market has control over the price. The competitive market price is determined by purely impersonal forces at work in an impersonal market—forces which no single participant can control. For this reason, we can say that in a competitive market all buyers and sellers are *price-takers*, not price-makers.

A second characteristic of a competitive market is that there is no obstruction or restriction placed on supply, demand, or the level of the price. Any demander or supplier is perfectly free to enter or leave a market. For example, in a competitive market a baker can sell cakes or cookies and use the revenue to buy labor or capital or flour at his or her own discretion. This decision can be made with regard only to the gains or losses which will result from it. Similarly, a laborer can leave one job market and enter another as he or she wishes. Such absence of restriction signifies that there is nothing in the economy, other than the market forces generated by individual choice, that can set prices. Governmental price supports or minimum-wage legislation or electrical equipment price fixers are absent. Because of the perfect mobility of resources and the absence of restriction, no single individual firm, or institution has what the economist calls *market power*.

The final characteristic of a competitive market is that only one homogeneous commodity is sold in any given market. One person's grade A corn is sold in the same market as all other people's grade A corn; every bushel of number 2 hard red winter wheat produced by one farmer is identical to the hard red winter wheat produced by every other farmer in that market.

II.   THE LAW OF SUPPLY AND DEMAND

A. Market Forces—Supply and Demand

The prime movers in our model market are the forces of supply and demand. They determine the price of the good and the quantity exchanged in any given market. To analyze how prices are formed, let us select one of the multitude of perfect and competitive markets in our theoretical system, say, the market for shoes. This market, like all markets, is established to permit an exchange of goods (or services) for money. Two kinds of participants operate in it: those with money who want shoes (demanders) and those with shoes who want money (suppliers). We already know the traders in this market. The households are the demanders and the business firms in the shoe industry are the suppliers.

The demand and supply relationships presented to this market by these groups are also known. For the demanders of shoes there is an inverse relationship between the price of shoes and the quantity demanded. Buyers will take more shoes at $22.95 per pair than at $54.95 per pair. Such a relationship is described by curve *DD* in Figure 5-1. This curve is a market demand curve and, as such, it incorporates the individual demands of all the households. Its negative slope reflects the Law of Downward Sloping Demand.

For the suppliers of shoes the relationship is somewhat different. Because of the Law of Diminishing Marginal Returns, a higher price induces a greater output than does a lower price. Consequently, a direct relationship exists between the price of shoes and the quantity that potential sellers are willing to supply to the market. This relationship, *SS* in Figure 5-1, reflects the Law of Upward Sloping Supply. At a price of $54.95 per pair, suppliers will offer to sell a larger quantity of shoes than at $48.95 per pair.

In representing the forces of supply and demand as a supply curve (*SS*) and a demand curve (*DD*), the quantities demanded and supplied are pictured as being dependent *only* on the price of the commodity. Many other factors, it will be recalled are hidden in such a simplification. In drawing the demand curve we have made the *ceteris paribus* assumption. The tastes and preferences of the household sector, its income level, the prices of other goods, and the number of demanders are *all held constant* in deriving the demand curve for, say, shoes. If any one of these variables should change, the demand curve for shoes would be altered. If everyone's income, for example,

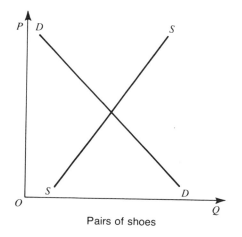

Figure 5-1

Pairs of shoes

doubled some night, the number of shoes demanded the next morning *at any given price* would increase.

The same *ceteris paribus* assumption applies to supply. The prices of the inputs, the input-output relationship, and the number of sellers are all assumed to be constant in drawing a single supply curve. As with the demand curve, if one of these variables changes, the supply curve itself changes. But let us save the analysis of these changes for later.

The demand and the supply curves are tools necessary for us to discover how prices and quantities in any given market are determined—why the price of shoes is $44.95 and not $60.95 or $20.95, why 5000 pairs of shoes were sold last month and not 7000 or 20,000.

B. Competitive Bidding and Equilibrium

In the establishment of any given market price, either demanders or suppliers will adjust to an undesirable situation by engaging in a process called *competitive bidding*. This process occurs as traders raise or lower the prices at which they offer to buy or sell. Consider the supply and demand relationship pictured in Figure 5-1 and reproduced in Figure 5-2. Assume that the going price of shoes is $50. At that price the demanders in the market want to buy *OA* pairs of shoes. This follows directly from the meaning of the demand relationship—a curve which relates the quantitites of a good which demanders stand ready to buy at all possible prices. For the same reason, the firms in the shoe industry want to sell *OB* pairs of shoes at a price of $50. Consequently, at the price of $50, the quantity of

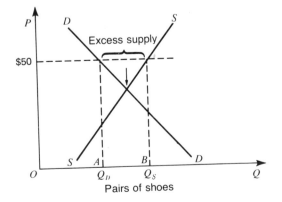

Figure 5-2

shoes supplied (Q_S) exceeds the quantity of shoes demanded (Q_D). Suppliers want to sell more shoes at a price of $50 than demanders wish to buy. The quantity *OB* minus *OA* exists as a *surplus* on the market; a situation clearly undesirable to some members of one of the two groups.

As a group, demanders are not the dissatisfied ones. At a price of $50 they desire to buy *OA* pairs of shoes and, because at least that many are available, they leave the market satisfied although perhaps grumbling about the high price of shoes. The suppliers of shoes react differently, however. At a price of $50 they desire to sell *OB* pairs, but can only dispose of *OA*. Those sellers who are unable to sell their goods are the unhappy traders. It is these would-be sellers, unable to find buyers for their commodities, who inaugurate the process of competitive bidding.

Rather than sell nothing at all, these suppliers begin to shave their price. They recognize that they can woo some buyers by charging a price slightly lower than $50. It is here that the process of competitive bidding starts. Suppliers, unhappy with the going price, begin to competitively bid it down. As long as quantity supplied exceeds the quantity demanded ($Q_S > Q_D$), competitive price bidding on the part of sellers will continue. Such a situation is a *buyer's market*. The suppliers scramble to search out buyers, and in their search they bid down the price, all of which is in the buyers' interest.

The reverse situation occurs if the going price of shoes is, say, $30, as in Figure 5-3. Now the quantity demanded exceeds the quantity

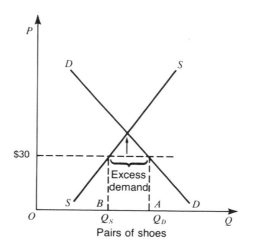

Figure 5-3

supplied $(Q_D > D_S)$. There are some would-be buyers in the market who desire to buy but can find no available supply. The excess of demand over supply in this case is equal to the quantity OA minus OB. In this situation, it is the would-be buyers who are the unhappy ones. In an attempt to attract some of the insufficient supply, these buyers will offer to pay more than $30 for a pair of shoes. They will bid up the price. This competitive bidding by demanders will continue so long as $Q_D > Q_S$. This is called a *sellers' market*. Buyers are the ones now scrambling and in the process the price is being bid up—a situation favorable to sellers.

From this analysis we can draw a firm conclusion. Whenever the price of a commodity is above the intersection of the supply and demand curves, competition among sellers tends to force it down; whenever the price is below the intersection, the competitive bidding of buyers forces it up. At the intersection, the quantity which suppliers are willing to offer (Q_S) equals the quantity which demanders desire to buy (Q_D). At this price $Q_D = Q_S$ and there is no reason whatever for it to change. This price is shown in Figure 5-4 as $39.95.

At the price at which $Q_S = Q_D$, all of the buyers of shoes are happy. They can acquire just the amount that they desire at this price. Sellers are also happy at this price, since they can dispose of the amount that they want to sell. This price, therefore, balances the force of supply with the force of demand: it causes OA pairs of shoes to be traded at the single and uniform price of $39.95. Point E, representing this price and quantity, is the supply and demand *equilibrium*. It is called an equilibrium because neither the price of

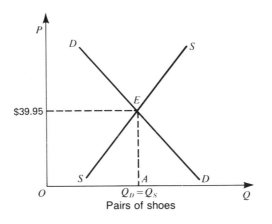

Figure 5-4

shoes nor the number of pairs exchanged has a tendency to change. There is no one to upset the market because the quantity supplied at this price equals the quantity demanded. The *equilibrium condition* for the market is $Q_S = Q_D$. This balancing of forces, this perpetual tendency toward equilibrium, is the *Law of Supply and Demand*.

C. Changes in Equilibrium

We have demonstrated that with given supply and demand curves in a market, the price and quantity will always tend toward equilibrium. As a matter of fact, in perfect, competitive markets, this "tendency" becomes an accomplished fact. Any deviation from equilibrium is instantaneously corrected by the process of competitive bidding.

However, an equilibrium will remain unchanged only under certain conditions. If any one of the many factors which have been held constant in drawing the supply and demand curves should change, either or both of the curves will shift. If, for example, all consumers should awake one morning to find their income to be twice that of the previous day, the original demand curve for shoes would no longer be appropriate. Each consumer would allocate some additional income to the available products which give him utility and, because shoes are not inferior goods, more shoes would be demanded at any given price than before the change in income. That is, the entire demand curve would shift to the right.

Thus, changes in (1) tastes and preferences, (2) the income level of the households, (3) the prices of other goods, and (4) the number of consumers in the market at each price level[1] all cause the demand curve to shift its position. Depending on the impact of the changes in these variables, the demand curve may shift up or down. It may increase as from DD to D_1D_1 in Figure 5-5 or decrease as from DD to D_2D_2.

The same type of *ceteris paribus*-related mechanism is present in the supply curve. If any of those variables assumed constant in drawing a single market curve—(1) the price of the inputs, (2) the input-output relationship, (3) the number of firms in the industry at each price level[2]—should change, the supply curve will shift. Again, depending on the impact of the change, the curve will either increase (shift to the right) or decrease (shift to the left). For example, if the number of firms selling shoes should increase, the supply

---

1. This is different from some consumers being priced out of the market as we move up a *given* demand curve.

2. This is different from firms leaving the industry as we move down a *given* supply curve.

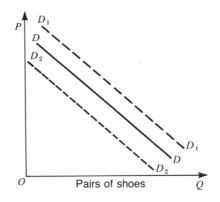

Figure 5-5

curve—being the sum of the firms' marginal cost curves—will shift to the right. It will increase from, say, SS to S_1S_1 in Figure 5-6. Or, conversely, if something should happen to decrease the output per unit of input for the firms in an industry—such as the impact of a moldblight in Florida on the output of oranges—the marginal cost curves of all the firms will rise, causing the industry supply curve to shift to the left—to decrease from, say SS to S_2S_2. If this is not directly obvious, the reader should go back to the cost curves of chapter 4 and ask: What will happen to the firm's marginal cost curve if the total product curve of the firm is shifted downward?

D. An Example of Changing Equilibrium—The U.S. Wheat Market

The question posed by these supply and demand shifts is clear: How will they affect the market equilibrium? To answer this question let us consider the recent history of the market for wheat in the United States.[3] During the past few years enormous changes have occurred in this market which have affected the supply and demand functions for wheat.

On the supply side, better seed, fertilizers and equipment have combined with improved methods of cultivation, planting and harvesting to increase the capacity of agriculture over the decades. Continual expansion of capacity has created a persistent problem of excess supply, depressing price and thereby depressing farm income.

---

3. The factual material in this section is drawn from the *Wall Street Journal* and from notes by Professor James F. Shepherd.

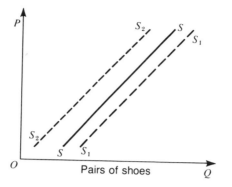

Figure 5-6

This problem has plagued agriculture in the United States since the 1920s. Government policy has provided for control of acreage to be planted and support of prices to farmers through a loan program. These policies aimed at control of supply have continued to be applied during periods of market glut.

On the demand side, efforts were made to expand the market for U.S. commodities by such programs as subsidies for the export of farm products. In the early 1970s, a major change occurred in the international demand for U.S. wheat which temporarily eased the chronic excess supply problem. During the late 1960s there was an increase in the demand for U.S. wheat from such countries as Japan, India, and the Soviet Union. The Soviet Union, for example, experienced a series of poor harvests which depleted their carry-over stocks of wheat. In the spring of 1972, the principal Russian wheat-growing areas had poor weather, and drought hit the Volga Basin in June of that year. A disastrously small harvest resulted.

On June 28, 1972, a trade agreement was concluded between the United States and the Soviet Union which provided for Russian purchase of wheat. However, the public announcement of the agreement provided no inkling of the sharp change in the demand for wheat that was in store. The price of wheat at the farm stood at $1.27 per bushel. Following the signing of the June trade agreement, Russian grain buyers began a carefully orchestrated program of wheat purchases (plus some corn and other feed grains) from a half dozen or more large grain exporting companies. The Russians succeeded in keeping each purchase secret from the other sellers. While these purchases expanded demand, a simultaneous program of restricting supply—the wheat control program—was announced by the Nixon administration in July 1972. It was a traditional program designed to step up support payments to farmers by about 10 percent and to restrict the amount produced. The Department of Agriculture, which had authority to approve the Russian sales, did not recognize that a large volume of sales was accumulating until well into the harvest season.

News of the sales broke in mid-July 1972, before some of the grain companies had covered their sales to Russia with purchases from U.S. farmers. Following the news stories, the market price for wheat rose rapidly. This prompted congressional debate. At a congressional hearing held to determine if the grain companies had profited at the expense of the American consumer, some of the grain companies claimed to have lost money on these sales. The price had risen between the time that they contracted for sales to the Soviet Union and then subsequently purchased wheat from farmers to cover the sales. Only those farmers who sold late in the season reaped unusual profits. The primary winners were the Russians who had managed their purchases so skillfully. Altogether the sales to the Soviet Union amounted to one-fourth of the 1972 U.S. wheat crop.

The effect of this sharp change in the demand for wheat on the equilibrium in the U.S. wheat market can be illustrated by the hypothetical supply and demand curves in Figure 5-7(a). Suppose that DD and SS are the demand and supply curves for U.S. wheat on July 1, 1972, before the institution of the program restricting supply and before the increased Russian demand. P_1 is the equilibrium price for wheat, represented by $1.27 per bushel.

When purchases by the Soviet Union between July and November 1972 are added to regular purchases, the demand curve shifts in successive steps from DD to $D'D'$. We can now evaluate the influence of only this change in demand on the equilibrium price and quantity. At a price of P_1, there would be substantial excess demand and competition among demanders would force the price to rise.

What actually happened to the price of wheat? Number 2 hard red winter wheat at Gulf ports increased in price by 10 percent between July 1 and August 1, 1972. By the 24th of August the price had climbed 31 percent over the July 1 posting. By November, wheat prices had reached the highest level in 25 years. Prices at the farm were now 55 percent higher than they had been at the time of the U.S.-Russian trade agreement five months earlier.

The new equilibrium price of P_2 illustrates the result of the bidding process. The higher price elicits some increase in the quantity supplied by inducing farmers and grain elevator operators to offer more stored grain to buyers. The quantity exchanged increases from

X_2 to X_2. The new supply and demand equilibrium occurs at E_2 where once again $Q_D = Q_S$.

Purchases continued and both buyers and sellers anticipated that the Russians would be back for more wheat in 1973. Later in that winter of 1972–73, the price of wheat went over \$3 per bushel and continued to climb. Retail food prices soared. Meat shortages became severe as cattle raisers were caught between price controls on meat and the inflation in grain prices accompanying the Russian purchases.

As a result of these changes, acreage controls were eased for 1973 and a record crop of 1.71 billion bushes was harvested in 1973. In Figure 5-7(b), this change in supply can be thought of as a shift in the supply curve from SS to $S'S'$. However, this expected supply curve shift was not realized as another change occurred simultaneously. Sellers' anticipations also changed. Because sellers expected prices to rise, they were willing to sell less from storage at existing prices, and less at each possible price level. The net effect of these two influences was to cause the market supply curve actually to shift to the left to, say, $S''S''$.

Expectations regarding future prices also affected buyers. Because they anticipated that the price would continue to rise they were willing to buy more in 1973 at each price level. As a result of this change, the demand curve again shifted to the right—to, say, $D''D''$ in Figure 5-7(b). A poor harvest in the USSR in 1973, led to further massive purchases from the 1973 U.S. wheat crop. By February 1974, wheat sold at \$6.45 per bushel. The February 1974 position might be represented by the intersection of $S''S''$ with $D''D''$ in Figure 5-7(b). $Q_D = Q_S$ at E_3, implying a price of P_3.

Following that time the price of wheat fell as acreage planted in wheat and feed grains increased substantially. Another record was set when a crop of 2.13 billion bushels of wheat was harvested in 1975. The U.S. government had completely relaxed the restrictions on the number of acres of wheat that could be planted. Suppliers responded to the high prices by shifting more land from the planting of other crops and by bringing more idle acres into production. Wheat fell from \$4.02 per bushel in October 1974 to \$3 per bushel in mid 1975.

In Figure 5-7(c), $S''S''$ represents supply in the fall of 1974 while $S'''S'''$ represents supply in 1975. $D''D''$ represents demand in 1975. Supply increased while demand fell off a bit. A new equilibrium of $Q_D = Q_S$ is achieved at E_4, implying a price of P_4.

Bumper wheat crops were harvested in the United States and in

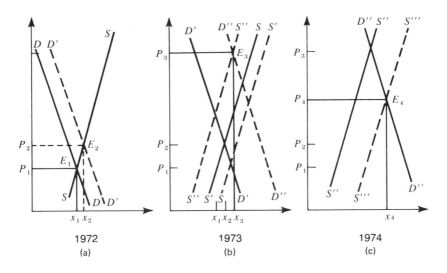

Figure 5-7

most producing countries around the world in 1976 and 1977. Price plummeted as the supply curve for wheat outraced the demand curve in shifting to the right along the quantity scale. Chronic surplus seemed to have returned to the U.S. wheat market, relieved only by occasional crop failures abroad.

During 1979, Russia again placed large orders for grains, and cash prices for wheat on the Chicago Board of Trade stood at $4.35 per bushel in December after having reached $4.76 in June. Demand for wheat was to be affected once again by events abroad when in December Russia invaded Afghanistan to prop up a pro-Soviet coup. On Friday evening, January 4, 1980, President Carter responded by announcing an embargo on grain shipments to the Soviet Union and offsetting purchases by the U.S. government. The market was shut down for two days to avoid total chaos. When trading resumed on January 10, prices closed at $3.95, reflecting the changed demand situation. There was promise of increased grain shipments to the poorer countries as foreign aid and promise of support for gasahol production from grain. These developments seemed to ease the threat of large stores of grain overhanging the market. Prices gradually recovered in succeeding weeks.

With shifts in supply or demand, new equilibrium positions replace old, prices rise or fall, and the quantity exchanged increases or decreases. Changes in the forces of supply and demand produce concurrent changes in prices and quantities—changes in observable

market data. Moreover, underlying the changes in supply and demand are a multitude of changes in other variables—some economic, some psychological, some sociological, and some technological. That is, changes in the *determinants* of demand and supply
cause the demand and supply curves to shift as described. These
shifts, in turn, cause the observable changes in the prices and quantities seen in the marketplace. When, for example, the wholesale
price of steel scrap first rises by 50 percent and then falls by more
than 30 percent in less than 12 months, as it has done in recent
years, we can be sure that either supply or demand, or both, were
shifting substantially and rather irregularly.

In Table 5-1, the direction of the changes in the equilibrium price
and quantity of various combinations of demand and supply shifts is
summarized. For example, in Box *A* it is seen that if both demand
and supply increase (shift to the right) the quantity exchanged will
also increase while the price may go up or down or may remain
constant. In attempting to understand fully the market mechanics
involved in supply and demand analysis, the reader would do well to
attempt independently to derive the many changes in the characteristics of the equilibrium as summarized in Table 5-1.

Table 5-1

	$D\uparrow$	$D=$	$D\downarrow$	
$S\uparrow$	*A* $P?Q\uparrow$	*B* $P\downarrow Q\uparrow$	*C* $P\downarrow Q?$	
$S=$	*D* $P\uparrow Q\uparrow$	*E* $P=Q=$	*F* $P\downarrow Q\downarrow$	
$S\downarrow$	*G* $P\uparrow Q?$	*H* $P\uparrow Q\downarrow$	*I* $P?Q\downarrow$	

III.   THE ELASTICITY OF SUPPLY AND DEMAND

Before concluding this discussion of market mechanics, we must
deal with one final concept. This is the responsiveness of the quantity of a good which is supplied or demanded to a change in its price.

In previous sections, we have seen how shifts in demand (with supply held constant) and shifts in supply (with demand held constant) change the equilibrium price and quantity. In analyzing an increase in the supply of agricultural commodities, we discovered that the equilbrium slid down the demand curve; the price decreased and the quantity increased. When the demand curve shifted to the right, as in the case of the Soviet grain deal, the equilibrium slid up the supply curve, causing the price to increase. In analyzing the effect of these shifts, the degree to which the price and quantity change is an important consideration.

When, for example, the equilibrium changes by sliding down a demand curve, it is the shape of the demand curve which determines the ext⌐nt of the price-quantity change. Thus, in Figure 5-8, the shift of supply from SS to $S'S'$ elicits a much bigger price change with demand curve DD than with $D'D'$. This is due to the different shapes of the two curves. Conversely, the change in quantity is larger in $D'D'$ than in DD. Because $D'D'$ is flatter than DD, the quantity variable responds more to the changed supply than does the price.

This matter of responsiveness was also an issue in the case of the Soviet grain transaction. The price of grain rose so precipitously because the supply of grain was almost completely fixed once the year's harvest was in.

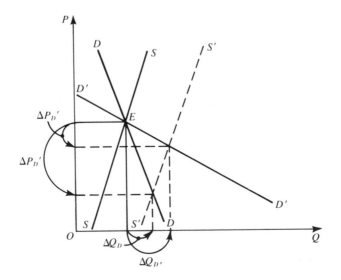

Figure 5-8

A. Elasticity Defined

The concept used to analyze these differing degrees of responsiveness is called *price elasticity*. Price elasticity is the degree to which the quantity demanded (or supplied) changes in response to a change in price along a single curve.

In the case of demand curves, this concept is referred to as price elasticity of demand; in the case of supply curves, it is known as price elasticity of supply. To evaluate the elasticity of a demand curve, the extent to which quantity demanded changes in response to a price change must be compared to the extent of the price change; to evaluate the elasticity of a supply curve, the response of quantity supplied to a price change is compared to the extent of the price change. Thus, in Figure 5-9, the price elasticity of demand describes the degree of responsiveness of *quantity demanded* to a change in price from, say, $12 to $10.

The degree of elasticity is measured by an *elasticity coefficient*. According to this measurement device, price elasticity is the *ratio* of the *percentage change in quantity* demanded (or supplied) to the *percentage change in price*.

$$\text{Elasticity} = \frac{\%\ \text{change in quantity}}{\%\ \text{change in price}}$$

or, in mathematical terms,

$$E = \frac{\Delta Q/Q}{\Delta P/P}$$

On the basis of this definition, we can compute elasticity if we know the change in quantity (ΔQ), the change in price (ΔP), a base quantity (Q), and a base price (P).

There is some confusion over which P and Q to use for the base when a discrete change occurs—the higher or the lower price involved in the change or the higher or the lower quantity involved in the change. To eliminate this confusion we shall take the average of the higher and lower price and quantity: $(P_1 + P_2) \div 2$. With this definition of the P and Q in the equation, we can rewrite it as follows:

$$E = \frac{\dfrac{\Delta Q}{\dfrac{Q_1 + Q_2}{2}}}{\dfrac{\Delta P}{\dfrac{P_1 + P_2}{2}}}$$

Employing this definition, let us run through a computation of
the elasticity of a demand curve segment. We will calculate the
elasticity of the demand curve segment BC in Figure 5-9. First, we
must find the change in quantity (ΔQ) for this segment. By inspecting the diagram, it is discovered that from B to C, quantity demanded changes from 100 to 150. Hence, ΔQ in the formula is 50.
Next, we have to determine a base quantity to be used in calculating
the percentage change in quantity. Following the rule of averaging,
we take the average of the higher and lower quantities, or the midpoint of 100 and 150. Hence, Q in the formula is 125. It follows that
the percentage change in quantity is 50/125 or 0.4. By identical reasoning, the percentage change in price is found to be 0.182. From
this procedure we calculate the elasticity of demand from B to C as

$$E = \frac{\dfrac{150-100}{150+100}}{\dfrac{12-10}{12+10}} = \frac{\dfrac{50}{125}}{\dfrac{2}{11}} = \frac{0.4}{0.182} = 2.2$$

Following the same procedure, the elasticity of the segment CD is

$$E = \frac{\dfrac{200-150}{200+150}}{\dfrac{10-8}{10+8}} = \frac{\dfrac{50}{175}}{\dfrac{2}{9}} = \frac{0.29}{0.22} = 1.3$$

From this calculation, we conclude that the first segment of the
demand curve (BC) is more elastic than the second segment (CD). In
percentage terms, the responsiveness of quantity demanded to a
price change in the first case exceeds the responsiveness in the second case. This is so even though the *slope* of the two segments—the
absolute response—is the same.

One might object, quite legitimately, that our computation here
is not correct—that, rather than 2.2 and 1.3, the numbers should be
−2.2 and −1.3 because the change in the quantity in the numerator
is negative if we subtract the new quantity from the original quantity demanded as price declines. By convention, however,

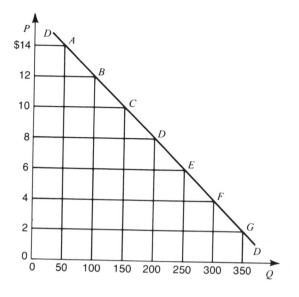

Figure 5-9

economists have decided to consider the absolute value to be the appropriate measurement of elasticity. This makes good sense. We are only interested in measuring the degree of responsiveness and not whether the response is positive or negative. Depending on the market curve with which we are dealing, we already know the direction of the response. If it is a demand curve the quantity response will be in the opposite direction of the price change, giving a negative value; if it is a supply curve the two variables will move in the same direction, giving a positive value.

It is also important at this point to emphasize that the use of "percentage change" is *not* merely excess baggage; that "absolute change" or the slope of the demand curve ($\Delta Q/\Delta P$) would not work as well. For two reasons the use of slope is unsatisfactory. First, if absolute change were used, the measurement of responsiveness would change whenever one changed the units in which either quantity or price were measured (for example, tons to bushels or dollars to cents). If percentage changes are used, the elasticity measurement is not altered when the price or quantity units are changed. Second, the concept of percentage (or relative) change permits the comparison of the responsiveness of the demand curves of different commodities. The measure of responsiveness using absolute quantities does not. If we would use absolute change as a measurement of responsiveness, we would have to compare tons of steel and tubes of toothpaste, for example—a meaningless comparison.

B. Degrees of Elasticity

Three distinct classes of price elasticity measurement can be distinguished: elastic, inelastic, and unit elastic. They are exhaustive classes so that every demand or supply curve segment must fall into one of them. Each class is defined by its relationship to the elasticity measurement of unity $(E = 1)$. As is clear from the elasticity formula, *unit elasticity* occurs where the percentage change in quantity just equals the percentage change in price. Similarly, all demand or supply curve segments in which the percentage change in quantity *exceeds* the percentage change in price possess an elasticity measurement greater than unity $(E > 1)$. Such segments are called *elastic*. All demand or supply curve segments in which the percentage change in quantity is *less than* the percentage change in price possess an elasticity measurement less than unity $(E < 1)$ and are called *inelastic*. In Figure 5-9, both segments BC and CD are elastic demand curve segments even though the former is more elastic than the latter.

In addition to these three classes, we should notice two special cases of elasticity: *infinite elasticity* and *zero elasticity*. In the irst case, the demand or supply curve is a horizontal line as displayed by DD in Figure 5-10. Here, if the price changes from P_1 to any other price, the percentage change in quantity is infinite.

Given the definition of elasticity, any infinite percentage change in quantity divided by a finite percentage change in price will yield

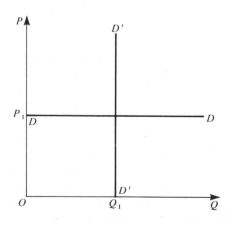

Figure 5-10

an infinite elasticity measurement. An example of infinite elasticity is the demand curve faced by any particular seller in a competitive market. If he sets the price of his output even 1 percent below the market price which is being charged by all of his competitors, the quantity demanded of his output will increase to infinity—all of the buyers would want to buy from him and not from other sellers.

The opposite situation occurs when a demand or supply curve has zero elasticity. This is pictured as the vertical line of $D'D'$ in Figure 5-10. Now, no matter what the price change, the demanders or suppliers of the commodity are willing to demand or supply only Q_1. Thus, the numerator of the elasticity coefficient in this case is zero and, consequently, so is the entire coefficient.

In the example of the Soviet grain deal, the supply was fixed once the harvest was completed if one defines supply as the visible supply in the market channels plus that stored by the growers. In this case one might conclude that the elasticity of supply is zero. However, growers do hold back quantities of grain in hope of higher prices later. They can be induced to sell more of the stored grain at high prices than at low prices, taking into account their expectations for future price movements. If a larger quantity will be supplied to the market at higher prices, the elasticity of supply is not zero but some positive number. Fresh produce, which can only be stored for short periods at high cost, provides a less ambiguous example of an elasticity coefficient of zero.

C. Elasticity and Total Revenue

The elasticity concept is more than a neat theoretical gadget with which economic theorists toy, although it is that too. A solid grasp of this concept is necessary if one is to understand how parts or sectors of an economy function and how the operation of some sectors of the economy affect behavior in other sectors. This is so because of the relationship of the *price elasticity of demand* to another concept with which we are already familiar, the concept of *total revenue*.

Until this point in our discussion we have considered total revenue to be the total sales income of a firm. We have defined it as the quantity of its product which a firm has sold times the price at which the sale was made ($TR = P \times Q$). The total revenue of a shoe firm that sells 10,000 pair of shoes at $20 per pair would therefore be $200,000. The total revenue concept, however, can be applied to an industry as well as to a firm. Indeed, an industry is simply a number of firms producing the same product. Thus, given a market price and a market demand curve, both the quantity demanded and the total revenue of the industry can be determined. In Figure 5-9, for example, given a price of $12 and the demand curve DD, 100 units can be sold, yielding a total market revenue of $1200. Or, at a price of $10, 150 units can be sold, yielding a total revenue of $1500. For an industry as well as a firm, $TR = P - Q$.

What, then, is the relationship of total industry revenue and the elasticity of demand? Because both total revenue and elasticity depend on the interaction of the price and the quantity variables, it is not surprising that this relationship exists. It can be stated as follows. If demand is *elastic, a decrease* in price will *increase total revenue;* if demand is of *unit elasticity, a change* in price *will not affect* total revenue. To verify this relationship, the reader would do well to compute the elasticity for each of the segments of the demand curve in Figure 5-9 and compare these measurements with the changes in total revenue over each of the segments.

In making these computations, it should be noted that even though this is a straight-line demand curve, the elasticity measurement is different for each segment even though the slope is the same throughout. Moreover, it will be noticed that the curve is elastic in all segments above the midpoint and inelastic in all segments below the midpoint. This phenomenon is true in the case of every straight-line demand curve. Thus, in Figure 5-9, demand is elastic from a price of $16 to a price of $8 and inelastic at any price less than $8. From this it follows that at the price of $8, total revenue must be at a maximum. If this last statement is not clear, one would be well advised to review the relationship between elasticity and total revenue.

The importance of this relationship between the elasticity of demand and total industry revenue must be stressed. We have seen that shifts in the supply curve alter the price-quantity equilibrium. We have not yet seen that shifts in the supply curve also have an impact on the sales revenue of the industry and therefore on the firms in the industry. An industry facing an inelastic demand, for example, would find that an increase in its supply curve would *decrease* its total sales revenue—a case of selling more units but earning less revenue. For the buyers of the industry's products, however, the impact is reversed. They obtain more units but give up less of their income for them. The opposite situation occurs for industries facing an elastic demand curve. Here, increases in the supply curve swell total revenue and decreases in supply trim total revenue in any given market. This relationship forms an important consideration in analyzing the behavior of both sellers and buyers.

D. Determinants of Elasticity

We are left with one final question about elasticity. Why do different commodities display different demand and supply elasticities? Let us consider demand first, since it is the most troublesome. One of the most notorious cases of demand inelasticity is that of agricultural commodities. Perhaps by seeing why the quantity demanded of these commodities is not responsive to changes in their price we can get a clue to the factors that cause differing degrees of elasticity.

Without question, a primary characteristic of farm products is that they are necessities. If life is to be sustained, food must be consumed. Consequently, even if the price of food changes a great deal, the quantity of food that people demand will remain relatively constant. If the price of food rises, people cut down on other things but keep their food intake about the same. If the price falls they will not generally consume a great deal more; the stomach, in this case, is a limiting factor. But necessity and limits to consumption are not the only reasons for the inelasticity of the demand for agricultural products.

Another consideration is that any given farm product accounts for a relatively small portion of a consumer's budget. For such small items price changes are absorbed and go largely unnoticed. The case of salt is a classic example. Even if the price of salt would double, few people would decrease their use of it.

The clear lack of substitutes for farm products is still another contributing factor. If there were a multitude of things that one could substitute for food intake, the elasticity of demand for food would undoubtedly be much greater—people would switch from food to other commodities if the price of food rose.

In general, then, *price inelasticity of demand* results when a good (1) has no close substitutes, (2) is a necessity, (3) has a physical limit to the amount of its consumption, and (4) is only a small item in the consumer's budget.

In discussing the determinants of demand elasticity, one must be very careful. The way in which a good is defined has a great deal to do with the elasticity of its demand. Liquid beverage, as a commodity, has a very inelastic demand. There are no good substitutes for drinking. The demand for soda, on the other hand, is much more elastic—a number of close substitutes come directly to mind. For the same reason, the demand for cola is still more elastic, and the demand for Pepsi-Cola is extremely elastic. If the price of Pepsi-Cola rose by two pennies while the price of Coca–Cola remained unchanged, a large shift of patronage would occur. They are rather close substitutes. There is not a 100 percent shift because consumers find some bit of real or imagined difference between the two drinks. The producers work hard to increase the difference between the drinks in the minds of the drinkers.

The reason for differences in the elasticity of supply are easier to handle than the reasons for differences in demand elasticity. Essentially, supply elasticity is synonymous with the flexibility of an industry's output, that is, the ease with which output can be adjusted to changes in price. This flexibility is related to the cost structure of the firms in an industry and, in particular, to the shape of their marginal cost curves. If the marginal cost curves are steep, the industry supply will be inelastic; if they are flat, the industry supply will be elastic. As one observer put it: "The supply of genuine paintings by a dead artist is highly inelastic, but the supply of copies is likely to be highly elastic."

E. Some Examples of the Price Elasticity of Demand

As might be expected, the importance of the price elasticity concept in economics has led to a good deal of effort by economists to measure the responsiveness of the quantity of goods demanded to their prices. Indeed, one of the most renowned of these measurement efforts was undertaken in the 1930s by Henry Schultz, who estimated the price elasticities of various agricultural commodities.[4] His estimates have been referred to numerous times in debates over government policies to alter the market price of farm products. Schultz found that, by and large, the demand for agricultural commodities was inelastic, suggesting that government policies to raise the price of farm products would lead to an increase in farm income.

A more recent study (1970) of the determinants of consumer demand also produced estimates of the price elasticity of numerous goods and services.[5] Table 5-2 presents these elasticity estimates for a selection of commodities and services.

All of these price elasticities measure the responsiveness of quantity demanded to price in the short-run—a period of time too short to allow consumers to fully adjust to the price change. Generally, the long-run price elasticity is greater than the short-run elasticity.

---

4. Henry Schultz, *Theory and Measurement of Demand* (Chicago: University of Chicago Press, 1938).

5. H. S. Houthakker and Lester D. Taylor, *Consumer Demand in the United States, 1929–1970* (Cambridge: Harvard University Press, 1970).

Table 5-2
Estimated Price Elasticities of Demand for Selected Goods and Services

COMMODITY OR SERVICE	PRICE ELASTICITY
Purchased meals	2.30
Shoes and other footwear	.39
Kitchen appliances	.63
China, glassware, and utensils	1.16
Physicians	.58
Medical care and hospitalization insurance	.28
Legal services	.48
New and used cars	.96
Tires and tubes	.63
Automobile repair	.36
Gasoline and oil	.16
Radio and television receivers	1.19
Radio and television repair	1.01
Newspapers and magazines	.10

Source: H. S. Houthakker and L. D. Taylor, *Consumer Demand in the United States, 1929–1970* (Cambridge, Mass.: Harvard University Press, 1970).

Indeed, the long-run elasticity may be very substantial if satisfactory substitutes for the commodity in question can be found over a period of time. In studying the elasticity patterns shown in the table, the previous discussion of the determinants of price elasticity should be borne in mind. Special note should be taken of the relationship of the elasticity measurements for the commodities and services related to automobile use.

In chapter 3, the importance of the price elasticity of demand for gasoline in framing effective energy policy was emphasized. It is worth noting that the price elasticity estimate for gasoline in the Houthakker-Taylor study is only 0.16, suggesting that a 10 percent increase in price would lead to only a 1.6 percent decrease in the quantity demanded. Because of the importance of this elasticity in the policy debate in the early 1970s several studies have attempted to improve upon this estimate. A number of these estimates are shown in Table 5-3. While the estimates vary, they support the earlier conclusion that, at least in the short run, the price of gasoline does not respond greatly to a change in its price. As noted earlier, this is one reason why the gasoline tax has been opposed by some as a means of reducing energy consumption in the United States. The very real possibility that the long-run price elasticity of demand for

Table 5-3
Estimated Price Elasticities of Demand for Gasoline in the United States

STUDY	PRICE ELASTICITY
Houthakker and Taylor (1970)	.16
Houthakker and Verleger (1973)	.30
U.S. Department of Transportation (1973)	.20
Greenspan (1973)	.40

Source: Business Week, December 15, 1973, p. 23.

gasoline is substantially greater than these values should not be overlooked. In the long run, consumers may well be able to find good substitutes for the continued driving of their existing cars. These include: buying smaller cars, buying cars with better gasoline mileage, constructing improved mass transit facilities, using bicycles, moving to residences which are closer to jobs, and so on. Indeed, dismissal of a gasoline tax on the basis of these very low short-run elasticities appears to have been premature. Consumers seem to be making precisely those kinds of shifts which one would expect over time.

IV. CONCLUSION AND SUMMARY

The objective of this chapter has been to develop a framework for thinking about the process of exchange in a market economy. Obviously, exchange can take place only if buyers and sellers are in touch with each other and it is this that the institution of the market makes possible. In the market, prices are established and the quantity of the good to be traded is determined by the interaction of buyers and sellers.

In analyzing this process of exchange, we developed several basic concepts. These included the supply and demand curves, equilibrium, supply and demand shifts, and elasticity. All of these concepts aided us in thinking precisely about the mechanism of the market. They enable any two people to discuss meaningfully the process of exchange and to analyze with consistency the effect of changes within the household and business sector on the price and quantity exchanged of particular goods and services.

Having analyzed the details of market mechanics, we must not lose sight of the larger role played by the tool of market analysis. Indeed, the primary functions of the market concepts developed in this chapter are that of integration or synthesis. For example, knowledge of the Law of Supply and Demand allows one to trace the

effect of a change in consumers' income on the profits of shoe manufacturers. It allows one to trace a change in the input–output relationship of producing, say, gasoline, to the quantity of cars which
will be purchased by consumers. Similarly, knowledge of elasticity
enables the analyst to discover how the sales revenue of an industry
becomes altered as the willingness of producers to supply increases
or decreases. In short, knowledge of market mechanics is necessary
to discover how economic changes in the household sector affect the
business sector and vice versa, and how changes in either sector
influence the prices of goods and services and the quantity of them
which is bought and sold.

QUESTIONS

1. The following two equations describe a market demand relationship and
   a market supply relationship for a particular good, say, granola bars. The
   price is measured in cents per package and the quantity is measured in
   hundreds of packages per unit of time:

   $$Q_S = -30 + 20P$$

   $$Q_D = 400 - 8P$$

   (a) Construct a table which relates the quantity demanded to the price
   (by 1¢ intervals) from 8¢ to 22¢. (Simply calculate the quantity demanded for each assumed price using the demand equation.) Construct a similar table which relates the quantity supplied to the price
   (by 1¢ intervals) from 8¢ to 22¢.
   (b) On a piece of graph paper, plot the supply and demand curves which
   are defined by the two equations.
   (c) From your graph, what is the equilibrium price of granola bars? What
   quantity will be exchanged per unit of time in equilibrium?
   (d) Assume that the government decreed that the price of granola bars
   could not rise above 10¢ per package. Describe the market situation
   in this case. What group(s) of traders would be displeased by this
   decision? What proportion of the total quantity demanded at this
   price would be satisfied?
2. Because of an exceptionally good harvest, the price of cereal grains (an
   input to granola bar producers) falls substantially. This decrease in the
   input price reduces the marginal costs of granola bar producers which
   ultimately influences the supply curve of granola bars. The new supply
   curve is defined by

   $$Q_S = -10 + 20P$$

   (a) Plot the new supply curve on the same diagram as was used for
   question 1.

(b) What would happen to the equilibrium price and quantity exchanged of granola bars because of the exceptionally good harvest of cereal grain?

(c) Describe the process by which the price would change from the original equilibrium level to the new equilibrium. What set of traders would initiate the process?

(d) What is the elasticity of demand between the old and new eqilibrium prices? On the basis of your calculation, what do you think happened to the total sales revenue of granola bar producers because of the shift in the supply curve? Check your conclusions by calculating total sales revenue at the old and the new prices.

3. Go back to the original equilibrium. Consider the following changes which might occur in the world. Evaluate how each of them would be likely to affect the equilibrium quantity and price. For each change, discuss whether the impact on the equilibrium would occur through a shift in the demand curve or a shift in the supply curve and state which determinant of demand or supply would be the vehicle through which the equilibrium would be affected.

(a) The managers in the granola bar plants become inefficient so that more inputs are required per unit of output than previously.

(b) Research findings demonstrate that the application of a particular kind of fertilizer used on cereal grains has serious adverse health effects through consumption of the grains.

(c) The manufacturers of chocolate bars wage a major nationwide advertising campaign entitled "A chocolate bar each noon means strength for the whole day."

(d) It is discovered that inhalation of the dust in the cereal plant reduces life expectancy. Because of this the managers of cereal plants find that they have to pay 30¢ more per hour in order to attract a labor force.

(e) The price of milk triples.

4. Describe carefully the difference between "supply" and "quantity supplied" and "demand" and "quantity demanded."

5. "Price is a rationing device." Discuss this statement showing how prices serve as signals in the allocation of spending and resources.

6. "When money is exchanged for goods at the equilibrium price, *both* the buyer and the seller are better off than if the exchange had not taken place." Do you agree with this statement? Can you show graphically (or logically) that this is so?

7. Which of the following are consistent with a perfect and competitive market?

(a) There is a limit to the number of taxicabs which a city can have and the only way to get to be a taxicab driver is to buy the medallion from an existing cabbie.

(b) In order to be a plumber you must get the permission of the existing members of the plumbing trade.

(c) In order to see, test, and get the price of the various automobiles you would consider buying, you must travel 65 miles and take an entire weekend.

(d) In order to sell used cars, you must sign an affidavit stating that you will deal honestly with your customers and potential customers.

(e) Sellers of granola bars would like to sell more of their available supply at existing prices than they are able.

(f) In order to buy circus tickets, you have to send in a filled-in form with your check or money order.

APPENDIX: WHAT, HOW, AND FOR WHOM—Some Basic Relationships

Thus far we have studied the private participants in the market system—households and business firms. We have analyzed their decision-making processes, and then we have introduced competitive markets as the structures which relate production and consumption decisions. Before we turn to chapter 6 to consider how well a perfect market system performs its task of answering the basic economic questions—what to produce, how, and for whom—let us return to those questions to understand them better.

We must remind ourselves that a market system provides only one of the ways by which a society may determine what goods and services to produce from the array of possibilities open to it, what combination of resources will be chosen from all of the combinations possible to produce those goods and services, and who will receive what quantities of the goods and services, that are produced. Choices must be made whether a society is organized to make them through tradition, command, or markets. Each economic system may be judged upon how well the basic choices are made according to standards of efficiency, equity and justice. Several diagrams will help us to understand the basic relationships involved in what, how, and for whom.

A. What to Produce: The Production Possibilities Curve

The social choice of what goods and services to produce requires that a vast number of alternative combinations be considered. However, to simplify the problem, suppose that we can choose between only two kinds of goods: capital goods and consumer goods. *Capital goods* are products that are used to produce other things. These include such things as factory buildings, shoe machines and barber chairs. *Consumer goods* are those final products which satisfy consumer wants, such as shoes and haircuts.

At one extreme we might choose to use all of our resources to produce only capital goods, a conceptual possibility, although not a very realistic one. In this event we could produce OA_1 of capital goods, an amount which is plotted on the vertical axis of Figure 5A-1. At the other extreme, if we were to devote all of our resources to the production of consumer goods, we might produce the amount OB_1, plotted on the horizontal axis of the figure. Realistically, a society must choose some capital goods and some consumer goods, since it must provide for both current and future consumption needs. All such possibilities lie along the curve joining point A_1 to point B_1. A society must decide where along the curve it is to produce, whether at point C, yielding A_3 units of capital goods and B_3 units of consumer goods, or at point D, yielding more consumer goods and fewer capital goods, or at some other point on the curve.

Shifting of the Production Possibilities Curve. The points on this curve represent possible choices of what to produce given a fixed amount of available resources and given the state of technology. Should the quantity of one or more resources increase, more of both goods could be produced. The curve would shift outward, for example, from A_1B_1 to A_4B_4, indicating that it is now possible to expand

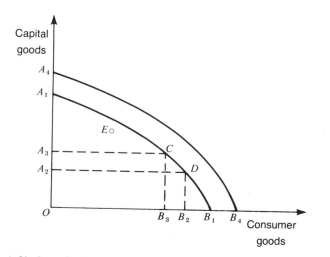

Figure 5A-1 Choice of what to produce: the production possibilities.

the production of both capital goods and consumer goods. The same type of shift would occur if new, more efficient techniques of production were discovered. Again, production of both kinds of goods could increase. Because of either of these changes, the economy would experience *economic growth*. Nevertheless, growth in quantity of resources and technological change occurs only over time and then often slowly. At any moment in society the choice must be made of what to produce but that choice is constrained by the position of the *production possibilities curve*.

A society that gives a high priority to economic growth will choose a point relatively close to the OA axis, for instance, point C on the production possibilities curve. This represents the production of a relatively large volume of capital goods and a relatively small volume of consumer goods. On the other hand, a community that assigns a high priority to present consumption and low priority to growth might produce at D. Because capital goods are a productive resource, expansion of their quantity will permit greater production in the next time period, causing the whole curve to shift outward over time.

Shape of the Production Possibilities Curve.   The production possibilities curve is concave to the origin at zero because of the *Law of Increasing Costs* (opportunity costs). Costs of producing one product will increase as resources are successively shifted to it from another product. This is so because some resources are rather specialized. Some are specialized in the production of capital goods and would be less efficient when used to produce consumer goods, while other resources are specialized in the production of consumer goods and would be less efficient when used to produce capital goods. If some quantity of both classes of goods is produced, those resources most suitable to each can be put to their most effective use.

Suppose that we start from point B_1 in Figure 5A-1 with all resources devoted to the production of consumer goods. Now let us take away some resources from consumer goods production and use them to produce capital goods. Naturally, we would select resources which are most advantageously used to produce capital goods. In doing so, we must give up B_2B_1 of consumer goods to get OA_2 of capital goods. The shift of resources will increase capital goods more than if no resources were especially efficient in capital goods production. As resources continue to be shifted, we will have to select those that are rather specialized in the production of consumer goods and of lower productivity in the prodution of capital goods. Hence, by giving up an amount of consumer goods B_3B_2, which is equal to the quantity B_2B_1, we gain an amount of capital goods A_2A_3, which is *smaller* than the previous increase of OA_2. Stated alternatively, we have to give up more consumer goods production to get an increase in capital goods equal to the first increase. The opportunity cost of the second increment of capital goods is greater than that of the first increment.

The existence of increasing costs and a bowed-out production possibilities curve can also be understood by recognizing that different products are produced most efficiently with different proportions of resources. For example, the production of food requires relatively more land, as compared to the production of electronic components which requires relatively more capital. Starting from a position in which all resources are devoted to the production of electronic components, the shift of some land to food production would involve very little sacrifice of output of electronic components. Successive shifts would eventually involve greater sacrifice of electronic component output as capital is moved from the production of components into the production of food. If resources were completely neutral in their use, the production possibilities curve would be a straight line, for example, between A_1 and B_1 in Figure 5A-1.

Production possibilities curves can illuminate many economic relationships. For example, point E in Figure 5A-1 represents a situation in which some resources are unemployed. It is not on the society's production possibilities curve because the curve is drawn on the presumption of full employment of resources. By employing the unemployed resources, the society can obtain more of *both* classes of goods, moving out to the production possibilities curve.

It is also interesting to note that if the labor force is inefficient because of poor diet, illiteracy, or other causes related to inadequate consumption, we might find a greater outward shift in the curve from one time period to the next if resources were shifted to consumer goods from capital goods. This would, in effect, increase the productivity of the labor output. From this it is clear that what to produce is a critical choice facing underdeveloped countries.

B. How to Produce: The Isoquant Curve

The discussion of the production possibilities curve indicated that the inputs to production could be substituted, one for another. This can be illustrated by a curve known as an *isoquant curve*. Each curve in Figure 5A-2 is made up of points representing all of the combinations of labor and machinery that will produce a specified output. In this hypothetical example, engineering information pro-

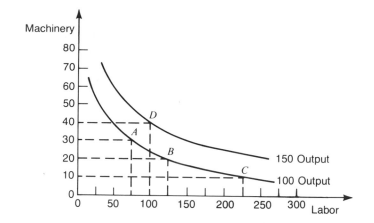

Figure 5A-2 Choice of how to produce: the isoquant curve.

vides us with the fact that 100 units of output can be produced with 30 units of machinery and 75 units of labor (point A), with 20 units of machinery and 125 units of labor (point B), with 10 units of machinery and 225 units of labor (point C), or with any other combination of machinery and labor described by a point on the same curve.

In the figure it can be seen that as labor is substituted for machinery—say, in moving from A to B to C and holding output constant at the 100 unit level—more and more labor is required to replace each machine. The isoquant curve is convex to the origin. This shape occurs because, while factors of production are substitutes for one another, *they are not perfect substitutes*. As labor is added and machinery subtracted, the additional labor has less and less machinery to work with. The effect of this change in proportions is to require more and more labor to replace each machine that is withdrawn. At the extreme there is so much labor relative to machines that an additional unit of labor would contribute very little to output, while one less unit of machinery would subtract a relatively large amount from output. Hence a very large quantity of labor must be added if output is to be held constant while a machine is subtracted.

Combinations of machinery and labor that could produce a larger output would be represented by points on a curve that would lie farther out from the origin. The curve in Figure 5A-2 labeled "150 output" is such a curve. Point D illustrates that it takes 10 more units of machinery and 25 more units of labor to produce 50 more units of output than the input-output combination represented by point A. It takes more resources to produce more output, but along the new curve representing 150 units of output, labor and machinery may again be substituted for one another to produce this output. The isoquant curve is similar to the indifference curve described in the appendix to chapter 3. Both illustrate the principle of substitutability.

We might digress here from the general proposition of social choice in combining factors of production to discuss the "best combination" in a price-directed economy. Suppose that the relative prices of machinery and labor are 6¼ to 1. Converting this ratio to dollar prices, one unit of labor will cost $10, while one unit of machinery costs $62.50. If total outlay on resources were $2500 it would be possible to spend it all on machinery and buy 40 units. If all were spent on labor one could buy 250 units. A straight line between those two points would describe all of the combinations of machinery and labor that could be bought for $2500. This straight line is a *constant outlay line* and is similar in concept to the *budget line* in the appendix to chapter 3.

In Figure 5A–3, this constant outlay line is tangent to the isoquant curve representing 100 units of output, the point of tangency being at *B*. The best combination of resources is 20 units of machinery and 125 units of labor so long as the firm faces these conditions of total outlay, techniques of production, and relative prices of resources. Any other combination of labor and machinery

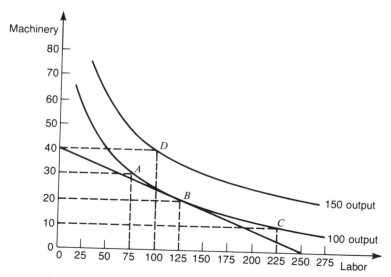

Figure 5A-3

involving a total outlay of $2500 will be a point on a lower isoquant curve representing a lower volume of total output. Point *B* represents the highest isoquant attainable—the maximum output attainable with $2500 worth of inputs.

A larger total outlay by the firm would be represented by a total outlay line farther out from the origin, and it would be parallel to the first outlay line so long as the relative prices of machinery and labor remain the same. There will be a tangency point between this total outlay line and an isoquant curve representing a larger output. That tangency will indicate the "best" combination of factors of production given the new and larger total outlay.

C. For Whom to Produce: The Lorenz Curve

The character of the distribution of total product (or income) may be visualized by reference to a *Lorenz curve* (Figure 5A-4.) If the curve is bowed toward the "people" axis, the distribution is shown to be unequal. For example, at point *A* on the Lorenz curve *OACBG*, the poorest 30 percent of the people are seen to receive only 10 percent of the income. At point *B* the richest 10 percent of the people are shown to receive 30 percent of the income. At the intermediate point, *C*, the richest 25 percent of the people receive 60 percent of the income. Clearly, the more bowed the curve, the more unequal is the distribution of income. The reader can satisfy himself that this is true by drawing a more bowed curve and reading the percentage of income associated with percentage of people at various points along it.

A straight line through the origin of Figure 5A-4, bisecting the 90-degree angle, represents perfect equality in the distribution of the total product or total income. It is evident from the line *ODEFG* that in a society with such an income distribution, each 1 percent of the people get 1 percent of the income, and so on. Again, the reader can test the proposition by reading off more points along the line.

Like the production possibilities curve and the isoquant curve, the Lorenz curve depicts a fundamental economic choice which all societies must make. Indeed, implicitly all societies—East and West, planned and unplanned—continually make such choices, which become reflected in their income distributions. If we were to draw Lorenz curves for many societies, we could see at a glance how societies have made different choices regarding for whom the product is produced, and which societies possess the more unequal distribution. We would notice that there was a substantial degree of inequality within *both* the planned economies and those which are primarily market economies. One recent study, for example, indi-

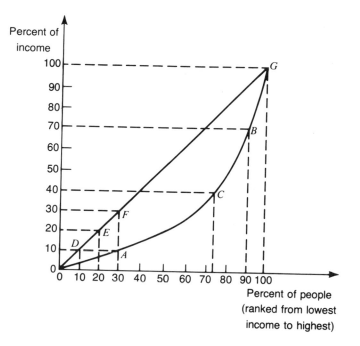

Figure 5A-4 Choice of for whom to produce: the Lorenz curve.

cated that the Soviet Union had a slightly more unequal distribution than the planned economies of Hungary, Czechoslovakia, Poland, and Bulgaria. The degree of inequality in these Eastern European countries, in turn, was about the same as that in the most egalitarian Western economy, Sweden. The United States and Canada had notably more income inequality than *any* of the other countries mentioned.[6]

QUESTIONS

1. How might the production possibilities curve be used to aid in deciding whether to extend, at substantial cost, a highway into the interior of Brazil? Use the notion of opportunity costs explicitly in your answer. Are there elements of the what-to-produce problem that cannot be handled by the production possibilities curve or a mathematical extension of it to more than two variables?
2. Consider the example of Figure 5A-3. Discuss what would happen if the price of labor were to double to $20 while the price of machinery stayed

---

6. See Peter Wiles, *Distribution of Income: East and West* (Amsterdam: North-Holland, 1974).

the same. Trace out the impact on total outlay, total output, and the "best" combination of resources.

3. Many people through the years have treated the distribution of income as a purely ethical question. Others have argued that the economic effects are so great that the decision on how to distribute income must be dominated by considerations of economic growth and productivity. Discuss. Will the shape of the Lorenz curve illustrate whether a society has adopted the equity or the economic growth basis for its decision?

6 | The Performance of a Market System

At this point in our analysis we must link together all of the markets in the economy. A market system, after all, entails more than the behavior of the household sector or the business sector or the process by which the supply and demand for a particular good or service becomes reconciled. A market system consists of the interactions of all of the component parts and processes in the economy. Because the only purpose of an economic system is to serve the needs of the people, it is the criterion of economic welfare which we shall use to judge the performance of the market system.

In this chapter, then, we will discuss the general equilibrium of the entire market system and investigate how and how well the market system answers the three basic questions: What? How? For Whom? We will be especially interested in the ways in which these answers are, from society's viewpoint, good or bad, and whether the market system serves or fails to serve the public interest.

I. THE CONCEPT OF GENERAL EQUILIBRIUM

In our study of households, firms, and markets, we have been doing what economists call *partial equilibrium analysis*. That is, we have taken these sectors one at a time and have analyzed their behavior under certain assumed conditions and in isolation from the rest of the economy. In our analysis of each of these parts of the economy, we have employed the *ceteris paribus* assumption and concentrated on the limited number of relationships in which we were most interested. In analyzing household behavior, for example, we obtained the relationship between the price of a good and the quantity demanded. We did this by assuming that all other relevant variables were constant. These included the consumer's tastes and preferences, the prices of other goods, and the consumer's income. It is the application of this *ceteris paribus* assumption in the study of individual sectors that has caused our analysis thus far to be "partial."

The world, however, does not operate on the *ceteris paribus* assumption. There are no real-world mechanisms for holding some variables constant while allowing others to change. In the real world, all variables are in motion simultaneously and, more important, they are all related. Thus, when an early frost destroys one-half of the orange crop and raises the prices of oranges and orange juice, it disturbs the equilibrium in the soft-drink market—the prices of other goods are no longer constant. The soft-drink situation, in turn, disturbs the equilibrium in the beer and ale market and so on, *ad infinitum*. An analogous situation holds in the factor markets; the discovery of a new technology influences the relative demands for labor and capital, the prices of labor and capital, and the incomes of those who supply labor and capital.

Because each market perpetually moves toward an equilibrium, the entire competitive system, being a composite of such markets, moves toward an equilibrium. Because the process of change is never ending, however, this sought-for equilibrium is never achieved. The study of a market system's perpetual tendency toward an equilibrium position is called *general equilibrium* analysis. This concept is of such importance to an understanding of how a price system works that we would be shirking our task if we skimmed over it lightly.

In order to understand the general equilibrium characteristic of a market system, we must grasp the system's quality of extreme interrelatedness, which, we must emphasize, is closely related to the term *economic adjustment*. We have seen that the decision maker in each sector of the economy is able to adjust his choices so as to move toward a partial equilibrium or optimum position—a maximum profit or maximum utility position. Moreover, in the marketplace, prices and quantities exchanged also adjust to form an equilibrium. In each market equilibrium position, there is no consumer who is unable to buy the good at the prevailing price, no seller who is unable to sell his product at this price, no surplus or shortage of any good or factor and, therefore, no tendency for price to change. With all of these conditions met we have what is called a general equilibrium, a situation of complete *economic adjustment*. With all of the goods and services markets in equilibrium, with all of the factor markets in equilibrium, with all of the households and all of the businesses in equilibrium, the economic system itself is in adjustment.

The interrelatedness of the parts of the market system can be further understood by observing the economic effects of a change in one of the economy's basic variables—say, a change in tastes, or a change in an input-output relationship, or a change in any one of the other variables that might shift some demand or supply curve. With such a shift, one market is thrown out of equilibrium and an adjustment in its equilibrium becomes necessary. The adjustment that must take place is clear; both the price and the quantity exchanged in this market will be altered. A new equilibrium will result.

This, however, is only the first step in a long chain of events. We assumed in deriving each demand curve that all prices other than the price to which it is related remain constant. If some price, therefore, is changed, this assumption no longer holds. The demand curves for all goods related to the commodity whose price has changed will shift. Because of these changes, succeeding adjustments are required in all markets and in all sectors—the outputs of various industries change, factor demands change, the prices of factors change, incomes change, and so on. The impact of the original change is ricocheted through the entire circular flow. Surely the statement of Schumpeter cited at the end of chapter 2 catches the essence of this elaborate system of linkages.

As a real-world example of this circularity, of this extreme interrelatedness, consider the following brief description of the English Cotton Famine of the 1860s after the disruption caused by the Civil War.

> The Civil War led to a near suspension of English imports of American cotton, which in 1860 had amounted to about four-fifths of the English supply. The price of cotton at Liverpool rose from 8 pence per pound in June of 1860 to a peak of 31½ pence in July of 1864.
>
> The [price caused by the] famine led to a great decrease in the demand for cotton fabrication, and hence in the demand for the services of cotton mills and their laborers. Wage . . . rates fell an unknown amount, and workers earnings fell much more when they were forced to work with the inferior Surat cotton.
>
> Of course a large expansion took place in rival fabrics. The production of flax quadrupled between 1861 and 1864 in Ireland, and yarn imports rose greatly; even so prices of linen goods rose about 60 percent between 1862 and 1864. Similarly, the wool industry experienced a great boom: imports of wool rose by a third during the period,

and raw wool prices rose more than 40 percent. . . . Some migration of cotton workers and entrepreneurs to Yorkshire (a wool fabricating center), and of weaving of woolens to Lancashire (a cotton fabricating center), helped the latter area.

The unemployment in Lancashire caused great distress. . . . The great decrease in consumer expenditure in the area hit shopkeepers hard, and landlords even harder. . . . By 1863 about one-fourth of the families requiring public assistance were not directly connected with the textile industry.

Of course the effects reached to industries for which cotton textiles was an important customer. The textile machinery industry had a bad slump until 1864, and warehouses of the region suffered also. The Lancashire and Yorkshire Railway . . . had a decline in both passenger and freight traffic in 1862 and 1863.

In Birmingham . . . , the button and needle industries had to discharge many workers, but the edged-tool industry expanded greatly to provide tools for new cotton plantings in India and Egypt.

It does not seem bold to conjecture that everyone in England was somehow affected by the cotton famine: as a consumer, in the price of clothing; as a laborer, in the altered directions of the consumer spending; in the effects on transport, banking, and commerce; as a capitalist, on the return on investments in textiles and other industries. [1]

A. A Simple Model

The extreme interrelatedness of the parts of a price system can be described in yet another way: by building a model and observing its operation. As before, we must make some simplifying assumptions in order to give the model substance and also make it manageable.

First, let us assume that the economy which this model describes is a competitive market economy which produces only two homogeneous goods. We will call them luxuries and staples. *Second,* let us assume there are only two factors of production used in producing these two goods, labor and capital. *Third,* let us assume that the production of luxuries is *capital intensive* (a high ratio of capital to labor in the production process) while the production of staples is *labor intensive* (a low ratio of capital to labor). *Fourth,* let us assume that the people in this economy can be divided into two groups, each of which earns income. We shall call these two groups labor suppliers (laborers) and capital suppliers (capitalists). *Finally,* let us assume that the economy is in general equilibrium. Every household and business is in optimum position and the price in

---

1. George Stigler, *The Theory of Price* (New York: Macmillan, 1952), pp. 288–89.

every market equates the quantity supplied with the quantity demanded.

Figure 6–1 depicts the structure of this model economy. The household sector is divided into two groups: laborers and capital owners. The group of laborers supplies labor services to the businesses and capital owners supply the services of capital. Both groups purchase luxuries and staples with incomes earned from supplying the services of their factors. The business sector, too, is divided into two groups: the luxury-goods industry and the staple-goods industry. Both produce their product by hiring the services of labor and capital. Therefore, there are four competitive markets in this economy: two product markets and two factor markets.

The market conditions conforming to the model's assumptions are indicated in Figure 6-2. Each of the four markets in this economy is seen in equilibrium (E). The equilibrium price in each market is P_1 and the equilibrium quantity is Q_1. In addition, the total revenue in each of the markets is depicted by the rectangle P_1EQ_1O in each diagram. In Figures 6-2(a) and 6-2(b), this rectangle refers to the total sales revenue of the staple and luxury goods industries, respectively. In Figures 6-2(c) and 6-2(d), it refers to the income received by the laborers and capital owners, respectively.

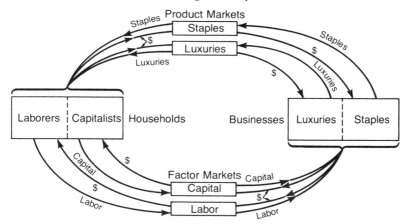

Figure 6-1

B. The Effects of a Change in Consumer Tastes

The best way to grasp the interrelatedness of the parts of our model economy is to watch it in operation. However, to put it into operation some basic change must occur to alter the existing general

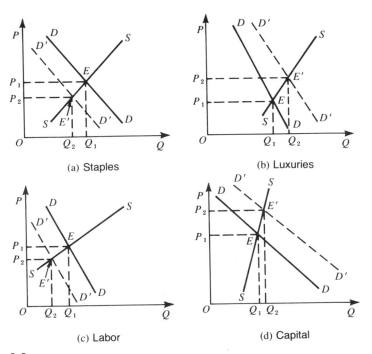

(a) Staples

(b) Luxuries

(c) Labor

(d) Capital

Figure 6-2

equilibrium. One of the forces determining the level of one or more of the supply or demand curves must change. To stimulate this change artificially, let us assume that consumers' tastes and preferences shift. In particular, let us assume that the tastes of both laborers and capitalists shift away from staples and toward luxuries. Such shifts in consumer tastes are common in the real world. People's preferences do change—compact cars do replace large sedans, miniskirts go out of style, calf-length skirts come in.

Let us now observe how our model economy adjusts to this disturbance in the general equilibrium. The first impact of this change in tastes is clear; the demand curves for both luxuries and staples shift. In the case of staples, consumers are willing to buy less at each given price after the change in tastes than before the change. The demand curve for staples shifts to the left from DD to, say, $D'D'$ in Figure 6-2(a). The opposite result occurs in the market for luxuries. There, because of the change in tastes, consumers desire to increase their purchases at any given price. The demand curve for luxuries shifts to the right from DD to, say, $D'D'$ in Figure 6-2(b). These demand shifts now elicit changes in a multitude of other economic variables as the system struggles to regain equilibrium. Let us trace some of these changes.

With the shift in demand curves, the change in tastes originating in the household sector makes itself known in the markets for goods and services. As seen in Figure 6-2, the price of staples falls and the price of luxuries rises. From these markets, the shock is then passed along to other sectors. To the business sector, the changed prices represent a modified set of signals for each of the industries. The firms in both the luxury industry and the staple industry react to these price changes by modifying the quantities which they produce and supply to the market. This is so because of the positive slope of the marginal cost (supply) curves of the firms in these industries. As each firm seeks its equilibrium where the marginal cost *(MC)* of producing the last unit equals the marginal revenue *(MR)* realized from selling that unit—so as to achieve the equilibrium condition, $MR = MC$—greater quantities will be supplied at higher prices than at lower prices. Therefore, the higher price of luxuries will elicit an increase in the quantity of luxury goods supplied and the lower price of staples will lead to a contraction in the quantity of staples supplied. From these changes a new equilibrium is depicted as E' in Figure 6-2(a) and 6-2(b). The price and quantity of luxuries increases, and the total revenue of the luxury industry rises. The price and quantity of staple goods decrease, and the total revenue of the staple industry falls.

Clearly, this is not the end of the chain of repercussions. As the output of one industry rises while that of the other falls, the demand for the factors of production, the inputs, is also affected. When output in the staple industry falls, the demand for both labor and capital decreases. However, because the staple industry is labor intensive, the decrease in the demand for labor is substantially greater than the decrease in the demand for capital.

Conversely, when the output of the luxury industry rises, the demand for both labor and capital increases. In this case, the demand for capital increases a great deal while the demand for labor only rises a little. The luxury industry is capital intensive.

In the case of labor, the combination of the large *decrease* in demand from the staple industry and the small *increase* in demand from the luxury industry decrees a *net decrease* in the market demand for labor. This is shown as a decrease in the demand curve for labor from DD to $D'D'$ in Figure 6-2(c).

For capital, the reverse occurs. The large *increase* in capital demand from the luxury industry coupled with the small *decrease* in demand from the staple industry decrees a *net increase* in the market demand for capital. The demand curve for capital rises from *DD* to *D'D'* in Figure 6-2(*d*). Because of these demand shifts, the price of labor, the quantity exchanged, and the income of laborers fall, while the price of capital, the quantity exchanged, and the income of capital owners rise.

The impact of the original change in tastes and preferences has gone full circle, arriving back at the household sector. But this is still not the end. The two groups in that sector, the laborers and the capital owners, have experienced a shift in incomes: the incomes of the laborers have decreased and the incomes of the capital owners have increased. Thus, relative to the laborers, the capital suppliers have become more well-to-do.

With this change in the distribution of income, the household sector's demand for goods and services becomes modified a second time. With a new set of incomes, consumers will again reallocate their expenditures between luxuries and staples. The demand curves will shift again. Thus, the original change in tastes has generated a secondary shift in demand which, like the first, is transmitted through the circular flow of the price system. Prices and outputs are again changed in all markets, and again the distribution of income is modified. And so the process continues as the economy adjusts and readjusts in its struggle to regain a new general equilibrium.

In this analysis, we have traced only a few of the many repercussions set in motion by the original change in consumer tastes. There are several lines of impact which we have purposely neglected or assumed away. They complicate our simple model significantly. Each of them, however, is present in the real world. None can be ignored in a complete analysis of the interrelationships of the parts of an economic system. Let us but mention several of these other lines of impact and deal with one longer-run repercussion in some depth.

First, we have seen that the original change in tastes and preferences changes the entire price structure in the economy. This change further modifies one of the independent variables which determines the demand for any good or service, namely, the prices of all other goods and services (P_n). When this variable changes in the demand equation of all consumers, it follows that all market demand curves are further jiggled. To analyze this effect, we would have to know the direction and size of the change in the demand for, say, good x because of a change in the price of y. This depends on whether goods x and y are complements to or substitutes for each other. We ignored this entire chain of impacts in our analysis.

As we saw in chapter 3, whether goods are *complements* or

substitutes becomes most important in analyzing the impact of changes in the prices of one good on the demand for other goods. A change in the price of one good will have different impacts on the demand curves for other goods, depending on whether they are complements to or substitutes for the good whose price has changed. If the two goods are complements, a change in the price of one will cause the demand curve of the other to shift in the opposite direction of the price change. If the price of good x decreases and good y is a complement of good x, the demand curve of good y will shift to the right (increase). The opposite occurs in the case of substitutes. If two goods are substitutes, an increase in the price of one results in an increase in the demand for the other. Examples of complementary goods are hamburger meat and buns. If the price of hamburger meat rises, people will cut back on their consumption of hamburgers and consequently fewer buns will be needed—the demand curve for buns will *decrease*. On the other hand, hamburger meat and pork chops are substitutes. The demand curve for pork chops will *increase* when the price of hamburger meat rises. The reader would do well to test these relationships with other pairs of goods which appear to be related, for example, candy and chewing gum, soap and water, beer and pretzels.

Another example: because of the original change in tastes, the price of luxuries rose from its original level. Consequently, the firms in the luxury industry begin making higher profits than they had previously. The price of luxuries begins to exceed the average cost of producing them. The reverse occurs in the staple industry. The firms in this industry experience losses. In a competitive economic system the factors of production are *mobile*. They can change their location or employment and do so as their self-interest guides them. Consequently, firms will leave the staple industry over time in order to avoid the losses. Because of the higher level of profits, resources will move to the luxury industry. In the long run, with fewer firms in the staple industry, the supply curve of staples would shift to the left and with more firms in the luxury industry, the supply curve of luxuries would shift to the right. The price of staples would tend to rise back toward its original level; the price of luxuries would tend to fall back toward its original level. The quantity of staple goods exchanged would continue to fall; the quantity of luxuries exchanged would continue to rise.

However, these are only the changes in the product markets which would be induced by the entry and exit of firms. The factor markets would also feel the impact. The demand for capital would show another *net* increase because of the entry of firms into the capital-intensive luxury industry combined with a decline in firms in the staple industry. The demand for labor would show another *net* decrease due to the exit of firms from the labor-intensive staple industry combined with the increase of firms in the luxury industry. With the shift in the number of firms as well as in their size, the price and quantity of labor (and, therefore, the incomes of laborers) would fall still further while the corresponding variables for the capital suppliers would continue to rise. We also ignored this entire long-run process in our original analysis.

(The reader would be well advised to work graphically through the analysis presented in the previous two paragraphs. Not only is it a good exercise in market mechanics, but it is also most helpful in gaining an understanding of how changes in market variables lead to succeeding changes in individual firm behavior.)

Furthermore, we said nothing about the relative use of the factors of production in the two industries. Perhaps as the output of the luxury industry increases, production in each firm would tend to become more labor (or more capital) intensive. This would have a further impact on the factor market and, in turn, on the market for goods and services.

Again, we said nothing about the likelihood that the households would change their willingness to supply labor and capital because of changes in their incomes. If their willingness would change, the supply curve of factors would shift, the prices of factors would change, and the incomes of factor suppliers would be modified. All of these changes would react through the circular flow of the economic system affecting businesses, commodity markets, and again households. We ignored all of these possibilities in analyzing the operation of our simple model.

C. A Change in Technology and the Loanable Funds Market

The tendency of the market system to adjust to a new equilibrium may be illustrated by yet another example, one which involves both economic growth and the operation of the loanable funds market. Consider the repercussions of a change in technology, a common source of disturbance to the general equilibrium.

Suppose that a new machine is invented which is expected to be much more efficient in processing wheat than the old technology. The new machine requires more resources to produce it than the old type. However, the entrepreneur who will produce the new machine expects that this increase in cost will be more than offset by the value of the increased output of processed wheat. The producer of the new machines, needing funds with which to buy the resources to build them, turns to the loanable funds market. In this market, too, prices and quantities are determined by supply and demand.

In seeking to borrow money, the firm joins other borrowers in the market for funds. Some are households who wish to shift their spending from the future to the present, perhaps because of an illness. There are business firms which expect an increased demand for their products. They may wish to buy more machinery and equipment, build a new factory, or merely expand their stock of goods in inventory. In each case borrowers wish to gain control over goods and services now, and are willing to pay for the money to gain that control. Each business firm, including our machine manufacturer, expects that the receipts from its action will be enough to cover the cost of production plus the cost of credit, and also provide a residual, a profit.

The price of loanable funds, *interest*, usually is expressed as a rate or percentage of the sums to be lent or borrowed. The interest rate is a cost for the borrower. The household which borrows will have to reduce future consumption spending more than it increases present spending in order to pay the interest. The business firm must add interest expense to its other costs in calculating its profit. The lower the interest rate, the lower the cost of funds and the more that borrowers will want to borrow. The demand for loanable funds fits the Law of Downward Sloping Demand.

The suppliers of funds are households which are willing to postpone spending for present satisfaction in order to consume in the future if they receive a payment for doing so. There are many reasons why households generally prefer present consumption to postponement of consumption for the future. We each face the uncertainty associated with the unknown—the chance that something may happen to us so that we may not live to enjoy future consumption. There is the further risk that prices of what we buy may rise so that less can be bought in the future with each dollar that we save.

If households lend money rather than hoard it in a mattress, there are additional risks. The borrower may be unable or unwilling to pay back the money. If he contracts to pay back the money only after a specified time, there is the risk that the lender may face an emergency and need the money in the interval but not be able to get it. Then, again, the market price of funds may rise before the end of the contract period and the lender would not receive this higher price for his money immediately. Suppliers of funds face risk and uncertainty of various sorts and will lend money only if they are paid for it.

The higher the interest rate, the more the lenders receive for accepting the risk of giving up control over their money, and the more they are willing to lend. The higher the price, the greater the quantity of funds that will be supplied in this market. The Law of Increasing Supply pertains to the loanable funds market just as it does to product markets.

Returning to the invention of the new wheat-processing machine, we may now trace the effect of this technological change through the various markets and observe the effect on the circular flow.

Producers enter the loanable funds market seeking additional funds needed to produce and install the new machines. These demanders (borrowers) are added to those already in the market so that demand for money to borrow has increased. The entire market demand curve shifts to the right. The demand curve now intersects the supply curve at a new higher interest rate (price). The price of money rises as does the quantity of it borrowed or lent. At a higher price for funds, lenders lend more money, forgoing some consumption and releasing productive resources. Borrowers borrow more funds to produce the new wheat-processing machines and, in spending it, attract resources. The decrease in spending by lenders decreases the demand for resources. The decrease in spending by lenders decreases the demand for resources, largely those used to produce consumption goods. Having obtained more money, borrowers increase the demand for capital goods and attract some of these additional resources. Productive resources have shifted from the production of consumption goods to the production of capital goods with the loanable funds market serving as the intermediary for this shift. Because of the new technology, a whole series of price changes are recorded, extending through labor and capital resource markets, and the markets for consumer goods and services. Through these changing signals and the responses of businesses and households to them, the market system moves toward a new general equilibrium.

In this section we have demonstrated how fundamental changes in a competitive economic system are transmitted from sector to sector, from market to market, and from individual to individual in a never-ending process as the economic system moves toward a new general equilibrium. We have shown how changing prices create profits for some and losses for others and how these profits and losses cause a shift in the flow of resources from one sector to another, a reallocation of resources. By isolating the factors leading to changes in the income of laborers and capital suppliers, we have illuminated the process by which society's income is distributed. We have shown how, in a market system, the decisions of consumers direct the entire system, changing outputs in the direction of the changed demand, changing profits, reallocating resources, and determining incomes. In general, what we have done is to show how a market system performs the basic resource allocation and income distribution functions; how it answers the questions of *what* to produce, *how* to produce it, and *how to distribute* it among the people.

II. THE MARKET SYSTEM AND THE WELFARE OF THE PEOPLE

To judge how good an economic system is we must be concerned not only with *how* it does certain basic things but also with *how well* it does them. To make a judgment on the quality of performance, we must have in mind some standard, some criterion, to which a given economic performance may be compared. We will claim that the primary goal of our economic system, the most important and basic task which a system must accomplish if it is to be a "good" system, is the *efficient production and distribution of the right kinds of goods.* The people of a society are served best if their economic system uses social resources in the most efficient way to satisfy the demands of consumers. We shall label *efficient* a system which performs in this way.

To attain this goal, an economic system must effectively perform three functions. First, it must produce the *right* goods and services. Second, it must produce these goods and services at the *least social cost.* Finally, it must *efficiently allocate* this output among the people. Let us take these tasks and, applying concepts already learned, investigate how a competitive price system stands up.

A. What to Produce

First, how well does a competitive price system determine *what* is to be produced? This question is perhaps the easiest of the three with which to deal. Stated most simply, the price mechanism assures that the collective body of consumers will get precisely that bundle of commodities that it most wants. It assures that the highest valued bundle of commodities will be the bundle that business firms find it worth their while to produce. How will this occur?

Given their tastes and preferences, their incomes, and the price structure in the economy, consumers make their desires known to the marketplace by offering to exchange their income for goods and services. As often stated, they enter the marketplace and vote for the goods they want, using dollars as ballots. If people want a good sufficiently, they will pay enough to make its production worthwhile. Their willingness to pay is reflected in the demand curve presented to the market and, hence, in the price of product. As long as the price exceeds the marginal cost of production, businesses will earn an additional profit on extra units and will be willing, indeed eager, to produce the extra units. The higher that consumers bid up the price, the more businesses will produce. Output will expand according to consumers' wishes. Surely, if the consumers in contemporary American society decided they wanted chateaubriand at every meal and were willing to pay the price, they could bid the price high enough to persuade businesses to produce the desired supply.

The principle of *price equal to marginal cost* is an important proposition in analyzing the operation of a price system. Not only does this principle demonstrate the process by which consumers' desires become fulfilled, but it also says something important about the effectiveness of the process. Because, in a competitive economy, the price of each good tends to equal its marginal cost, we can say that the production of the last dollar's worth of *each* good uses up exactly a dollar's worth of society's productive resources—its labor, capital, and natural resources. This principle of $P = MC$ was discussed in chapter 4, section VI. That is, the last dollar's worth produced of any given commodity uses up resources which would never produce more than an extra dollar's worth of another product, no matter where they were shifted. Consequently, society could not be made better off by allocating its resources any way other than that generated by the price system. Since market prices establish the relative value of different commodities to the society, the resources producing these commodities could never produce anything that consumers would rather have than the goods that a smoothly functioning, competitive market system distributes to them.

Through prices, then, a perfect market economy assures that the production of goods and services will conform to the desires of consumers. It carries out this assurance in the most efficient manner. It allocates resources so that the basket of goods produced is superior in consumers' eyes to any other which could be produced through some other allocation of resources.

B. How to Produce

Through our discussion of the "What" question, we have begun to answer the second question: How well does a market economy produce those goods it has decided to produce? That is, how well does it allocate the different factors in the production of these goods? Just as a competitive system regulates what to produce through prices, it also regulates how to produce through the pricing mechanism. In dealing with the problem of what to produce, we saw that the right goods are produced in the right amounts when the price of each good equals the marginal cost of its production. This same relationship must exist if the goods are to be produced properly, that is, if the right combination of inputs is to be used in the production of each of them. Here, however, we must look at this relationship from the other side—from the viewpoint of the producer instead of the consumer.

In our analysis of firm behavior, we built a simple model in which labor was the only variable factor of production. In that model the marginal cost of the firm was the cost of the additional labor necessary to produce an additional unit of product. Conversely, the marginal product of labor was the additional output which the firm obtained from hiring an additional unit of labor. We saw that as long as the marginal revenue product of any input exceeded its price (the wage in our model), the firm continued to hire additional units. The reason for this behavior was that an additional profit was earned by hiring those additional inputs for which the marginal revenue product exceeded the price of the input. In equilibrium, then, each firm in a competitive system uses each input up to the point at which its *marginal revenue product equals the price of the factor.* (This $P_F = MRP$ equilibrium was discussed in chapter 4, section VII.)

The implications of this equality are important for society. What it means is that the society can gain nothing by shifting any factor of production to a use different from the one determined in the competitive market system. The allocation of resources resulting from a competitive pricing mechanism is the most efficient possible. It is an optimum allocation. Because of the decreasing marginal revenue product of additional units of a factor employed in any use, the reallocation of resources to a new sector would, *at best*, produce additional output that would match the value of the loss of output in the sector from which the shift was made. There would be no net gain. Thus, the factor prices determined by the *pricing mechanism* guide each unit of each factor to produce that output which is of *the greatest value to society,* namely, those products consumers most desire. By leading each factor to the use in which the value of its marginal product is the highest possible, the price system, through free markets, efficiently produces each of the goods. The price system must also be judged to be an excellent performer of the *how* task.

This conclusion—that the price system allocates the right amount of resources to any particular industry and in the right proportions, and that the industry produces the optimum value of output with these resources—has a corollary. This corollary is that the industry produces its output by using the fewest possible dollars' worth of inputs. That is, the industry produces the output at *least cost*.

C. For Whom to Produce

The final task facing an economic system is the distribution of the goods produced among consumers. How efficiently does the price system answer the question "For whom?" As with the previous tasks, the price system makes this allocation in a particular way. It again uses market prices as rationing devices.

In thinking of the allocation of a quantity of goods and services among a number of households each of which possesses unlimited wants, we must have in mind some idea of an optimal or efficient distribution. Such a concept does exist. It was first set out in the late nineteenth century by an economist named Vilfredo Pareto. According to Pareto's proposition, a distribution of goods is surely an optimum if it is not possible to find another distribution which would make some households better off without making others worse off. Thus, if a given number of apples and oranges were distributed between two people and if, after the distribution, the two people were willing to trade some of the apples and oranges with each other, it would be clear that the original distribution was not ideal. By trading, *both* of the parties are benefited with no one being harmed.

The principle that derives from this is that any given good is properly allocated if it is in the possession of the consumer who wants it more than anyone else *and* whose desire for it is backed up by a willingness to pay more for it than anyone else. A good is distributed efficiently if the consumer who is willing to give up more of his income for it than anyone else—who is willing to "pay the price"—gets it. Let us see if a price system secures such a distribution and if it does, how.

We have already discovered that there exists only one equilibrium market price for each good and service in a competitive system. Given these prices, any consumer is free to choose whatever quantity of any given good he or she desires. This choice is made by each consumer according to the dictates of his or her tastes and income. Given an income, tastes and preferences, and the prices of the goods in the market, a consumer will increase the purchase of any good as long as the loss of utility from the other goods which are forgone is less than the gain in utility from the additional unit of the good. This will be recognized as the opportunity cost concept, which we considered earlier.

Put another way, the consumer will continue buying additional amounts of an item as long as the value to the consumer of an additional unit exceeds the value of the other things that could be bought with the same money. Operating in this way, the consumer will maximize utility. (This utility-maximizing equilibrium for the consumer was discussed in chapter 3.) Because prices come from the interaction of market supply and demand and because the demand comes from consumers' operating according to the maximizing principle just mentioned, market prices regulate the allocation of supply so that those who are willing to pay the price, who are willing to give up more of their incomes than anyone else, acquire the goods. This, according to Pareto's principle, describes an efficient allocation of the goods which society has produced.

How a society finally divides up the goods and services that it has produced among its members is a most crucial question. It should be emphasized that other important considerations besides efficiency are used to judge the merits of any particular income distribution. Equity or justice come immediately to mind.

In a market system, the distribution of the society's output depends ultimately on (1) how the ownership of the factors of production is distributed among the people and (2) the prices of the services of these factors. From this, it follows that if all of the capital in society were held by just a few people, their incomes would be exceedingly high; they would bring to the product market a very great willingness to pay for goods and services and, consequently, they would go home with the lion's share of the output. In our discussion of the allocating power of the price system, we have taken this distribution of the ownership of the factors of production as a given. We have only asked if a price system allocates its current output *efficiently* among the people, given their original endowment of factors; we have not asked if it allocates this output *equitably*. Hence, when we judge the distribution to be an efficient one, we must realize that it might also be an inequitable (some would say unjust) one. Because the already wealthy have the ability to secure a large share of society's current output, while the existing poor, possessing but few factors of production, obtain little, an equity standard may well not be satisfied by the price system.

In economics, the equity problem has traditionally been divorced from the operation of the market system. Economists have, for decades, argued that if efficiency is to be attained, equity will have to be achieved outside of the pricing mechanism. The claim is that, if society objects to a particular distribution of its current output (income), a *public* decision to rearrange the existing pattern of factor ownership (or the rewards earned from selling the services of particular factors) could be made through taxes and subsidies. Then, given the rearranged income pattern, the price system, through its multitude of *private* decisions, could again proceed to the *efficient* answering of the "what," "how," and "for whom" questions.

III. CONCLUSION AND SUMMARY

In this chapter, we have attempted to place the spotlight on the market system as a whole. It has been argued that markets are the cement which binds the various sectors of the economy together. Markets take the demands and supplies of businesses and households and convey prices—market signals—to each sector. As the system adjusts to any basic change in tastes or technologies, it is the complex of markets which conveys the impact of these changes to every household and business. Because of the extreme interrelatedness of the parts of an economy that is made possible by markets, the economy as a whole tends to a general equilbrium as each household, business, and market seeks its equilibrium.

In our discussion, we have shown that a competitive, free market system does answer all three of the questions faced by all societies. Moreover, we have demonstrated that the answers to each of these questions lead a society to an efficient and optimum position, given its unlimited wants, its limited resources and a particular distribution of income. The answers to all of the questions are determined by the preferences of individual and free consumers as these preferences are made known by the willingness of people to spend their money—to cast dollar ballots—on alternative goods and services. As one writer has stated:

> The market performs the democratic task of bringing about a distribution or allocation of goods that takes into consideration the preferences of all the individuals. ... It is as if it allowed each individual to vote, with dollars, as to which of the available goods and services he wanted to have, and then fulfilled all of the election promises—giving him the things he voted for. The market also permits each individual to vote in different degrees for different items, and in different degrees for additional amounts, in a way which is as much beyond the possibilities of the [political] ballot as a modern skyscraper is beyond a simple mud hut. ... This is called

consumers' sovereignty, *and forms an essential part of economic democracy.* [2]

However, while the market system does promote efficiency, it does not necessarily promote equity or justice in the distribution of the social income. Indeed, many have argued that it sustains—or even promotes—inequity and injustice. This is the most serious charge which has been leveled at the market system, and will be evaluated later.

QUESTIONS

1. Assume a perfect and competitive market system with all markets in equilibrium except the market for, say, shoes. In the market for shoes, the price is above equilibrium for some unexplained reason.
   (a) Without someone or something to artificially hold the price of shoes above equilibrium, what will tend to happen to it? Why?
   (b) Because of the change taking place in question (a), what would you expect to happen to the demand for shoe repair services? Why? How about the demand for bread? Why?
   (c) What would you expect to happen to the demand for labor and its price as the system adjusts? How about the demand for capital and its price? Why? What kind of additional information would help you to answer this question?
   (d) What would you expect to happen to the income of the households? Why?
   (e) What would you expect to happen to the number of shoe manufacturing businesses? Why?
2. Consider the following sentences from this chapter. In each case, prepare a brief paragraph describing the reasoning which allows the statement to be made.
   (a) "It is the application of this *ceteris paribus* assumption in the study of individual sectors that has caused our analysis thus far to be 'partial.' " (Section I.)
   (b) "Thus, the original change in tastes has generated a secondary shift in demand which, like the first, is transmitted through the circular flow of the price system." (Section I.B.)
   (c) "The demand for labor would show another *net* decrease due to the exit of firms from the labor-intensive staple industry." (Section I.B.)
   (d) "Output will expand according to consmers' wishes." (Section II.A.)
   (e) "[T]he production of a dollar's worth of each good uses up exactly a dollar's worth of society's productive resources." (Section II.A.)

---

2. Abba P. Lerner, *Everybody's Business* (New York: Harper and Row, 1964), pp. 62–63.

(f) "[S]ociety could not be made better off by allocating its resources any way other than that generated by the price system." (Section II.A.)

(g) "Market prices regulate the allocation of supply so that those . . . who are willing to give up more of their incomes than anyone else acquire the goods." (Section II.C.)

3. "The Pareto proposition argues that a society has not achieved maximum welfare as long as there are two people in society who would be willing to trade some goods or services with each other." Do you agree? Why?

4. Distinguish between equity and efficiency in the distribution of income. Why it is impossible to argue that the market system performs well on the "equity of distribution" questions? Does it necessarily perform badly?

5. Discuss why the $P = MC$ condition implies that the right answer to the "What?" question is being given by the market system.

6. Why is mobility of factors necessary for a general equilibrium to occur?

7 | Interference in the Adjustment Process—The Problem of Economic Power

If supplies and demands were not artificially manipulated, if the quantities of goods and services exchanged and their prices were free to vary according to the dictates of market forces, if consumers were free to choose among these goods and services as they please, if businesses were free to react to market conditions as they please, we should truly have a competitive economic system. But these are very big "ifs." Few things in life possess such freedom, few things run so smoothly and without obstruction. The market system is no exception. The real world simply does not work in the unconstrained fashion described by the model we have analyzed. Real-world market economies are often obstructed to some degree. Something or someone often interferes in the process of economic adjustment.

Interference is an exertion of *economic power*. When a group of firms in the electrical equipment industry conspires to fix the price of their machinery, they are exercising economic power. When Alcoa sets the price of aluminum where it pleases, as it did earlier in this century, it exerts market power. When labor unions create a situation in which wages can only rise, market power is being exercised. When the federal government fixes the price of farm products, or subsidizes the housing industry, or regulates the rates charged by railroads, it is exercising economic power. In each of these cases the circular flow is obstructed; in each case, the competitive price system's optimum allocation of social resources is subverted. The impact of these obstructions on the operation of a competitive price system is the concern of this chapter.

I. TYPES OF MARKET POWER

Before discussing the influence of market power on the price system, we must distinguish the different kinds of such power. Although market power takes on many guises, there are three basic types. Two of them deal with control over the supply or demand of a product. The third deals with control over its price.

A. Monopoly and Monopsony Power

To control the supply or demand of a good or service is to possess market power. Free markets are rigged and the market system obstructed when either or both of these forces are controlled. Those who control *supply*, who determine how much of a good or service is to be brought into the market, possess *monopoly power*. Those who control *demand*, who determine how much of a good or service will be taken off the market, possess *monopsony power*.

To possess either is to possess much more than that power alone. Given a market demand curve, control over the supply curve automatically conveys the power to determine the market outcome: the quantity exchanged, the price and, perhaps most important, the total revenue which accrues to the sellers. And the ability to control total revenue conveys the power to determine profits. Similarly, given a market supply curve, the power to manipulate the demand curve conveys this same power over market outcomes. Indeed, if the competitive system can be called economic democracy in which individuals choose freely by casting dollar ballots, the power over either market demand or market supply is equivalent to stuffing the ballot box.

Just as the outcome of a fixed political election benefits the fixers, so does this occur in economic elections. By violating the principle of consumer sovereignty, by interfering with the operation of the pricing mechanism, the exercise of market power yields a gain to a particular interest at the expense of the rest of society. Monopoly and monopsony power, therefore, have both an *efficiency impact* through their effect on resource allocation and an *equity impact* through their effect on the income of the owners of factors of production. Indeed, both of these effects are present even if it is government which is exercising the market power.

B. Power of Price Control

Both monopoly and monopsony power derive from a deficiency within the structure of a market. The third kind of market power, however, is imposed on the market by an outside force. Monopoly and monopsony power control price through control of either supply or demand, but this kind of market power controls the price directly, irrespective of the forces of supply and demand. Of its many names, we prefer to call it simply the *power of price control*. In the real world, its pervasiveness and importance may well exceed that of monopoly or monopsony power. Governments, by subsidizing and taxing and regulating, are probably the primary exercisers of this form of market power.

C. Market Structure and Market Power

Monopoly and monopsony power result from a particular kind of market structure. Their existence implies the absence of competition.

Competitive markets, we have seen, have a unqiue set of buying and selling conditions. There are so many independent buyers and sellers that no one can affect the price; the commodity exchanged is homogeneous; business and households can enter and leave markets at will. Indeed, a competitive market can be defined as one in which monopoly or monopsony power is nonexistent. Each firm and each household is so minute compared to the market that no such power is possible.

If a market does not possess these characteristics, if there is one supplier instead of many, if the product is differentiated instead of homogeneous, if entry is blocked and not free, it is not a competitive market. It follows that there are many different market structures possessing many degrees of monopoly or monopsony power. It further follows that each structure generates a different market outcome. In the following sections, we will investigate a number of these structures, each of which possesses some degree of market power. In our analysis, we will only deal with the effects of monopoly power. Because monopsony power has the same impact as monopoly power—operating on the demand instead of the supply side of the market—the general conclusions which we derive in analyzing monopoly also apply to it. We will first analyze the extreme case of pure monopoly and then proceed to intermediate market structures called oligopoly and monopolistic competition.

II. THE PURE MONOPOLY MODEL

Pure monopoly lies at the opposite end of the spectrum from pure competition. Indeed, it implies the absence of everything for which pure competition stands. Whereas a competitive industry has a large number of firms producing the identical product, *a monopolistic industry has but one firm*. Consequently, while a single competitive firm cannot influence the supply of goods coming onto a market, a monopolist can. Firms move into and out of a competitive industry with ease, but entry into the monopolistic industry is effectively blocked. The competitive firm sees only the market price, is unable to affect it and, consequently, seeks an optimum position by adjusting its output to that price. The monopolistic firm, on the other hand, sees the entire market demand curve and is able to pick and choose the price and quantity that best serve its interests. The distinction between what the monopolist and the competitor see when they look at the market is clarified in Figures 7-1 and 7-2.

Figure 7-1 shows the position of the pure competitor and the market in which such a firm operates. The price of the commodity in the competitive market is determined by the forces of supply and demand. Figure 7-1(a) depicts such a market with its supply and demand curves. The equilibrium price in this market is automatically transmitted to the individual competitive firm pictured in Figure 7-1(b). Indeed, this price is the only communication which the individual competitor receives from the market. Because the firm's actions have a negligible effect on the market, the competitor views the market price as the demand curve for its output. The market demand curve does not appear relevant. Indeed, the demand curve the competitive firm faces is the horizontal line at the market price illustrated in Figure 7-1(b). Any quantity that the competitor might decide to sell would be taken at the market price; that is, the market will "demand" any quantity from the firm at that price. Because the firm earns an additional revenue equal to the price for each additional unit supplied to the market, the market price is also the firm's marginal revenue. To reach an optimal position the

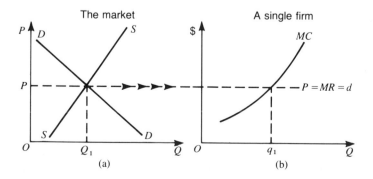

Figure 7-1

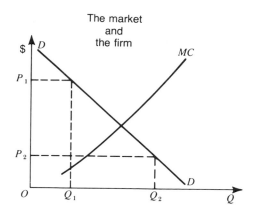

Figure 7-2

competitor equates marginal cost and marginal revenue (the market price) and supplies a quantity equal to q_1. As a *price taker*, the competitor operates by adjusting its rate of output to the going market price. The firm's output is the only thing over which the pure competitor has control.

Figure 7-2 represents a pure monopoly. Because the monopolist is the only firm in the market, there is only one diagram. The marginal cost curve of the monopolist is labeled MC. In monopoly, the forces of supply and demand are not the impersonal forces that establish competitive equilibrium. Market supply is now controlled by one firm. As the only firm in the market, the monopolist faces the entire market demand curve and is free to choose any point on it. The monopolistic firm can charge any price or supply any quantity which would be in its interest, which would maximize its profits. If the monopolist charges P_1, consumers stand ready to buy Q_1: at P_2, consumers stand ready to buy Q_2. Conversely, if it supplies Q_1 units, a price of P_1 will clear the market; when the quantity supplied is Q_2 units, a price of P_2 will clear the market.

A. Marginal Revenue and Monopoly

The monopolist is a *price maker*, not a price taker. In view of this freedom of choice, we must develop a model which will explain how much the monopolistic firm will supply and the price it will charge. These are the same variables that the competitive model explained for that market structure. In developing a monopoly model, we will again adopt the assumption of profit maximization. We will observe the same marginal principle in action. In the competitive situation, we found that the individual firm is required to accept that price which is determined in the free market and to choose that output which maximizes profits. To find this output, the firm equated its marginal cost with its marginal revenue (which was also equal to the price). Applying the same marginal principle, the monopolist also maximizes profits by equating marginal cost with marginal revenue. Here, however, an additional complication arises. *The monopolist's marginal revenue does not equal the price of the product.*

Marginal revenue diverges from the price in a monopoly situation because of the kind of signals the firm receives from the market. The monopolistic firm is not given a single price; it faces the entire demand curve. For this reason, the price of the output does not remain stationary when a monopolistic firm alters the amount which it supplies. If a monopolistic firm sells a larger quantity, the price falls; if it decreases the quantity supplied, the price rises. Moreover, no matter what output the monopolistic firm is producing, it will have to lower its price to sell an additional unit.

Here, then, is the clue. When the monopolist increases its rate of output by one unit, the price must be lowered if the product is to sell, and this lower price is attached not only to the additional unit but also to the units of output which the firm was producing at the lower output rate. Thus, in selling the additional unit, the monopolistic firm gains additional revenue equal to the price at which the unit is sold but *loses* revenue because of the decrease in the price attached to the prior number of units which were being produced at the lower output rate. This revenue loss is equal to the number of previous units sold multiplied by the decrease in price necessary to sell the additional unit. Consequently, the marginal revenue gained from the sale of the additional unit is the *additional revenue* from the sale of that unit *minus the loss in revenue* owing to the sale of the prior number of units at a lower price. Marginal revenue to a monopolist is, therefore, less the price. This is illustrated in Table 7-1.

The first two columns of Table 7-1 produce the demand curve shown in Figure 7-3. At a price of $1, 0 units are demanded; at a price of 90¢, 1 unit is demanded; and so on. The monopolist's total revenue at each price is found by multiplying each price-quantity pair in the first two columns. This is displayed in column 3. Thus, as the monopolist moves down the demand curve, total revenue rises, reaches a maximum of $2.50, and then falls. From the total revenue schedule of columns 1 and 3, the *change in total revenue* owing to the sale of additional units can be found. It is the marginal revenue and is represented in column 4. In going from 0 to 1 unit of output,

Table 7-1

P	Q	TR	MR
$1.00	0	$ 0	
			$ 0.90
0.90	1	0.90	
			0.70
0.80	2	1.60	
			0.50
0.70	3	2.10	
			0.30
0.60	4	2.40	
			0.10
0.50	5	2.50	
			−0.10
0.40	6	2.40	
			−0.30
0.30	7	2.10	
			−0.50
0.20	8	1.60	
			−0.70
0.10	9	0.90	

the marginal revenue is 90¢, in going from 1 to 2 units, the marginal revenue is 70¢, and so on. The information in the marginal revenue schedule is also depicted as *MR* in Figure 7-3. From this schedule and the *MR* curve, it is seen that the marginal revenue at each level of output lies below the price and, in fact, deviates farther and farther from the price as the output level rises. At two units of

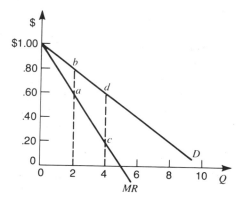

Figure 7-3

output, for example, the graphic deviation is *ab*; at four units of output, the deviation is *cd*, a substantial increase.

Let us derive this marginal revenue concept more concretely. Assume that the monopolist facing the demand curve of Figure 7-3 is currently selling two units of output at a price of 80¢ and earning a total revenue of $1.60. Assume further that the firm decides to increase output by one unit—from two units to three. From the shape of the demand curve, the price will clearly have to be decreased from 80¢ to 70¢ to sell the additional unit. What, then, is the marginal revenue? From the sale of the third unit, the monopolist receives 70¢ as an addition to revenue. However, to obtain this additional 70¢, the price on the prior two units must be reduced from 80¢ to 70¢. The firm, therefore, loses 10¢ on each of the first two units or a total of 20¢. What now is the monopolist's *net gain* or *net marginal revenue* from selling the next unit? Considering both the gain in revenue from selling the additional unit and the loss in revenue from selling the previous units at a lower price, the *net* marginal revenue to the monopolist from selling three instead of two units is 50¢, that is 70¢ minus 20¢.

From this example, the *increasing* divergence of the marginal revenue curve from the demand curve can be readily understood. This increasing divergence phenomenon occurs for two reasons. First, because of the shape of the demand curve, the price charged decreases as output increases. Therefore *gross marginal revenue*— the revenue from the sale of the additional unit of output—is greater at low levels of output than it is at a larger level. Second, because the price reduction necessary to sell an additional unit affects more units when output is large, the revenue loss is greater when output is large than when it is small. This revenue loss, it will be recalled, is subtracted from gross marginal revenue in order to obtain *net marginal revenue*. For both reasons, marginal revenue drifts farther and farther away from price as output increases. Graphically, the marginal revenue curve displays a steeper slope than the demand curve. Moreover, after the output level at which total revenue begins to fall, the marginal revenue curve becomes negative.

On the basis of this relationship, let us redraw the demand and marginal revenue curves of Figure 7-3 and add the marginal cost curve of Figure 7-2. These are shown in Figure 7-4.

B. Rational Choice and Monopoly Equilibrium

The questions which we asked earlier can now be repeated: "What is the quantity of output which the monopolist will produce, and at what price will it be sold?" Remembering the marginal principle,

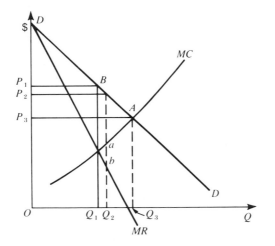

Figure 7-4

the answer follows directly. The monopolist facing the demand and cost situation of Figure 7-4 will produce that level of output at which marginal cost equals marginal revenue—output Q_1. Having chosen this output, the monopolist will sell it at the highest price possible—P_1 in Figure 7-4. At this price demanders are willing to buy quantity Q_1. Therefore, P_1 and Q_1 are the equilibrium price and quantity for the monopolist. There is no tendency for the monopolist to change either; they are the best attainable.

Why is this true? Why should not the monopolist attempt to increase output to, say, Q_2 in Figure 7-4? In answering this question, the effect of such a change on the monopolist's profit must be considered. If the change increases total revenue more than total costs, it would clearly be worthwhile for the monopolistic firm to increase its output to Q_2. Let us observe the impact on profits from producing beyond Q_1. By increasing output to Q_2, the monopolist sees that total revenue would rise; marginal revenue is positive. This is so even though the firm has to sell its output at a lower price. But costs would also rise. The firm's decision, therefore, can be reached only after considering how these two variables move in relation to each other. If the additional revenue exceeds the additional cost, profit will rise and the monopolist will produce the additional unit; if the additional revenue is less than the additional cost, profit will fall and the additional unit will not be produced.

As can be seen in Figure 7-4, marginal cost equals marginal revenue at output Q_1. As output increases beyond Q_1, marginal cost rises and marginal revenue falls. Consequently, for any additional output beyond Q_1, say, Q_2, marginal cost exceeds marginal revenue and the firm would add more to its total cost than to its total revenue. A decision to produce that unit would be most unwise. For example, if the firm produced Q_2 in Figure 7-4 its marginal cost on the last unit would exceed marginal revenue by ab. By the same reasoning, a reduction in output from Q_1 would decrease total revenue more than total costs and profit would again decrease. Since either an increase or a decrease in output from Q_1 would decrease the monopolist's profit, output Q_1 sold at a price of P_1 is the optimum position. Hence, *equilibrium monopoly output occurs where marginal cost equals marginal revenue: MC = MR.* And the equilibrium monopoly price is the highest price which can be charged for that output, and is given by the level of the demand curve at the equilibrium output level. The equilibrium price clears the market.

C. Monopoly, Competition, and Social Welfare

With $MC = MR$ established as the equilibrium position in both monopoly and competition, how does the price and output solution of a monopolistic industry differ from that of a competitive industry? What is the impact of monopoly power on the process of economic adjustment and thereby on the level of well-being of the citizens of the economy? The first of these two questions will be answered in two steps covering two periods of time—the short run and the long run. Later, we shall analyze the impact of monopoly power on the adjustment process in the entire economy.

The difference between the *long run* and the *short run* must be distinguished before the two market structures can be compared. In economics, neither the short run nor the long run is a calendar period of time. Rather, both are distinguished by whether certain events have sufficient time to occur. The short run is a period which is insufficient for new firms to enter an industry or for existing firms to expand or contract their capacity. The long run is a period of time which is sufficient to permit existing firms to change their size or additional firms to enter an industry.

D. A Short-Run Comparison

In the short run, then, how does the competitive market equilibrium differ from the monopoly equilibrium? In competition, we have seen that both the price of a commodity and the quantity exchanged are determined in the market by the forces of supply and demand. Competitive equilibrium is established where the supply curve, being the sum of the firms' marginal cost curves, intersects the demand curve. Hence, were the situation in Figure 7-4 a picture of a competitive market, the curve labeled MC would be the supply curve and an equilibrium would be achieved where it intersects the market demand curve. An equilibrium price of P_3 would be observed and a quantity of Q_3 would be the equilibrium quantity exchanged.

In monopoly, however, the equilibrium is not established in the market by impersonal forces. The monopolistic firm has the power to regulate the flow of output coming onto the market and, with this power, it can set the price. The monopolistic firm has the power to pick an equilibrium which is more beneficial to its private interests than the competitive equilibrium. The profit-maximizing solution will be chosen by the rational manager. By restricting the amount supplied, the monopolist can raise the price of the commodity. The firm secures a greater profit by producing a *smaller output* and selling it at a *higher price* than would be the case in a competitive industry. As we have seen, the monopolist produces Q_1 and sells it at a price of P_1.

In Figure 7-4, the short-run price-quantity solution of the two market structures can be analyzed by comparing point A, the competitive solution, and point B, the monopolistic solution. First, a greater quantity is exchanged in the competitive industry than in the monopolistic industry. Q_3 exceeds Q_1. This reflects an important facet of the monopolist's behavior; output is restricted. Second, the price charged in the competitive case is a lower price than the price charged by a monopoly. P_1 exceeds P_3. Because the monopoly firm restricts output, it is able to sell at a higher price. Third, because of the restricted output and the higher price, the quantity of resources or outputs which are used in the monopoly firm is smaller than the quantity used in the competitive industry. Production in the competitive industry is carried up to the point at which the price of the product equals the marginal cost of production $(P = MC)$, while production in the monopoly case is halted before this equality is attained.

Short-run equilibrium for a monopoly is achieved *where the price of the commodity exceeds the marginal cost* of producing it. Although $MR = MC$, $P > MC$ in the short-run monopoly equilibrium. As we will see later, this results in either the unemployment or the misallocation of society's resources or both.

Strangely, we have not yet mentioned profitability. Surely, this is a relevant consideration. If the monopolist possesses market power and the competitive firm does not, the monopolist should be more profitable than the competitor. However, this is a long-run rather than a short-run question. Because industry profits may be eroded over a period of time by entering firms striving for a slice of the high profits, abnormal profits in the short run are not relevant. In the short run, even competitive firms may make abnormal profits.

To discuss the profit of either a monopolist or a competitor requires a familiar concept but one which we have not yet introduced into this discussion—the average cost curve. In Figures 7-5 and 7-6, the average cost curve is drawn on the graphs of both the competitive and monopoly models.

Let us assume that both Figures 7-5 and 7-6 show hypothetical short-run equilibrium positions in the two models. The *total profit* of the firm in each case is equal to the *difference* between the *price* and the *average cost times the number of units sold.* $TP = (P \cdot x) - (AC \cdot x)$.

Thus, in Figure 7-5(b), the shaded area represents the total profit of a single firm among many in a competitive industry. The shaded area in Figure 7-6 represents the total profit of the monopolist. In both cases the shaded area equals the amount by which price exceeds average cost, multiplied by the output. In both models large profits are being made; not an unusual short-run situation in either case.

E. The Long-Run Competitive Solution

How will these short-run equilibriums be modified in the long run? It will be recalled that we have defined the long run to be a period of time sufficient for both the entry and the exit of firms and for existing firms to expand or contract. Let us first consider the competitive model. One of the primary characteristics of a competi-

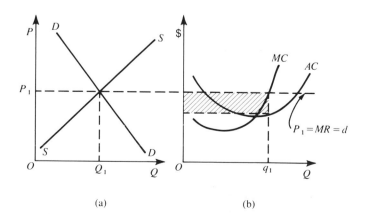

(a)   (b)

Figure 7-5 Competitive model.

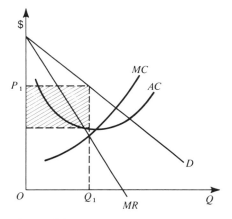

Figure 7-6 Monopoly model.

tive industry is that there is free movement of resources and firms into and out of the industry. Clearly, the desire to earn a profit or avoid a loss provides the motive for such movement. Thus, when the firms in a competitive industry are earning a large profit, as in Figure 7-5, additional resources and firms will be attracted into the industry. On the other hand, if the firms were losing money— average cost greater than price—resources and firms would tend to leave the industry. Because of this entry and exit, the long-run equilibrium in a competitive industry will be quite different from the industry's short-run equilibrium.

If, because of large profits, additional firms enter the industry, the number of marginal cost curves will increase and the supply curve will expand. This is so because the supply of a competitive industry is the summation of the marginal cost curves of all of the firms in the industry. The opposite occurs if firms leave the industry. With substantial profits existing in our model (Figure 7-5), additional firms and resources will enter the industry and the supply curve will shift to the right. As it shifts, the market equilibrium slides down the demand curve, the price falls, and the quantity demanded and exchanged rises. In fact, additional firms will be attracted to the industry and the supply will continue to shift to the right until the price falls to equality with the average cost of the firms in the industry. At this point abnormally large profits become eliminated from the industry. Figure 7-7 shows this process of long-run adjustment.

In Figure 7-7(a), the additional firms and resources entering the industry because of large profits increase the supply curve from S_1S_1

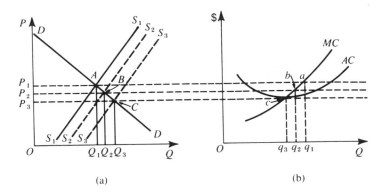

Figure 7-7

to S_2S_2 to S_3S_3. Because of the increasing supply, the equilibrium moves from A—the original position—to B to C. The price of the product decreases from P_1 to P_2 to P_3 and the quantity exchanged expands from Q_1 to Q_2 to Q_3.

In this process, the individual competitor (Figure 7-7(b) is also affected. As the price falls, the competitive firm continues to equate marginal cost with the price (marginal revenue). The firm's equilibrium changes from a to b to c and output decreases from q_1 to q_2 to q_3. The level of profit is also affected by the influx of resources into the industry. Because the price is forced downward by the increased supply, the margin between the price of the product and the average cost of producing it decreases. When the price has fallen to P_3, average cost equals price. Abnormal profits have withered away through competition. At this point, there is no motive for additional resources to enter the industry. Nor will existing firms be forced out. Point C in Figure 7-7(a) and point c in Figure 7-7(b) represent the long-run equilibrium for the competitive industry and firm.

Two things stand out from this analysis. First, in long-run competitive equilibrium, only a *normal* return to capital would exist. If returns were above this level (referred to as *abnormal returns*) or below this level, firms would be entering or leaving the industry, a sign that long-run equilibrium had not yet been attained. Therefore in *long-run* competitive equilibrium, *price equals average cost*. $P = AC$ is the long-run competitive equilibrium condition.

As we have discussed previously (chapter 4), this equilibrium should not be interpreted as entailing a zero return to either management or capital. Returns to these factors are normal competitive returns and are already counted and included in the average cost curve. After all, these returns do have an opportunity cost. The equilibrium is to be interpreted as entailing *zero excess* or *abnormal* returns to capital and management.

Finally, the efficiency at which an individual competitive firm is forced to operate in the long run must be mentioned. As additional firms, attracted by large profits, enter the industry; as the price of the product falls because of the increased supply; and as abnormal profits are eroded, the firm is driven to the minimum point on its average cost curve. It is forced to produce at minimum average cost in order to survive. As can be seen in Figure 7-7, *long-run equilibrium* finds the competitive firm producing at *minimum average cost*—at *maximum efficiency* for the firm.

F. The Long-Run Monopoly Solution

But what about the process of long-run change in a monopoly? Indeed, because of the very nature and definition of a monopoly market, there need be no long-run change of the type we observed in competition. In monopoly, there is no free entry or exit of firms and resources; entry is foreclosed. There is, therefore, no tendency for prices or profits to fall or for supply or efficiency to increase. The absence of competitive pressure from entering firms implies that the short-run monopoly equilibrium need not be modified in the long run.

There is, however, one kind of long-run adjustment which can be made. The monopoly firm can change the size of the plant, expanding or contracting its physical facilities. The drive for maximum profits is again the motivation for such change. If the monopoly firm changes plant size, both average and marginal cost curves change. This change may increase output or decrease it; it may increase the price charged or decrease it; it may increase average costs or decrease them; it is impossible to say. What can be said, however, is that the profit of the monopolist will increase because of the change. Were it otherwise, the change would not be undertaken.

For the monopolist, the solution in the long run is not substantially different from that in the short run. In *long-run monopoly equilibrium*, the *price* of the product remains substantially *above* the competitive price; the *output* remains *restricted;* ·*too few resources* are channeled into *production* of the product; *large profits* remain *unchallenged;* and there is no need for the firm to produce at the *lowest average cost*. In short, the misallocation of resources noted in the short-run monopoly equilibrium persists into the long run because of barred entry and the consequent lack of competitive pressure. Thus, Figure 7-6 pictures both the short-run and long-run equilibriums for the monopolist.

While this analysis portrays the outcome of a pure monopoly, it should once again be emphasized that no such purity exists in the real world. In reality, if a monopolist's customers can switch to products which are not produced by the monopolist, his power may be severely undermined. This "competition of substitutes" is an important form of competition in a real economy. We will elaborate this point later.

QUESTIONS

1. Consider the demand curve equation used in the questions at the end of chapter 5, $Q_D = 400 - 8P$. Assume that this demand curve is for a commodity which is sold by only one business firm.
   (a) Plot this curve on a graph and construct a demand schedule (a table) based on this equation. Again, use 1¢ price intervals from 8¢ to 22¢ plus 30¢ and 40¢.
   (b) Calculate a marginal revenue schedule using the demand schedule which you constructed in (a). Plot this marginal revenue schedule as a curve on the demand curve graph. (Again, plot the marginal value at the midpoint of the interval over which it is measured.)
   (c) On this graph, draw in a set of marginal and average cost curves of a monopolist supplying this market. Make sure that these curves have the shape decreed by the Law of Diminishing Marginal Returns and that they relate properly to each other. The relationship of the four curves—D, MR, AC, and MC—should resemble that of Figure 7-6.
   (d) What are the equilibrium price and quantity in this market? Why is this an equilibrium?
   (e) Is the monopolist pictured in your graph making a profit? Can you calculate how much profit is made? What is the profit per unit of output?
   (f) How would the equilibrium price and quantity for the monopolist compare with the short-run price and quantity if this were a competitive industry meeting the demand?
2. "The difference between monopoly and competition is characterized by the difference between the shapes of the demand curves facing individual sellers in each of these markets." Discuss this assertion, and if you conclude that there is a difference in demand curves, describe it.
3. "The most serious economic impact of monopoly is that there is little or no tendency for abnormally high profits to be eroded over the long run." Do you agree with this assertion? If you do not, how would you describe the most serious economic effect of monopoly?

4. "You can always distinguish a monopolist from a competitor on the basis of their motivations." Do you agree? What questions would you ask to determine whether an industry is competitive or monopolistic?
5. "How in the world can you claim that the monopolist produces 'too little?' Why, consumers are not willing to buy even one more unit of output at the price at which it is selling." Evaluate this statement.
6. In competitive equilibrium, the following equalities hold for the individual firm: $MC = MR$, $P = MC$. How would you have to amend these to describe the equilibrium of the monopolist? Describe the significance of the amendment in evaluating the economic performance of a monopoly.
7. "The trouble with a monopoly in an otherwise competitive full employment economy is that it makes the quantity produced of all other commodities excessive." Do you agree? Why, or why not?
8. "It is not possible for a monopoly to be in equilibrium when the price it charges is at a point on the demand curve which is inelastic." Is this statement true? Why or why not?
9. "A monopoly is like a government—it has the power to levy taxes." In what sense is this a true statement? If there is a sense in which it is true, what distinguishes a monopolist from a government?

III. OLIGOPOLY

To find any real-world industry with the characteristics of either pure monopoly or pure competition is no easy task. The agriculture industry is as close to the competitive norm as any but, for reasons which we shall see later, it fails to function competitively. The aluminum industry some decades ago was an example of a pure monopoly with effectively barred entry. It is no longer. To be sure, the vast majority of contemporary industries lie somewhere between pure competition and pure monopoly, possessing elements of both. The term *oligopoly* applies to a large number of these real-world industry structures. Indeed, several economists have claimed oligopoly to be the prevailing market structure in the American economy, and one economist has gone so far as to call it "ubiquitous."

The primary characteristic of oligopoly is described by the word *fewness*. Instead of a multitude of firms producing and selling a product as in competition, or a single firm as in monopoly, there is an intermediate number—a few. Moreover, the product which oligopolists sell need not be homogeneous as in competition and monopoly; it may be *differentiated*. Both kinds are common. The steel of any firm in the steel industry is identical to the steel of any other steel producer. As one economist put it: "Steel bought from stock is standardized. . . . One firm's steel is as good as another's."

The steel industry, therefore, is a *homogeneous oligopoly*—a small group of firms producing an identical product.

The automobile industry is another oligopoly. However, its output is not homogeneous. Although a Ford and a Chevrolet—or a Volkswagen and a Fiat—sell for much the same price, perform much the same service, and have a similar appearance, they are not identical. Rather, they are differentiated. Nevertheless, they are closely substitutable commodities. Most people are relatively indifferent between them and a few hundred dollars either way will sway their buying decision. Therefore, the automobile industry is a *differentiated oligopoly*—a small group of firms producing a differentiated though highly substitutable product.

A. The Causes of Oligopoly

Before we investigate oligopoly performance and compare it with that of monopoly or pure competition, we must ask: If oligopolies are so prevalent, how did they come to be? What caused their development in the United States?

Many reasons have been given for the development of oligopoly in the American economy. Because many of the prominent oligopolistic industries also contain the nation's largest firms, these reasons explain the growth of big business as well as oligopoly. A close relationship between the growth of oligopoly and changes in certain explanatory variables can be observed in data. Other reasons are not empirical, but logical. It makes sense that oligopoly should result from these factors even though the relationship between them cannot be demonstrated by data. Of the many causes of oligopoly, let us discuss two: *economies of scale* and *mergers*.

B. Economies of Scale

Economies of scale (sometimes called economies of large scale) occur when the average costs of a firm decrease as it grows larger. This may occur when the firm finds that it can utilize new technologies which will make it more efficient only if it expands. Consider, for example, the firm pictured in Figure 7-8. Assume that this firm possesses average cost curve AC_1. The firm produces at lowest cost with AC_1 when it produces output A. AC_1 is a familiar kind of curve. It relates the average cost of producing different outputs when the size of the firm does not change—when at least one factor of production is fixed. AC_2, AC_3, and AC_4 are additional fixed-size average cost curves. They refer to the firm's average costs at sizes B, D, and D. All of these curves are *short-run cost curves*

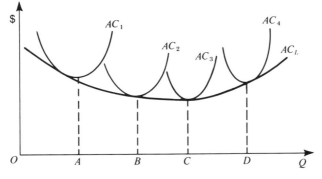

Figure 7-8

because each depicts the average costs of a firm in a period of time too short for the firm to change its size.

By enlarging the size of its plant from A to B to C, the firm pictured in Figure 7-8 experiences lower and lower costs of production. Its short-run average cost curve changes from AC_1 to AC_2 to AC_3. These curves, it should be noted, shift down as they move to the right. The firm is able to incorporate the technology of mass production by growing bigger. It gains the economies which go with this technology. However, as expansion proceeds beyond C, the economies of scale become exhausted. AC_4 is higher than AC_3. *Diseconomies* set in. Beyond some size, larger firms may be less efficient than smaller firms because of management and communications problems. The curve AC_L is made up of the lowest cost point for each output level (or scale) and is, in effect, a lower boundary of the whole family of short-run cost curves. Because the change of firm scale is a long-run concept, this curve is the *long-run average cost curve.*

Assume now that the firm of Figure 7-8 has the short-run cost curve AC_1. This firm equates its marginal cost and its marginal revenue, determines the output which maximizes its profits, and supplies that quantity to the market. If, by looking at a larger size, the firm sees that its average costs can be decreased to AC_2 or AC_3, it may not be satisfied with its short-run position. It will tend to enlarge, and to attain lower costs, larger output, and consequently higher profits. When economies of scale exist, the profit motive gives incentive to exploit them. By making such a move, the firm absorbs a larger share of the industry's market. It does so at the expense of its competitors. As a result, the output of the industry becomes concentrated in fewer and fewer hands. If carried far enough, oligopoly results.

Two questions arise: Have sufficient economies of scale existed so that large size and fewness can be attributed to them? And, if they have existed, what factors caused them?

As to whether such economies exist and have existed, there seems to be little doubt. The most comprehensive investigation of this issue by Joe S. Bain reviewed 20 prominent manufacturing industries in the United States, ranging from petroleum refining to steel to automobiles.[1] Defining an "optimal firm" as one just big enough to exploit the economies of large-scale production in its industry, Bain found that about one-half of the 20 industries were able to absorb 10 or fewer such optimal firms. That is, if each firm in these industries were big enough to attain minimum long-run average cost (scale C in Figure 7-8) there would be room for only 10 or fewer firms in each of these industries. In these industries oligopoly is natural due to the existing economies of large scale.

Since this study, a number of investigations of costs in particular industries have been undertaken.[2] These studies imply that the contribution of economies of scale to oligopoly may not be as great as the early study indicated. This is so, in part, because the U.S. economy has expanded sufficiently to allow numerous very large firms to exist in a single industry—hence reducing the tendency to oligopoly. Professor Leonard Weiss summarized this result as follows:

> The general finding [on economies of scale] is that the American economy is so huge that it can support many firms of efficient size in most industries. ... [A] common situation is like that in steel or petroleum refining. There, plants of the most efficient scale account for less than two or three percent of total output each. These plants may produce hundreds of millions of dollars of output, but our economy is ... large enough to have both the economies of scale and competition.[3]

Why have such economies of scale occurred? The most straightforward answer is one word—technology. From the beginning of the industrial revolution to a few decades ago, the vast

---

1. Joe S. Bain, *Barriers to New Competition* (Cambridge: Harvard University Press, 1956).

2. A number of them are reviewed in Edwin Mansfield, *Microeconomics*, 2d ed. (New York: W.W. Norton, 1975).

3. Leonard Weiss, *Economics and Society* (New York: John Wiley and Sons, 1975), p. 154.

majority of technical innovations and inventions worked in the direction of increasing the economies of large scale—the economies of mass production. The change in the source of power from muscle to steam with its required *in loco* steam plant line, the change in materials used for production from wood to iron and steel, the change in processes from labor-intensive to large, single-purpose machines, and the change in transportation from the ox cart and the canal to the railroad with its opening up of nationwide markets—all of these technological changes made production substantially more efficient in large firms than in small ones.

These changes did not occur overnight. Rather, they developed over a long period of time, as one innovation succeeded another. As they became known, market structures in industry after industry began to reflect them. Between 1880 and 1900, the changes in technology took their toll in radically transformed market structures. Where there had been many producers of each product, there remained only a few. Highly competitive markets turned into oligopolies. This was the period of the Great Combination Movement in the American economy. Robert L. Heilbroner describes it this way:

> In the early 1800s . . . no single plant controlled as much as 10 percnt of the output of a manufacturing industry. By 1904, seventy-eight enterprises controlled over half the output of their industries, fifty-seven controlled 60 percent or more, and twenty-eight controlled 80 percent or more. . . . By 1904, . . . 300 . . . giants controlled over two-fifths of the industrial capital of the nation and affected four-fifths of its important industries.[4]

C. Merger

While changed technology is one of the most important causes of oligopoly, other forces have also converted many firms into mass producers, and many industries into oligopolies. The most common of these is the *merger*, the joining together of two existing firms to form a single, larger one. Although merger has undoubtedly resulted in economies of scale, it is not clear that these economies motivated most mergers. In fact, some economists claim that the existence of a merger is evidence that such economies of scale do not exist; the firm would have grown internally if they did. This argument holds that the real reason for the merger is the desire to obtain market

---

4. Robert L. Heilbroner, *The Making of Economic Society*, 3rd ed. (Englewood Cliffs, N.J.: Prentice-Hall, 1970), p. 105.

power, to achieve the ability to control price and thus overcome a major pressure plaguing firms in competitive markets.

Aside from the motive for merger, the fact remains that the merging of smaller firms to form bigger ones is one of the most significant causes of big business, high industrial concentration, and oligopoly market structure. Indeed, it is estimated that from 1895 to 1929, the period of the most intense merger activity, more than $20 billion dollars of corporate wealth was merged into larger business firms. The industries that were transformed into oligopolies through such merger, activity form an impressive list: steel, automobile, tobacco, petroleum, agricultural equipment, biscuits and crackers, and many more.

In a classic study of the influence of mergers on industrial structure, 74 large firms in 22 prominent industries were analyzed.[5] It was found that in 6 of the industries, merger accounted for more than 50 percent of the total growth of the firms analyzed; in 13 of the 22 industries, merger accounted for more than 30 percent; and in 18 of the industries, merger accounted for more than 20 percent of firm growth. Mergers, whether motivated by the desire to take advantage of economies of scale or the desire to secure monopoly power, are important contributors to the creation of oligopolistic industries.

D. Oligopoly Behavior

Unfortunately, there is no standard theory of oligopoly behavior such as exists for pure competition and pure monopoly. Each oligopoly operates in a particular milieu, surrounded by a unique set of circumstances. Moreover, each new set of conditions elicits a different pattern of behavior. Consequently, no single model can universally explain oligopoly behavior. For example, in some oligopolistic situations a pattern of *price leadership* arises. In the steel industry, U.S. Steel usually sets the industry price, and the other firms follow it. In other situations, a pattern of *market sharing* evolves, as in the meat packing industry. In still other cases, a tacit understanding not to compete in price exists with the rivals wooing business through advertising, sales effort, and other forms of *nonprice competition.*

One basic pattern of behavior is common to all oligopolies. Noticed by many observers, this pattern has been described in

---

5. J. F. Weston, *The Role of Mergers in the Growth of Large Firms* (Berkeley: University of California Press, 1953).

several ways. The Supreme Court has called it "conscious paral-lelism of action." Others have referred to it as "tacit oligopoly collusion," or "oligopolistic rationale." Because of the size and closeness of the firms in an oligopoly, each is forced to react in some way to any action of its rivals. Thus, any action considered by an oligopolist will be taken only after the expected reaction of its rivals has been weighed and evaluated. If the firm should anticipate a violent response to its action, its decision to go ahead would not be the same as if it expected a quiet acceptance. This process of each firm's weighing its rivals' response to every anticipated action distinguishes oligopoly behavior from that of all other market structures.

E. A Simple Oligopoly Scenario

To demonstrate this "oligopolistic rationale," this mutual inter-dependence, let us analyze two oligopoly situations. We shall call the two situations the *price leadership case* and the *"live and let live" case*. Both are common patterns of oligopoly behavior.

Figure 7-9 contains a three-by-three matrix, which shows all possible combinations of the actions of an oligopolist and its rivals' response to them. The entries on the left-hand side of the matrix describe the three possible *actions* which any given oligopolistic

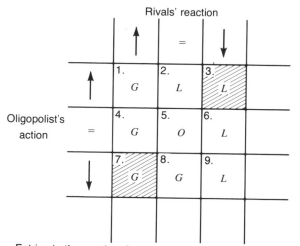

Entries in the matrix refer to changes in the *oligopolist's* profits.
G stands for gain and L stands for loss.

Figure 7-9

firm might initiate: the firm might raise price ($\uparrow$), keep it the same
($=$), or decrease it ($\downarrow$). The entries along the top refer to the *response*
of a rival firm to any of the oligopolistic firm's actions. The rival
firms can increase their prices ($\uparrow$), decrease prices ($\downarrow$), or keep prices
unchanged ($=$).

To fill in the boxes of the matrix, we must determine how each of
the nine possible combinations of action and reaction influences the
oligopolistic firm's profits. To do this, we shall make three assumptions about the state of affairs in the market.

1. Both the oligopolistic firm and its rivals are selling the product at the
   same price, say P.
2. If the oligopolistic firm raises its prices and all of the rivals raise theirs,
   the profits of the firm initiating the change will rise. That is, the price at
   the beginning of the analysis is below the *industry's* profit-maximizing
   price.
3. If the oligopolistic firm lowers its price and none of the rivals lowers
   theirs, the initiator's profits will rise. Some sales which previously went
   to rivals will now be attracted to the oligopolist. However, if the rivals
   match the oligopolist's price reduction, the profit of the oligopolist will
   fall.

On the basis of the particular situation defined by these assumptions, we can fill in the cells of the matrix. Each entry will display
the effect on the oligopolist's profit of any combination of action and
reaction—G referring to gain, L referring to loss, and O referring to
no change.

Let us begin with the status quo. If neither the oligopolistic firm
nor its rivals change price, nothing happens to the oligopolist's
profits—no gain, no loss. We place an O in the center cell of the
matrix. However, if the oligopolistic firm were to keep its price
unchanged and its rivals were to react to this by either raising or
lowering their prices, the situation would be different. Were the
rivals to raise their prices, sales would shift from them to the
oligopolistic firm and its profits would rise. On the other hand, if the
rivals lowered their prices, they would induce customers to shift
from the oligopolist and the oligopolist's profits would fall. We place
a G in cell number 4 and an L in cell number 6.

By the same token, were the oligopolistic firm to raise its price
while the rivals kept theirs unchanged, the oligopolistic firm would
lose sales and its profits would decrease. Conversely, were the
oligopolistic firm to lower its price while the others kept their
constant, the oligopolist would gain both sales and profits. This

latter case follows from assumption 3. Hence, we place an *L* in cell number 2 and a *G* in cell number 8.

This leaves only the four corner cells unfilled. They present no problem. Surely, if the oligopolist's profits rise when rivals keep their price constant as the oligopolistic firm lowers its price, its profits will also increase if the rivals raise their prices as a response. We place a *G* in the bottom left-hand cell of the matrix. By the same reasoning, if the oligopolist loses when rivals keep their prices unchanged as the oligopolist raises price, even more will be lost if the rivals lower their price in response. An *L* is placed in the upper right-hand corner. The entries in the remaining cells 1 and 9 follow directly from assumptions 2 and 3, respectively.

From the matrix, we can already isolate two important and basic characteristics of oligopoly behavior. First, it is obvious that an oligoplistic firm's profit is not determined by its behavior alone but also by the behavior of its rivals—by their reactions to its actions and vice versa. Second, because of this interdependence of profit among oligopolists, the action of any rational oligopolist is determined by the expected reaction of rivals. Understanding these characteristics of oligopoly behavior, we can use the matrix to analyze two particular oligopoly patterns: price leadership and "live and let live."

F. Price Leadership

Patterns of price leadership often develop in oligopolistic industries, especially those in which a group of smaller firms compete with one very large producer. This is the case in the steel industry. Not eager to antagonize the giant, the smaller firms permit it to set the industry price and follow its every move. Recognizing this pattern of reaction, the leader behaves on the assumption that every action it takes will be imitated by the followers.

The firm which behaves as price leader, therefore, faces only three of the nine possibilities represented in the matrix. If it raises price, the others will too; if it keeps price constant, so will its rivals; if the leader decreases price, the rest of the firms will follow suit. Only cells 1, 5, and 9 are relevant to this case.

Facing these three choices, a rational price leader firm has a clear course of action. If it raises price, the entire industry price will rise and the leader's profits will increase. Either of the other actions will hold the leader's profits constant or reduce them. Recognizing that the other firms will follow, the price leader will raise price until its profits are maximized. The net result of this behavior could be called *collective monopoly*—the firms in the industry behave as if they had formed a cartel and had agreed to follow a common price policy. They behave like plants of a single firm under a single manager. As a result of *price leadership*, the *oligopoly* tends to charge *monopolistic prices*, earn *monopolistic profits*, and *restrict output* as does a pure monopolist. This tendency is apparent even though there is no overt agreement among members of the oligopoly, but only a tacit acceptance of one of them as price leader.

In addition, it is clear from the model why such arrangements should exist in the real world and, indeed, feed on themselves. By following the leader, the other oligopolists increase their profits as the price rises toward the monopolistic level. They have incentive to strengthen the relationship rather than weaken it. Attempts to pursue an independent price policy are abandoned with little reluctance. Consequently, many economists have concluded that the "monopolistic solution," with all of its adverse consequences, does not require the existence of a monopolist. It may occur through a tacit agreement of the members of an oligopoly to a policy of price leadership.

G. Live and Let Live

The second oligopoly situation is characterized by the phrase "live and let live." Although this behavior pattern also arises out of an oligopoly market structure, it holds little resemblance to price leadership. In the case of price leadership, the oligopolistic firm was certain of its rivals' reaction pattern. Every change in price becomes imitated. In this case, however, there is no tacit agreement among the oligopolists and little knowledge of rivals' reaction patterns. The high degree of uncertainty concerning reaction patterns causes the oligopolist to proceed cautiously. A bad move can have serious consequences.

We shall also analyze this case using the matrix. In referring back to the matrix, again recall the three assumptions on which it is based—especially the assumption that the initial single price is below the industry's profit-maximizing price. First, let us see if there are any of the nine possibilities in the matrix which can be eliminated in this oligopoly case. From the matrix, it is clear that were an oligopolist to keep the firm's price unchanged, there would be no indication at all of the rivals' reaction. They might lower their price, raise their price, or keep it the same. However, if the oligopolistic firm lowered its price, the rivals would either lower their price or keep it unchanged but, in all likelihood, would not raise it. Finally, if an oligopolistic firm raised its price, the rivals would either raise their price, or keep it unchanged but, in all likelihood, would not lower price. With this likely pattern of rivals' behavior, all of the cells in the matrix become possibilities except the two corner cells that have been shaded.

When an oligopolistic firm is uncertain of rival reactions and wants to play it safe—to live and let live—which price policy will it pursue? Will it raise its price, lower price or keep it unchanged? From studying the matrix, it is clear that the firm may suffer a loss, regardless of its choice. It all depends on the reaction of its rivals. Likewise, it may gain no matter which policy is chosen. Assuming that the oligopolistic firm desires to maximize profits and, above all, to avoid losses, what policy should it choose? Let us take the possibilities one at a time.

First, what is likely to happen if the firm keeps its price unchanged? The rivals can raise or lower their prices or keep them unchanged. If they lower their prices the oligopolist will clearly incur a loss. Profits will decrease. Even if the oligopolist attempts to remedy this by matching the price cut (moving to cell 9 after the rivals cut prices), the firm will still lose. Thus, a decision to keep price unchanged can result in an irremediable loss of profit.

Second, what will likely happen if the oligopolistic firm lowers its price? This policy can also result in a severe loss. If the oligopolistic firm lowers price and the rivals follow its action, the oligopolist will be in the same situation as in the first course of action. Moreover, if the oligopolist attempts to correct the situation by again raising price, there is no assurance that the rivals will follow. The oligopolist may simply shift from losing cell 9 to losing cell 6. Again, the loss may be permanent and irremediable.

Third, only if the firm raises its price will the situation be different. Even if it loses in this case (because its rivals keep their prices unchanged), the loss will not persist. By cutting its price back to the previous level, the oligipolstic firm could recover its earlier rate of profit.

This same situation can be viewed somewhat differently. From Figure 7-9, it is clear that at all costs the oligopolist must avoid choosing that policy which will cause rivals to lower their prices. As seen in the right-hand column of the matrix, if they should lower their prices the oligopolist can only lose. On the other hand, the oligopolistic firm will be best off if it can induce the rivals to raise their prices. This can be seen in the left-hand column of the matrix. The question is: What should the oligopolist do to encourage rivals to raise their prices and to discourage them from lowering their prices?

The best policy for the firm is clearly to raise its own price. Not only does this prevent its rivals from lowering their price, but it encourages them to increase it. The worst loss that the oligopolist could sustain in this case would occur if the rivals kept their price unchanged. But even then, the firm can avert a persistent loss by again reducing its price.

Raising price, therefore, is the safest policy for the oligopolist to adopt. It is the policy least likely to unsettle conditions. Indeed, and this is the importance of this case, if every oligopolist in the market believed in playing it safe, in living and letting live, the result would be the *same as in price leadership. Prices* and *profits* would *rise* and *output* would be *restricted*. The solution would again tend toward that of pure monopoly.

Although we have considered only two cases out of a multitude of possibilities, the general pattern of oligopoly behavior is clear. Because the interdependence of one rival on another is recognized by all, because any rival's behavior is anticipated, reacted to, and countered by the rest, because each rival desires maximum profits and recognizes that vicious warfare will harm all, the oligopoly solution will not be the competitive one. It will, in fact, tend toward the monopolistic solution.

IV.   CARTELS

In our discussion of oligopoly, we have used the terms "conscious parallelism of action" and "oligopolistic rationale." These terms emphasize the point that oligopolists need not engage in overt collusion or conspiracy in order to establish abnormal profits and monopoly-like prices. They need not meet together to raise prices; all that is required is that they be conscious of one another's actions.

However, the fewness of firms in an oligopoly gives both the incentive and the ability for more concrete collaboration. Such overt cooperation in setting prices or organizing other aspects of market control is called *cartelization*. It is attractive to producers in an oligopolistic setting because it reduces the uncertainty which often accompanies more tacit understandings.

Although collusion is outlawed in the United States, prominent examples of it have occurred. During the late 1950s, for example, manufacturers of electrical equipment—including General Electric, Westinghouse, and Allis Chalmers—regularly engaged in overt collusion or cartelization. Arrangements on prices, market shares, and bidding procedures were made at meetings held during conventions and through circulated memoranda; indeed, a rather elaborate code system was developed to hide the arrangements being made.

This cartel was finally broken by government investigations and, after an extensive trial, the defendants were found guilty, fines were imposed, and a number of high-level executives served jail terms.

Outside of the United States, the formation of cartels is more prevalent. For example, under the auspices of the International Air Transport Association, air lines which service trans-Atlantic customers meet regularly to fix the prices for such flights. Indeed, this cartel not only fixes prices but also allocates routes among its members. At times, for example, during the financial difficulty of Pan-American Airlines during the mid-1970s, routes and prices were adjusted to keep a member of the cartel from financial failure. Interestingly, this cartel has had the support of the U.S. government, which on occasion has been a quasi-participant in it.

Perhaps the most well-known cartel is that fomed by countries who are the major producers and exporters of oil. This international collaboration, called the Organization of Petroleum Exporting Countries (OPEC), is composed of the 13 major oil-producing nations.

As our models suggest, such a cartel has an incentive to increase the price of oil toward the monopoly level. Since the early 1970s, it has done this with remarkable success; it has managed to boost the world price of oil from $4 per barrel in 1973 to a figure over six times that amount by 1980. Because of this result, it is estimated that these countries have secured an increase in their oil revenue of about $120 billion per year. Through regular and now well-publicized meetings, the governments of these countries regularly collaborate to set prices and to work out other arrangements for securing monopoly profits.

While substantial incentives exist for the creation of cartels, there are also inherent reasons why such organizations contain the seeds of their own collapse. Because the price set by a cartel will be above the free market equilibrium, the quantity demanded will be restricted and some means has to be found to divide up this limited demand among the members. But after the division of the market, it will be in any individual firm's interest to increase its sales and its share of the market. Indeed, the higher the cartel price relative to marginal cost, the greater will be this incentive. An individual member of the cartel can take advantage of this situation by making secret price concessions or in some other way cheating on the cartel agreement. To counter the loss of markets due to this behavior, other participants in the cartel are also likely to deviate from the agreement—and as the number of those who deviate expands, the cartel will become less effective. Ultimately, unless the cartel has the ability to punish those who cheat on the agreement, the cartel is likely to completely disintegrate.

This "self-destruct" character was present from time to time during the electrical equipment conspiracy, as excess capacity of one or more of the participants would often lead to independent action. Instability would result and the members of the cartel would have to regroup to establish a new collusive agreement.

Many observers of the OPEC cartel believe that ultimately it too will be undermined by one or more countries who will "chisel" on the agreement. Except for the role of the multinational oil companies, OPEC has little structure to enable it to punish price cutters or to otherwise keep them in line. Indeed, prior to 1970 OPEC was generally regarded as an ineffective organization and the current optimistic view (at least from the point of view of consumers) is that the effectiveness of OPEC will be eroded over the long run by such price cutters. One observer has stated the basis for this view as follows:

> [The] *huge discrepancy between the price [of oil] and the long-run marginal cost . . . of 15 to 20 cents [will] result in an irresistible expansion of production. . . . [This] means that surpluses will inevitably emerge, producing countries will begin jockeying for position in world markets, OPEC will break up in the classic manner, and prices in the long run will fall.*[6]

After nearly a decade of success for OPEC, most observers would find this conclusion overly optimistic, or at least based upon a view of the long run which must be measured in decades rather than years.

V.   MONOPOLISTIC COMPETITION

A. Market Characteristics

The final market structure we will consider is *monopolistic competition*. As the name implies, this form of industry structure possesses characteristics of both competition and monopoly. Although it is characterized by many firms like competition, each firm does not produce and sell a uniform or homogeneous product. Rather, each firm has a monopoly for its own unique commodity. However, the product produced by each firm is highly substitutable with the

---

6. James W. McKie, "The Political Economy of World Petroleum," *American Economic Review* (May 1974), pp. 51–57. See also, M. A. Adelman, "Politics, Economics, and World Oil," in the same issue, pp. 58–67.

products produced by the other firms in the industry or group which is the competitive element. This high degree of product similarity is what distinguishes the monopolistically competitive market from either monopoly or competition. Thus, monopolistic competition occurs where a *large number of firms* produce *highly substitutable commodities* and *other firms are free to enter the market* with a *differentiated* or similar product. While in oligopoly there are a few firms producing a product, here there are many. While in competition the product is homogeneous, here it is not. While in monopoly there are no close substitutes for the product of a firm, here there are many.

The next time you go into a drug store, spend a few moments studying the plethora of cold remedies. Each of the many remedies bears a claim for its own particular effectiveness—the product is differentiated. Nevertheless, all of them presumably perform one primary function—relief from cold symptoms. Thus, they are closely substitutable products. Moreover, anyone can develop a new remedy and sell it over the drug counter. The market for cold remedies is, therefore, monopolistically competitive as are the markets for most household items. As a matter of fact, in all likelihood, the drug store is itself a monopolistic competitor. If prices on each item here were a few cents higher than those of other drug stores in the neighborhood, this druggist would lose business. The service rendered is a close substitute for the service rendered by the many other drug stores in the area.

The highly substitutable product characteristic of monopolistic competition is incorporated into the demand curve facing the individual monopolistic competitors. Figure 7-10 pictures two demand curves. The curve labeled *DD* in Figure 7-10(a) is the *market demand curve*. It represents the relationship of total quantity demanded to price in the market. As the market curve, it may be elastic or inelastic depending on the nature of the demand for the product. If the quantity demanded is responsive to changes in the price, the market demand is elastic; if the quantity is not responsive, market demand is inelastic.

In Figure 7-10(b), the demand curve facing the individual monopolistic competitor is labeled *dd*. This curve displays a very high degree of price elasticity. Any individual monopolistic competitor knows that if the price of the product changes even a little, the quantity that can be sold changes a great deal. This is due to the close substitutability of the product with those of the firm's competitors. While an individual firm has some control over the price of its product, it does not have very much. Were it to raise its price a

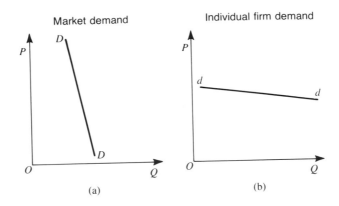

Figure 7-10

little, many customers would shift to a competitor; were it to reduce its price slightly, it would gain some of its competitors' sales.

This situation is substantially different from either pure competition or monopoly. Because of product homogeneity, the firm in a competitive market has *no* control over the price charged. The demand curve that a pure competitor faces is an infinitely elastic horizontal line. The monopolist, on the other hand, produces a product with no close substitutes. Being the only firm in the market, the monopolistic firm faces the entire market demand curve. Its control over price is *total*.

B. Behavior and Performance

To analyze the behavior and performance of monopolistic competition, we will again build a model. As with our other models, we must make assumptions before we can draw conclusions. First, let us assume that there are a large number of firms producing a differentiated but very similar product. Second, we will assume that all of these firms are in the position pictured in Figure 7-11: they all have costs represented by MC and AC; they face an extremely elastic demand curve for their product dd; they are in short-run equilibrium $(MC = MR)$; they produce Q units of output and sell them at a price of P; and they are earning a large profit. With these assumptions, the question is: In an industry with this structure, what will happen in the long run—will the equilibrium pictured in Figure 7-11 be modified or will it not?

In monopolistic competition, as in pure competition, ease of entry and exit is a primary characteristic. In each case, it is the presence or absence of expected profits which provides the motivation. If abnormal profits exist, new firms and resources will move

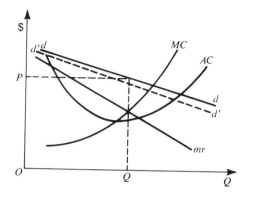

Figure 7-11

into the industry to take their slice; if the industry is experiencing losses, firms and resources will leave the industry.

In our model, large profits are being made $(P > AC)$ and new firms will enter the industry. The short-run equilibrium pictured in Figure 7-11 will be modified. Each of the new entrants, by placing its somewhat differentiated product on the market, will carve out a segment of the market for its own. Significantly, the market segment which is carved out by the new entrants is composed of sales which the other firms in the market would have made if no entry had occurred. By gaining a share of the market for themselves, the new entrants decrease the market for each of the existing competitors.

Figure 7-11 depicts this process of market erosion for one of the existing competitors. Because of the large profits in the industry, new firms enter the market, carve out a part of the market for their own product, and cause the market of the existing firms to be eroded. Whereas the demand for the products of the existing firms was dd before the new firms entered, their entrance has the effect of reducing the existing competitors' demand curve to, say, $d'd'$.

As long as profits are being made in this industry—as long as the dd curve lies above the average cost curve—entry into the industry will occur. And every time entry takes place, the dd curve of the existing firms shifts down toward the average cost curve. The nature of the long-run equilibrium in monopolistic competition now becomes clear. As long as entry takes place, the dd curve decreases until profits are eliminated. This situation is pictured in Figure 7-12. The dd curve of existing firms has fallen until it is tangent to the average cost curve. Figure 7-12 pictures the long-run equilibrium of the monopolistic competitor.

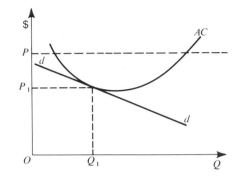

Figure 7-12

In moving from short-run to long-run equilibrium, several things happen to the industry. Because of entry there are more firms than before. As the demand curve of the individual producers is whittled down, the price falls from P to P_1. In long-run equilibrium, profits are forced toward zero.

Having defined the long-run equilibrium, we can compare the performance of a monopolistically competitive industry to that of pure competition and pure monopoly. It appears that the performance of monopolistic competition lies somewhere between these two extremes. It is not as desirable as competitive performance but not as undesirable as the monopoly solution.

As Figure 7-12 shows, the price charged by a monopolistic competitor in long-run equilibrium is higher than the price charged by a competitor. The competitor's price, it will be recalled, is forced down to the minimum point on the average cost curve in long-run equilibrium. For the same reason, the quantity produced by a monopolistic competitor is smaller than that produced by a competitor. In monopolistic competition, each firm in long-run equilibrium has some excess capacity. We can conclude that because of the small degree of monopoly power present in this market structure, the quantity produced is somewhat smaller and the price somewhat higher than in competition.

However, because of the excess capacity which exists in each firm, a more serious inefficiency arises. To produce a given output, *a greater number of firms is required in monopolistic competition* than in pure competition. This clearly represents misallocated resources and economic waste.

Finally, it should be noted that the long-run monopolistic competition solution is similar to that of pure competition with respect to profitability. In both cases, profits are eliminated as free entry forces price down to average costs. This is substantially different from the long-run monopoly solution.

C. Advertising

The description of the performance of a monopolistically competitive industry (and, in fact, some oligopolies) would be incomplete if we failed to mention the problem of advertising. Clearly, advertising and other forms of *nonprice competition* are the main techniques used by firms to gain entry into monopolistically competitive industries. Advertising is the chisel used to carve out a share of the market.

The reason such nonprice competition is present in this market structure is clear. The existence of differentiated products spawns such expenditures. Because the allegiance of customers can be shifted from one product to a close substitute with a little persuasion, the individual firm has incentive to use advertising to gain or maintain a market share.

In a very real sense, expenditures on advertising which try to differentiate close substitutes—expenditures which support one of the nation's largest service industries—can be considered a *social waste*. Since their primary effect is simply to shift business from one firm to another, with the consuming public paying the cost (which is reflected in increased product price), advertising expenditures yield little or no net social gain. Such a result cannot be ignored in evaluating the performance of monopolistic competition as a market structure.

This is not to claim, however, that *all* advertising expenditures are wasteful. Those expenditures that inform the consumer of products, prices, and services of which one would otherwise be unaware provide real economic benefit. They increase the mobility of resources in the economy and make markets more perfect by augmenting the knowledge of consumers. This is a benefit which must be compared with the cost of these expenditures. However, those advertising expenditures whose sole purpose is simply to shift trade from one firm to another with a slightly differentiated product do not yield such a benefit. Although they may provide a substantial private gain to the firm doing the advertising, their social gain is nonexistent.

QUESTIONS

1. In what sort of market structure do you think four-year, coeducational, liberal arts colleges operate? Why? How about supermarkets? automobile

companies? cigarette companies? computer manufacturing companies? tie manufacturing companies? toy retailers?

"The key difference between an oligopolist and a monopolistic competitor is that the oligopolist produces a homogeneous product." Do you agree? Why or why not?

3. "In some industries, the Law of Diminishing Marginal Returns does not hold. That is why they have become oligopolistic." Discuss and evaluate.

4. Why is "conscious parallelism of action" or "rivalry" present in oligopoly when it is not present in monopolistic competition?

5. Discuss the relationship between the elasticity of the demand curve facing a firm and the degree to which its product is substitutable with the product of other firms. Is this relationship positive or negative? Why?

6. What would have to happen to transform a differentiated oligopoly into monopolistic competition? Would the existence of substantial economies of scale indicate anything about the probability of such a transformation occurring?

7. Explain why "excess capacity" is often cited as a characteristic of monopolistic competition. "Excess capacity" in a monopolistically competitive industry often has two components—"excess industry capacity" and "excess firm capacity." Distinguish between these two and describe why both kinds tend to be associated with monopolistic competition.

8. "Collusion" is often thought of as businessmen meeting in hotel rooms to rig the price of an industry's output. Is this the way "tacit oligopoly collusion" works? Describe the basic differences in the two types of collusion. Is there likely to be any difference in the final outcome of the two types?

VI. PUBLIC POLICY AND THE MARKET ADJUSTMENT PROCESS

Early in this chapter, we noted a type of market power different from monopoly or monopsony power. We called this power the power of *price control*. The distinguishing characteristic of this power is that it is imposed on a market by some outside force. This force ignores supply and demand considerations and manipulates the market price directly.

In the U.S. economy, this force is often exercised by some form of government regulation or control. Often governments are induced to intervene directly into the economic system to protect some (often, powerful) economic interest or to provide higher prices or incomes for some producer group. In many cases of such intervention, governments impose direct controls over certain prices, either in the market for goods and services or in factor markets. Examples which will be considered are price floors for agricultural products, minimum wages, price ceilings during war or high rates of inflation, and support of minimum prices by manufacturers through "fair trade" laws. When such direct price manipulation occurs, the market adjustment process is eliminated and distortions and misallocations of resources occur. Often these effects are unintended, in the sense that government policy didn't plan them. Indeed, they often reflect the fact that policy makers failed to understand the operation of the market system when they went about their legislating.

Before looking at some examples of government interference in the market mechanism, let us analyze the economic effects of efforts to manipulate prices in general.

A. The Economic Effect of Government Price Setting

In a free and competitive market, prices are determined by the forces of supply and demand. As in Figure 7-13, the market price of a good or service attains equilibrium where the supply and demand curves intersect. In such a free market, if the price were higher than P, excess supply and competitive selling would force it down toward P. This is a buyer's market. If the price were lower than P, excess demand and competitive buying would force it up toward P. This is a seller's market. The price and quantity in such a free situation vary according to the dictates of supply and demand.

Assume now that a law is passed, ignoring the forces of supply and demand, which decrees the price at which each unit of a product shall sell. By chance, this price might be the market equilibrium price. In this case, the law might as well not have been passed at all. The free market conforms to its intent. However, the legislation is likely to stipulate a price different from the market price—a price

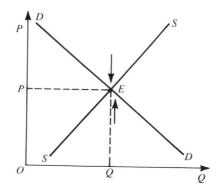

Figure 7-13

either higher or lower than P. In Figures 7-14 and 7-15, these possibilities are presented.

Figure 7-14 depicts the first of these possibilities. Whereas the free market would establish a price of P, we shall assume that the law decrees a price higher than P, say, a price of P_1. At this price, the quantity which buyers will take from the market, the quantity demanded (Q_D), is less than the quantity which suppliers will bring to the market, the quantity supplied (Q_s). Because the price is maintained above the equilibrium price, a surplus equal to $OQ_s - OQ_D$ develops. The market simply cannot be cleared at a price of P_1.

Such a legislated price affects consumers of the product in two ways. They are not only forced to pay a higher price for the product but, what is equally serious, they are unable to buy as large a quantity as under the free market equilibrium.

The opposite situation occurs if the legislation decrees a price lower than the market equilibrium price. This is pictured in Figure 7-15. Again, the market equilibrium is at E, yielding an equilibrium price and quantity of P and Q. If the price were set at P_1, a disequilibrium would again occur. The quantity demanded (Q_D) would exceed the quantity supplied (Q_s) and an insufficient supply (or excess demand) would plague the market. A *shortage* equal to the amount that consumers desire to buy at this price (Q_D) minus the amount that sellers are willing to supply (Q_s) would result.

Clearly, the impact of this situation differs from that in Figure 7-14. While consumers had to purchase the product at a price above equilibrium in that case, here they secure the product at a price below the market price. In both cases, however, the quantity exchanged is restricted. Because sellers are willing to bring only Q_s

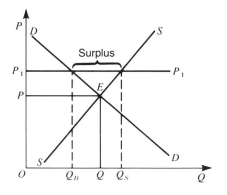

Figure 7-14

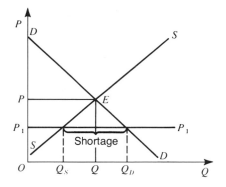

Figure 7-15

to the market, only that amount will be exchanged at the below-equilibrium price.

From this discussion, the economic effect of interfering in the market adjustment process by directly setting price can be summarized:

1. For any price other than the market price, the quantity produced and exchanged will be reduced and resources will be diverted from the sector with the controlled price to other sectors, where they will be less productive. This loss of efficiency is economic waste.
2. When the price is set above the market price, a surplus appears on the market, and those suppliers who manage to sell their output experience an increase in revenue and profits. Buyers of the output lose.
3. When the price is set below the market price, a shortage appears on the market. Those buyers who manage to purchase some of the restricted supply are the gainers. The sellers of the output lose.

Hence, while government price setting benefits some groups and hurts others, it always leads to a misallocation of resources and economy inefficiency.

B. Some Examples of Government Price Regulation Policies

In the American economy, the direct setting of prices by the federal, state, and local governments is not at all uncommon. In the following paragraphs, we shall describe a few instances of such direct price controls. Numerous other examples could have been cited and described, and all of them would have the same economic effects as those we have discussed. Among the omitted examples are:

- The payment of a below-market-wage rate to military forces, with the consequence of having to impose a draft;
- The establishment of a legal ceiling on market interest rates with the consequence that lenders have to ration funds;
- The fixing of a zero price on facilities with a limited capacity—such as highways—with the result that congestion and delays result;
- The setting of rent ceilings on rental housing by some cities, resulting in serious housing shortages and a low level of new construction.

Example 1—U.S. Farm Policy.   For certain farm commodities all of the time and for almost all commodities at some time, direct setting of minimum prices by the federal government has been an accepted procedure. Because of low farm income and deteriorating farm prices, the agricultural interests demanded that government support the price of certain agricultural products. And, from the 1940s on, the government has done just that. The prices were inevitably set above the free market price and, as would be expected from Figure 7-14, the market did not clear—a surplus accumulated which was purchased by the federal government. With the quantity of farm products supplied exceeding the quantity demanded, further measures were necessary to avoid the physical destruction of food. Being responsible for the creation of the surplus, the government did the next best thing. During this period, it bought the surplus and placed it in massive storage bins. The government also set acreage restrictions for the crops whose prices have been supported.

In the early 1970s, the large and rising international demand for U.S. farm produce reduced the pressures for governmentally supported prices. When foreign grain harvests have improved and when bumper crops have been produced, pressures for government price supports have returned. Such events as the embargo of grain shipments to Russia at the beginning of 1980 also produce market interference.

Example 2—Minimum Wage Legislation.   Minimum wage legislation has much the same impact as the direct setting of farm prices. Again, a price—this time a wage rate for some lower skilled workers—is fixed above the market price. The setting of an above-equilibrium price may again create a surplus. In this case, however, there is no special provision for the purchase (or support) of the surplus labor. Whatever labor is displaced simply enters the ranks of the unemployed. By artificially raising wages, such legislation may, therefore, increase the level of unemployment. Perhaps more important, it will tend to increase the unemployment of those workers who can least afford it—the workers who, when they were employed, earned the lowest wages.

While minimum wage legislation is often defended as helping those workers in the society earning the lowest incomes, our theoretical discussion suggests that it may not do so. And, as is often the case in economics, it is not easy to measure empirically the true impact of such legislation. Some studies indicate no clear tendency for workers to be laid off or unemployment to increase after changes in the minimum wage. Other studies have indicated quite the opposite result—especially for teenagers, household workers, and others with low skills and little training.

There are many reasons why our theoretical outcome may not be clearly observed in the real world. Let us mention just a few. First, because of a lack of precise knowledge in the real world and a reluctance to abandon the status quo, adjustments to economic change are neither precise nor instantaneous. Rather than crisp response, adjustment has the character of broad, somewhat uncertain tendencies. We should not be surprised if we are unable to get instantaneous readings of the labor market effect of minimum wage legislation. Second, if firms have some market power in purchasing labor, the government price fixing (minimum wage legislation) may merely offset private market power. In this case, the minimum wage law may actually result in resource allocation closer to that which pure competition would provide. This, too, limits our ability to make any certain claims about the effect of the minimum wage legislation. Third, if there are other forces in the economy which are inducing expansion of employment at the same time that the minimum wage legislation works in the opposite direction, the impact of the wage legislation alone may be impossible to filter out and measure. This is the danger in using partial equilibrium analysis in appraising the impact of public policy on the economy. The *ceteris paribus* assumptions of the partial analysis simply may not hold in the real world.

Example 3—Price Controls in National Emergencies. Minimum wage legislation and agricultural price support legislation reflect the ability of suppliers to persuade legislators to alter how the price system allocates income. Price control during war reflects public dissatisfaction with the way the price system allocates resources when social demand must take precedence over private individual demand. In a national emergency, the supply of most consumer goods is cut back to allow for the production of war materials. The cutback in the supply of consumer goods tends to cause the market price of these goods to rise with no prospect of a response in supply. To avoid these rising prices and the accompanying inflation, the government has commonly instituted a system of price control. It did so during World War II and again in 1971–1973. A ceiling price is set on a broad range of goods above which the price is not permitted to rise. This ceiling is clearly established below the market equilibrium and, hence, results in a situation similar to that pictured in Figure 7-15. The buyers wish to purchase more than the sellers are willing (and, in the case of a national emergency, able) to supply. A shortage results.

In World War II, the government attempted to solve the resulting problem of shortages by rationing the available supply of consumer goods through a system of coupons and stamps. This rationing program accomplishes what the society desires during wartime. It eliminates the danger of inflation and restricts the use of particular nonessential kinds of goods. In doing this, it frees resources for wartime outputs. It should be emphasized, however, that this form of social control directly substitutes the judgments of political leaders for the freely expressed tastes of consumers. Consumers are prohibited from using dollars as ballots in buying the goods and services they desire. And prices are prohibited from serving their traditional role as rationing devices.

Another example of price control occurred with President Nixon's announcement on August 15, 1971, of a 90-day price and wage freeze. Inflationary pressures had built up for manufactured goods during the Vietnam war. The pressures worsened as a corn blight hit the Midwest in 1970, reducing cattle and hog herds during the winter of 1970–71. Meat prices soared. Poor growing weather occurred in Russia, China and India, resulting in increased demand for U.S. agricultural products. Such a confluence of events seemed to the President and many in Congress to call for drastic action.

The 90-day price and wage freeze gave the federal government time to organize a systematic control program. In November, Phase Two of the program commenced. Farm prices were not controlled in the freeze and continued to rise rapidly. The Cost of Living Council permitted wages to rise a maximum of 5.5 percent (plus 0.7 percent for fringe benefits) during the year. Nonfarm prices were tightly controlled by the Cost of Living Council according to profit-margin ceilings. Wholesale prices rose only 4.3 percent, with industrial commodities rising only 2.8 percent.

A Phase Three wage-price stabilization program was announced early in January, 1973. It represented a shift toward more flexibility, and more voluntary policing. Price increases over authorized levels had to be justified by higher costs. Once again the rationing function of prices was reduced. Unlike the program of World War II, ration coupons were not introduced to carry out the rationing function. Rather, as in Figure 7-15, there was unsatisfied demand and rationing occurred on a "good friend" or "old customer" or "first come, first served" basis where shortages occurred.

In the fall of 1973, the OPEC countries imposed an oil boycott on Europe, the United States and Japan. The United States was presented with yet another dramatic example of how supply and demand analysis can illuminate the problems of price control. The retail gasoline market became especially chaotic as consumers scrambled for a sharply reduced supply. While gasoline prices rose, they were constrained from reaching their market equilibrium levels because of both pressures from the federal government and the fear by oil companies of consumer reactions to the enormous profits which market-clearing prices would imply. And, again, shortages resulted—for the reasons illustrated in Figure 7-15. Gas stations attempted to ration gas by reducing the hours that they remained open. Some stations discriminated in favor of their old customers. Most sold gas on a first-come, first-served basis. Long lines of cars waiting for a turn at the gasoline pumps were the rule. No matter what their relative willingness to pay, customers well back in line failed to get gas as the pumps ran dry.

Wage and price guidelines were imposed in the fall of 1978 to combat rapidly spiralling inflation. Despite some compulsion through the withholding of federal contracts, the guidelines were unsuccessful and prices soared, powered by market forces such as very large OPEC oil price increases, a rapid increase in household formation, and widespread expectations of continued spiralling inflation. Here, market forces were not restrained, but when they were in previous periods of price control, prices rose rapidly for a time following removal of control as prices once again took over their rationing role.

Example 4—"Fair Trade." One final example of how government action can lead to the control of prices is what is called "fair trade" legislation. In past years, both state and federal governments have had such legislation. Since 1975, however, the federal government no longer permits this practice, although several states still do. Although disguised under the title of "fair trade," this legislation has the same impact as direct governmental price fixing. Through fair trade legislation passed by either state or federal governments, individual *producers* are permitted to establish the *retail* price of the goods which they produce but do not sell at retail. For example, the manufacturers of men's shirts would be allowed to determine the price at which the haberdasher must sell the shirts under fair trade legislation. There is only a slim chance that producers will choose the market equilibrium retail price. For obvious reasons, they will set the price in their own interest and above the free market price. Hence, the impact of fair trade is similar to that of the monopoly solution: the price is raised, the quantity exchanged restricted, the price structure distorted, and resources misallocated. Because the producing firm can restrict its own supply in this case, the problem of the surplus is automatically eliminated.

QUESTIONS

1. Consider the demand and supply functions for granola bars in question 1 of chapter 5. Assume that the government decreed that, because granola bars were such a vital food, they would not be permitted to sell for more than 10¢ per package.
   (a) Presumably the government's objective would be to encourage the consumption of granola bars. Would its decree have that effect?
   (b) What would be the shortage of granola bars?
   (c) What would you expect to happen to the number of firms in the granola bar industry?
   (d) What steps could the government take if it wanted both to encourage the consumption of granola bars and to keep the price below 10¢ per package?
2. Setting prices above and below equilibrium hurts some people and helps others. Assume that the rent of apartments in Chicago was set by the government at a below equilibrium level. How would you feel about this decision if you were:
   (a) A poor apartment dweller.
   (b) A rich apartment dweller.
   (c) A slum landlord.
   (d) A homeowner.
   (e) A newly married couple looking for an apartment.
   (f) A black family moving from Georgia to Chicago.
3. Perhaps the dominant example of governmental price control in the U.S. economy was the military draft. During the period of the draft, the maximum price that the Defense Department could pay military personnel was set by law. At the legislated price, the quantity of men demanded often exceeded the supply of men willing to work in the service at that price—there was a shortage. Diagram this situation. How did the

government resolve this situation? Who gains and who loses if the men required for the service are obtained by hiring in the open labor market at the prevailing wage rate rather than by being drafted? Describe what would happen to: taxes, the prevailing wage rate in the economy, and the defense budget if the necessary labor is hired at the prevailing wage rates. What are the economic and noneconomic reasons why you would favor (or diaspprove of) this free market system of meeting military manpower requirements?

VII. THE IMPACT OF ECONOMIC POWER: CONCLUSION AND SUMMARY

In this chapter, we abandoned our analysis of how a competitive market system works. We were interested in how the efficient performance of the competitive system becomes modified when market power is substituted for competition. The two basic types of market power were discussed in this chapter: market or industry structures in which the requirements of competition were not met, and markets in which some external force arbitrarily sets the price. In the first category, we discussed the market structures of monopoly, oligopoly, and monopolistic competition. In the second category, we analyzed the effect of arbitrarily setting a price both above and below the market equilibrium. We illustrated this kind of market interference by discussing four public policy measures involving direct price control.

In studying the competitive system, we learned that the optimum allocation of national resources requires the free movement of all goods and services, including the factors of production. Any good, service, or factor must be permitted to move freely if prices, including wages, are to perform their resource-allocating duties with efficiency. Indeed, because of the elaborate interdependence of the system's parts, a restriction imposed at one point in the economy is an indirect restriction on the entire mechanism.

Only when businesses have no power over prices or markets is the output of an economy adjusted so that the marginal cost of each commodity is equal to its price ($P = MC$). This adjustment occurs because the single, competitive producer faces a price which is equal to his marginal revenue ($P = MR$) and produces where his marginal cost equals this price.

In each of the market structures observed in this chapter, the $P = MC$ relationship does not hold. Under conditions of imperfect competition (monopoly, oligopoly, monopolistic competition), the single firm has control over price. It faces a demand curve for its product which slopes downward and to the right. For this reason, marginal revenue to the imperfect competitor is less than the price $(MR < P)$. By producing where marginal cost equals marginal revenue $(MC = MR)$, the imperfect competitor restricts output below what it would be if market power were lacking. It halts production while the cost of producing the next unit—the marginal cost—is less than the value of the next unit to the consumers, as represented in the market price. When market power is present, $MC < P$.

> The effect of this market power, whether held by buyers (monospony power) or sellers (monopoly power), is to restrict output, to reduce the movement of goods, services, and factors, and to cause a misallocation of resources. Much the same result was seen to occur when the market price was arbitrarily set by governmental legislation or some other external force.

This, then, is the most basic result of market power. It results in restricted outputs in the controlled sectors as judged by the preferences of consumers and evidenced by the casting of their dollar ballots.

Such restriction excludes resources from activities in which consumers wish them to be employed and forces them either into alternative employments which are not as desirable in consumers' eyes or into unemployment. Consequently, these resources either produce products which are less urgently desired or produce nothing at all. This results in a reduction in the value of their marginal product, which is synonymous with *economic waste*.

We conclude, then, that the most important impact of market power is its restrictive ability, its forcing of some sectors of the economy to be too small relative to others as judged by the preferences of consumers. Such restriction has many implications. Prices are no longer determined by the market, resources become misallocated, the productivity of factors is lower than otherwise, and social waste results. The prices of restricted outputs are higher than otherwise, abnormal profits accrue to the firms in the restricted sectors, and society's income is redistributed by those private interests doing the restricting. Moreover, inefficiency and excess capacity are created within individual industries, costs are higher than otherwise, and again social waste results. We have, therefore, studied market power because of its impact on allocative efficiency and the economic welfare of people. In a comparison with competitive performance without market power, it comes off badly.

8 | Market Failures and Public Policy

The presumption in a market-directed society is that, in pursuing their own self-interest, individuals will act to maximize social welfare if they are subjected to the discipline of competition. The model of competitive markets that we have presented demonstrates the logic of this conclusion. In contrast, the models of noncompetitive markets (chapter 7) illustrate how market power or the control of supply or demand leads to misallocation of resources and a consequent failure to achieve maximum social welfare.

In addition to a lack of competition in some markets, there are a number of other reasons why the market system may not perform in the way our models have indicated. These include problems of immobility and imperfect information, and difficulties caused by what economists call "public goods" and "spillovers." In all of these cases of "market failure," society must look for means to either correct the problem in the market or to replace the market with some other kind of resource allocation system if one can be found that is superior in its outcome. In addition, the market system produces a particular distribution of income which may not be acceptable to the society. In this case, additional correctives must be sought. The collective efforts of society to modify the way markets work or to modify the outcomes of market operation are, by and large, undertaken by governments. They are termed *economic policies*.

In this chapter, we will describe a few of the most important problems which lead to public sector action. First, we will continue the discussion of chapter 7, showing both the social dilemma which market power poses and how public policy has responded to this dilemma in the United States. Then, another set of problems will be discussed—imperfect information, immobility, and irrationality—and the kinds of policy measures these have brought forth. Third, the problems of public goods and spillovers will be introduced and illustrated by policy responses to them in three areas. Finally, the problem of income distribution and policies to modify it will be briefly mentioned. Books could be—and have been—written on all of these problems and policies. We can only briefly introduce them here.[1]

I. LACK OF COMPETITION—MORE ON MARKET POWER

A. Conspiracy and Market Power

If competition serves as a disciplinary force for self-interest, we can expect that market participants will try to escape it; they will attempt to gain market power. Over 200 years ago, Adam Smith recognized this tendency when he wrote, "People of the same trade seldom meet together, even for merriment and diversion, but the conversation ends in a conspiracy against the public, or in some contrivance to raise prices."[2] Or, again, "Masters are always and every where in a sort of tacit, but constant and uniform combination, not to raise the wages of labour above their actual rate. . . . Masters too sometimes enter into particular combinations to sink the wages of labour even below this rate."[3] In the 200 years since Smith wrote, both workers and employers have constantly sought to combine. Labor unions have developed into strong institutions whose primary purpose has been to raise the price of labor through control of its supply. Oral agreements have been reached among competitors in the electrical equipment industry in recent years more covertly than among assembled steel industry magnates at the famous "Judge Gary dinners" earlier in the century. In addition, manufacturers have sought shelter from competition by organizing trusts, cartels, and mergers.

    If the only force leading to the control of supply or demand were cupidity, society might merely formulate and enforce rules prohibiting various forms of noncompetitive behavior. This is the basis of

---

1. See Robert H. Haveman, *The Economics of the Public Sector, 2d ed.*, in this series, for a more complete discussion of public policy in a market system.

2. *The Wealth of Nations.* Modern Library ed. (New York: Random House, 1937), p. 128.

3. Ibid., pp. 66–67.

antitrust legislation which aims to maintain competition by forbidding certain kinds of mergers, conspiracies for price fixing or division of markets, and predatory practices that are designed to destroy competitors.

B. Economies of Scale and Oligopoly

Efforts to enforce rules for competitive behavior through antitrust policy are complex and often ineffective because the cupidity of businessmen has an ally in technology. The continuing and accelerating technical revolution has created production units whose minimum efficient size (measured in units of output) is very large. We pointed out in chapter 7 that economies of scale decree oligopoly in a number of industries. Sometimes these economies occur because a single key machine, in its smallest efficient size, will produce an enormous output. In 1931, for example, a small Banbury mixer used to mix rubber compound for automobile tires produced 118,000 pounds of rubber compound per day. This one machine produced enough rubber compound for 6700 tires per day if used in standard passenger car tires of the period. If 51 such machines had been in use in 1933, they would have accounted for the entire capacity of the industy. In that year there were 44 plants and 33 firms in the tire industry, probably enough to ensure competitive performance. But these numbers disguised the concentration into large firms. Four of the 33 firms owned 64 percent of total industry capacity. The nine largest firms had a capacity of 6000 or more tires daily, accounting for 84 percent of the capacity of the industry. All of these firms made use of the productive, large-scale Banbury mixer. The remainder of the firms, 24 of them, shared the remaining 15 percent of capacity, using old-fashioned, high-cost technology. In the years since 1931, virtually all 24 have disappeared. The Banbury mixer reinforced the tendency toward market power in the tire industry.

Economies of large-scale operation may occur for other reasons as well. Sometimes machines used in sequence do not each produce an output that meshes with the others in a 1-to-1 ratio. In that case it is necessary to seek the lowest common denominator for the most efficient size of output. Suppose three different machines, used in succession on the production line, had capacities of 100, 500, and 600 units per day, respectively. To utilize all machines to capacity a firm would need 30 of the first type, 6 of the second, and 5 of the third. Minimum efficient capacity would not be 600 units (the capacity of the largest machine) but, instead, 3000 units per day.

Plants may have to be very large if they are to use the most efficient means of production, but that is not the end of the story.

Great gains may be had through specialization and division of labor within management. Firms may grow to be larger than the size established by one efficient plant and one firm may control many plants.

Large-scale operation may also occur when firms react to uncertainty. A firm may wish to produce a variety of products which are sold in different markets in order to spread the risks. If the demand curve for one product shifts downward because of a change of tastes, business cycle variations, or other reasons, the demand for other products may not be affected in the same way, and the firm as a whole may continue to prosper. Some of the impetus for the merger of firms in completely different fields—called *conglomerate mergers*—in recent years stems from this incentive to spread the risks.

While technological change has created large-scale enterprise, it has also reduced the isolation of small towns and has enlarged effective market areas. Such market expansion brings additional firms into contact, and hence stimulates competition. For example, when transportation innovations brought New England shoe manufacturers into competition with those in St. Louis for the Great Lakes markets, the possibility of competition serving as an effective regulator was enlarged.

In many industries in the American economy we do not find markets large enough and efficient producers numerous enough to have a market-determined, competitive price. A high proportion of production is carried on by firms that operate in oligopoly situations due primarily to economies of large scale. This should not be taken to mean, however, that existing firms must be as big as they are. The profit motive may lead to size greater than that implied by technical efficiency. The gains from market power are indistinguishable in the firm's balance sheet from the gains due to technical efficiency. Some of our industrial giants might be broken down into smaller firms without sacrificing a significant amount of managerial or production efficiency. This step would make it easier to prevent outright collusion. However, in most of these cases the larger number of firms would still find themselves in situations of oligopoly with both the desire and the necessity to act like oligopolists.

It appears that we are on the horns of a dilemma. If we insist on efficiency in the allocation of resources by requiring purely competitive markets, we must accept some inefficiency in the techniques of production. Costs will remain above the minimum. If we want efficient production, however, we must live with less than sufficient competition to allocate resources efficiently.

C. The Market Power Problem—Some Policies and Approaches

Dilemmas are frustrating. When there are both costs and benefits associated with any changes that might be made, recommendations for policies may be inconsistent—indeed, contradictory. This is true in the case of the big business and market power problem. Some economists urge that competition be created by the passage of strong antitrust legislation and its vigorous enforcement. This would include the breaking up of big firms which have substantial market power such as General Motors and U.S. Steel. Other economists urge that the federal government reform its mechanisms for directly regulating businesses and then include more industries in the regulated sector. Still others argue that technology changes will automatically undermine market power—or that monopolists facing each other across the market will neutralize the effects of market power—and that we shouldn't worry so much about the problem. We shall briefly present three of these positions.

1. Innovation—"The Perennial Gale of Creative Destruction." Joseph Schumpeter, in his *Theory of Economic Development,* saw a force at work in the capitalist economy which is different from the price competition of our model.[4] In this important work, Schumpeter placed the entrepreneur or innovator at the center of his theoretical structure. By introducing new things, or new ways of doing things, the innovator puts pressure on already existing products and methods. The new competes with the old in a process of *creative destruction.* It is not inevitable that the new displace the old; sometimes the new is not a close substitute for anything existing at the time of its introduction. The only effect may be the generalized one of competing with all other things for a share of the consumer's income. But more often than not, the new destroys some or all of the utility of the old. The old must adapt if at all possible, or die.

The internal combustion engine, applied to the automobile and bus, destroyed the electric street railway. It seriously cut the passenger traffic of railroads for short hauls. The truck reduced the high-grade freight traffic of railroads. While the internal combustion engine of the car, bus, and truck introduced a new, flexible dimension to our transportation system, its innovative character also pro-

---

4. Joseph Schumpeter, *The Theory of Economic Development* (Cambridge: Harvard University Press, 1934).

vided a direct and effective challenge to rail transit. Indeed, the railroad may well have faced a fatal blow to its long-distance passenger traffic from the competition developed since World War II by the commercial airline.

Innovators have a temporary monopoly when they introduce something new, and if they are successful they will receive a flow of monopoly profits. But if the competition of our model now comes into play, they will attract a host of imitators who will compete away their profits. Secrecy, patents, the requirements of large-scale financing, or the advantage of an early start may hold imitators at bay, but innovators cannot rest, since another firm, perhaps in another industry, may introduce something new which will displace their process or product.

What are the results of this process of innovation? There is no question that the development of aluminum processing created a substitute for many products that had been made of steel. This reduced the market power held by steel firms. Plastics compete with both steel and aluminum as a material for many products. Wherever new products are introduced which can be substituted for existing products, control of supply is weakened and the public benefits. But substitutability does not always develop, and where it does not, a few firms may continue to control supply. For example, there are many uses of steel for which other materials are not close substitutes. In these markets, steel companies control supply. All in the steel industry recognize that because of an oligopolistic market, standard competitive behavior—price reductions to produce and sell more—would be detrimental to their interests. Thus, prices are held up (sometimes even increased when demand is low) through oligopoly behavior of "live and let live" or price leadership.

Innovation does substitute for price competition in many cases where technology has decreed an oligopoly market structure. Innovations may stimulate rivalry among businesses in two dimensions: product differentiation and cost reduction. *Product differentiation* may add to social welfare when product quality is improved or new useful products are developed. It may subtract from social welfare when a large volume of resources is devoted to creation of superficial differences among commodities and their promotion. Innovation in the production process is in the public interest because it reduces production costs. Innovation also stimulates *interindustry competition*. This form of competition is in the public interest even though each industry is an oligopoly. Because of such competition, it is more difficult for firms to establish mechanisms for market control. These firms may be under constant threat from firms in industries other than their own.

2. Countervailing Power.   Thus far we have considered two kinds of "built-in" economic forces that protect the public interest in a market economy; one is our model of competition which illustrates protection by intraindustry competition, and the second is innovation which enlarges this form of competition and creates interindustry competition. A third force which may protect the public interest is countervailing power, identified by John Kenneth Galbraith. In *American Capitalism; The Concept of Countervailing Power,*[5] Galbraith develops the thesis that the existence of power on one side of a market creates a tendency for a countervailing power to develop on the other side. Thus, he claims that if a group of sellers exercises control over supply, we might expect that a group of buyers will try to develop control over demand to offset and neutralize the sellers' power.

There is a strong incentive to develop countervailing power for self-protection. Moreover, the monopoly profits on one side of a market give incentive to develop offsetting power on the other side of the market in order to share in the profits. According to Galbraith, this is why powerful labor unions are most often found in highly profitable, concentrated industries. Likewise, chain stores have developed to counter the power of concentrated manufacturers. Sears, Roebuck, and Company, for example, was able to obtain substantial price concessions from the Goodyear Tire and Rubber Company in the 1920s, when Sears negotiated with Goodyear to produce a private brand tire.

Countervailing power tends to develop only where there is an initial power that produces high prices and high profits. This appears to be a necessary condition because creation of power on one side of the market without power on the other side would constitute the creation of an initial, as opposed to countervailing, power. Moreover, if prices and profits of the initial power were just sufficient to draw the flow of products, nothing could be gained from the exercise of countervailing power. Such power may be most effectively exercised against oligopolies rather than monopolies because, with several firms, one firm may be played off against another. In a booming fully employed economy, it will be difficult for *buyers* to organize effective countervailing power. An individual firm, even though a giant, will not be able to exercise power as a buyer if there are other buyers eager to absorb all of the output that sellers can produce. However, if a group of *sellers* (for instance, labor) seeks to counter the established power of buyers (for example, a group of business firms), they are likely to be most successful during a full employ-

---

5. 2d ed., rev. (Boston: Houghton-Mifflin, 1956).

ment period, when businesses are having difficulty filling job vacancies. But—and this is the rub—in this case consumers continue to pay because higher labor prices are passed on in higher product prices. Higher wages are carved out of high profits, and consumers do not benefit.

What are the conditions under which countervailing power will produce public benefits? When countervailing power is effective, it changes prices and the distribution of income. Whether these changes are a social benefit depends entirely on the individual circumstance. If farmer cooperatives can bring down the prices charged by concentrated farm suppliers, farmers will use more supplies and resources will tend to be allocated more efficiently. This will happen because the farmer sells in a competitive market and the lower costs will be passed on to the buyers of farm products. If a manufacturing firm (or retailer) brings down prices charged by its suppliers, and absorbs the gain rather than passing it on, one economic power group has gained at the expense of another, and there is little improvement in the public welfare. Nothing has been passed on to the consumer.

There must be a broad distribution of the gains from countervailing power for there to be public benefit. Generally, the gains must be passed on to the ultimate consumers. Whether this will happen depends on the degree of market control by sellers through each transaction all the way into the consumer markets.

It should be noted that some public policies forestall this potential public benefit rather than encourage it. This happens because the policies do not distinguish between countervailing and initial power. The Robinson-Patman Act, for instance, prevents price concessions that can be substantiated by lower costs for that transaction. This prevents the exercise of countervailing power.

"Fair trade" laws, passed in the name of competition, have the same effect. By destroying price competition at the retail level, they remove any pressure on this source of countervailing power to pass its gains on to the consumer.

3. Enforcing Competition—The Antitrust Approach.   While it may be reassuring to believe that the innovation process or the tendency to countervailing power will reduce the inefficiencies and misallocations caused by market power, few economists are content with these approaches. Neither are many policy makers. For 90 years now, the U.S. government has passed and sought to enforce laws which would maintain competition in markets, or restore competition to markets that had become controlled.

The first act passed was the Sherman Antitrust Act of 1890. It was passed shortly after an enormous series of mergers and combinations of firms which left many major industries in the control of one, two, or three businesses. The Sherman Act has two main provisions. First, it prohibits agreements by competitors—such as on price or shares of the market—which "restrain competition." Second, it prohibits acts that are meant to maintain or to create monopoly.

The agency which is charged with enforcing this law is the U.S. Department of Justice, which maintains a division of lawyers and economists for just this purpose. This agency conducts investigations into the structure and behavior of industries, and every year numerous court suits are brought against business firms. Some of these suits cite evidence of overt conspiracy on prices or market shares; others cite patterns of tacit collusion such as price leadership; and others seek to forestall mergers which threaten to reduce or eliminate competition. In all cases, these suits look to the courts for remedies, interpretations of the law which will stop the action cited.

The Clayton Act of 1914 was the second major piece of antitrust legislation. It bars specific practices which might "substantially lessen competition." These practices include certain kinds of mergers, certain kinds of restrictive contracts (such as when a company tells its customers that they must carry the full line of company products, and not just one or two, or that they are prohibited from carrying the products of competitors), and certain kinds of pricing and advertising practices. This act also established the Federal Trade Commission (FTC) to enforce the act.

This legislation has been most effective in eliminating certain overt kinds of activities, such as direct price fixing, and in restraining certain kinds of mergers. Because the law so clearly prohibits overt conspiracies, the Justice Department and the FTC are able to turn up relatively few instances of this sort each year. And these are typically minor. While business executives rarely meet in hotel rooms to set prices nowadays, they do engage in an enormous amount of oligopoly-type collusion—tacit, unwritten and uncommunicated. While this sort of behavior may be just as destructive of competition as the more formal kinds of conspiracies, the law has had little effect in reducing such patterns of action.

With respect to mergers, the laws have also been rather effective, especially after the 1950 amendments strengthening the Clayton Act. Because the antimerger portions of the acts were stripped of some of their teeth through court decisions, strenuous enforcement of them was not attempted from 1900 to 1950. During this time, two major merger movements—one around the turn of the century and the other in the 1920s—caused some industries to become near-monopolies (steel and tin cans, for example) and other industries to become more concentrated and oligopolistic. With the 1950 amendments, however, the effectiveness of the antimerger provisions was increased and enforcement has been more effective. Today, most businesses know that attempted acquisition of a rival or of a major supplier or customer will quickly bring on a court suit and they don't attempt such mergers. This is so even for businesses in industries which are not clear-cut monopolies.

There are a number of ways in which the legislation has not been effective in enforcing competition. It has not led to the break-up of the nation's biggest and most powerful companies. This is so even though the Department of Justice has tried on a number of occasions. Since World War II, cases or threats of cases have been brought against Alcoa, IBM, and General Motors. Only in the Alcoa case was any divestiture accomplished.

The legislation has not been effective in curbing the merger of businesses in quite different lines of production either. These mergers are called *conglomerate mergers*. Although the Justice Department brought several suits against such mergers, their results have not been conclusive and the Supreme Court has not had to rule definitively on the applicability of the law to such mergers. Thus, while the threat of a suit does constrain some potential conglomerate mergers, many of them still occur. Such mergers do have the ability to create enormous corporations with huge assets and substantial economic power. On the other hand, such mergers may also create competition (or at least rivalry) where little existed previously. This can happen if, through acquisition, a small company can gain the resources to effectively compete and to challenge larger producers, or if weak and ineffective managements can be dislodged through such combinations.

All in all, the antitrust laws have been effective in eliminating overt collusion and curbing mergers which could lead to monopoly or oligopoly power. They have been less than effective in breaking up big corporations or in reducing their economic power, and they have only mildly restrained conglomerate mergers.

And perhaps this is as much as is necessary. If moves toward monopoly and oligopoly are stopped, the growth of the economy and the process of innovation may lead to more effective competition over time. In any case, we have seen that it is impossible to enforce anything like pure competition in large areas of the economy without significantly reducing technical efficiency. While this may create a void in the protection of the public interest, the forces of innovation and countervailing power which create different forms of "competition" may come into play. Where none of these private regulators are effective, government may be required to regulate business directly if the public interest is to be protected.

4. Regulating Businesses—The Regulatory Agency Approach. Over the years the U.S. government has created a number of agencies to regulate business. They have developed a vast array of rules and regulations to control prices, regulate behavior and fix rates. The Interstate Commerce Commission, the Federal Communications Commission, the Federal Aviation Agency, and the Federal Trade Commission are among those agencies which have been substituted for markets as regulators of economic activity. Their charge is to regulate the behavior of firms and individuals in the public interest because markets fail to do so properly.

Regulatory agencies also exist at the level of state government. For example, public utilities commissions regulate prices of electricity and natural gas and telephone service. State highway commissions control the length and weight of trucks using the state highways. At the local level building inspectors enforce building codes which stipulate such standards as the materials that may be used in construction or the character of electrical wiring. Planning commissions enforce ordinances that restrict the location of businesses by zoning. Other agencies regulate the quantity of pollutants that may be released or license practitioners of particular activities such as taxi companies, electricians, or plumbers.

Much of the regulation at each level of government succeeds in protecting consumers from fraud in advertising, in materials, and in workmanship. Some agencies hold prices below what would exist under the free reign of market power using concepts of a "fair rate of return" as their standard.

Some agencies by their regulatory powers prevent price wars and other forms of "destructive" competition which might drive out of business some of the small firms whose limited assets prevent their accepting losses for as extended a time as larger and more powerful firms. This helps to maintain a larger number of firms, and thus competitive behavior may be maintained in the nonprice rivalry of firms.

Regulatory agencies often provide for the protection and well-being of the public where markets cannot or will not do so, but several difficulties arise in the operation of these agencies. To be effective, an agency should be staffed with experts on the operation of the industry to be regulated. Such experts most often are to be found at work in that industry. When they are recruited for public service, the experts carry old loyalties or industry ways of thinking into their public office along with their expert knowledge. It is not surprising that at times the rate of profit of firms in the regulated industry is better protected than the interest of an amorphous mass of consumers. Regulated firms may prefer such a status to the "destructive competition" which it replaces. Whenever a public agency replaces markets in regulating economic activity, the public faces a predicament in determining how to call upon the experts without turning regulation over to those who are to be regulated.

Another difficulty arises because of the imperfection of the regulatory process. Economic relationships in a modern economy are complex and intricate. Very competent people are nevertheless unable to predict many of the ramifications of the regulations they propound. For example, we have seen above that antitrust legislation has outlawed agreements, collusion and trust arrangements as methods for limiting competition between firms. The Federal Trade Commission Act supplemented the antitrust legislation by creating an agency to control "unfair" competitive practices. The result was that for many years a single, merged company could do what two competing companies could not do. As a result of government regulation, then, mergers had become the most common method to reduce competition. Antitrust regulations then had to be extended to prohibit certain types of these anticompetitive mergers. It is clear that legal regulation is not simple, often requiring an apparently endless web of rules to try to accomplish its purpose.

Since regulation tends to prevent merger of competing firms, conglomerate mergers of noncompeting firms have become numerous in response to yet other financial-legal considerations. Because of our tax laws, it often is advantageous for a highly profitable small firm to sell out to a larger firm to convert income into capital gains. Tax law also enables an acquiring firm to chare off over a number of years the losses of an unprofitable firm which it has purchased. Policy makers have been striving, with some little success, to develop a legal basis for proceeding against some of these conglomerate mergers.

When complexity is added to simple bad judgment, it is not surprising that analysts urge that we weigh the costs of imperfection in government regulation against the costs of imperfection in markets. The choice for public policy may at times boil down to selecting the least imperfection—that in a particular market as compared to that in a proposal for government regulation. Generally, business structure and performance must be studied industry by industry if one is to understand the factors on which such public policy choices must be based.[6]

II.   IMPERFECT INFORMATION, IMMOBILITY, AND IRRATIONALITY

For a realistic view of how the market system functions we must understand many problems in addition to that of market power. One such group of problems may be identified as *frictions*. In chapter 1, it was noted that the price system works best if all buyers and sellers are *well informed* of the choices they face. We also emphasized that buyers and sellers had to be *mobile*. Buyers had to be able to shift from one seller to another if a price differential developed, and workers had to be able to shift from one job to another in the face of wage differentials. Finally, behavior designed to maximize utility or profits—we called it *rational behavior*—was necessary.

In real-world markets, these characteristics are often not present. In this section, we will discuss these market failures and the efforts of public policy to correct them.

A. Problems and Policies Regarding Imperfect Information

The gap between the information required in the market model and the situation in the real world is so large that it hardly needs to be documented. There are basically two kinds of information required by the model for markets to function smoothly and efficiently. The first is information on *current* prices and buying and selling opportunities. Buyers and sellers must be fully aware of the range and quality of goods and services available, and of the market prices of these goods and services. The second kind of information concerns *future* conditions in markets and prices. Because many kinds of economic decisions do not produce their effect until several months or years later, an accurate estimate of future conditions is essential to make efficient decisions.

Even with respect to information on current opportunities, the world deviates far from the model's requirements. How often, for example, are workers fully aware of the range of job opportunites available to them—even in their own communities? Even when actively searching for employment, the typical labor supplier will

---

6. *Case Studies in American Industry*, by Leonard Weiss, in this series, provides such a study.

assemble information on only a handful of options—and then only in his immediate neighborhood or community. Similarly, prior to equal employment opportunity and affirmative action regulations, employers usually filled a vacancy after considering only a few applicants for the position. And while careful comparative shopping may be common for some households, most purchase out of habit, paying little attention to price differences and the availability of different suppliers. In this regard, it should be added that when obtaining information is costly, the economic optimum is something less than perfect knowledge.

The information required for decisions which have an impact over time are even more demanding. Consider for a moment the prices of agricultural products which are produced (harvested) at one time in the year but sold throughout the year. It is easy to see why prices for agricultural crops would experience wide swings over time without data collection. In the absence of data for forecasting, supply curves in these markets would be based on quantities in storage. The supply curves would shift more and more to the left as the last harvest became more remote. They would move to the right at harvest time. With a relatively stable demand curve over time, prices would be high just before harvest and low just after harvest. The speed and amplitude of the price movement would depend upon how perishable the product is. Regular forecasts of the growing crops, however, help to reduce these price swings. With reliable forecasts, buyers and sellers are better able to anticipate changes in the future supply. Price stability is further enhanced by selling and buying contracts for future delivery, for instance, several months hence. Some of these future contracts are for the harvested crop held in storage by growers, while some of the contracts are for delivery from next year's harvest. Crop forecasts are essential for these transactions.

Another example concerns manufacturing firms, which often require a lead time of as long as six months in planning production schedule changes to meet short-run shifts in demand. Mistakes in forecasting lead to unintended increases or decreases in inventories. As inventories are worked off, or efforts are made to enlarge them, there will be shifts in demand for raw materials and for labor. Where factor prices do not move quickly to clear the markets, there will be unemployment.

A lead time of many years may be required to meet long-term shifts in demand. Often it will require two or three years to build new plants, order new capital equipment which must be manufactured, and install that equipment. If errors in forecasting are made, the firm may face excess capacity with high fixed costs for many years before either demand shifts to the right or some capital goods are fully depreciated and no longer contribute to cost. Losses from such errors may take many years to absorb.

The "Edsel debacle" was an example of the serious effects of a bad forecast. To place this automobile on the market, the Ford Motor Company required a long lead time for planning and many millions of dollars for capital equipment even though many component parts were common to other Ford products. Ford had planned for the Edsel to be the principal competitor to Buick, then in third place in total automobile sales. But the company failed to forecast the decline in this automotive price line and consequently experienced gigantic losses.

Provision of market information tends to increase knowledge and thereby tends to reduce price instability, periodic unemployment, and a misallocation of resources because of errors in forecasting. To accomplish these results, both government and private enterprise strive constantly to gather more complete data for more accurate market forecasts. But despite these efforts, some uncertainty will persist as long as production plans must anticipate future sales rather than respond to special orders already received. Errors can be costly because capital is durable. Consequently, business managers will expect a higher return on capital than they would if there were no risks. Some capital goods would produce an adequate return without consideration of these risks, but would not be profitable if the risks were included in the calculations. If such capital goods were to be purchased and installed, this lack of knowledge would adversely affect the allocation of resources. More accurate information will reduce uncertainty and the magnitude of error, thereby contributing to a more smoothly functioning and efficient market economy.

As several of these examples suggest, the information required for smoothly functioning markets is substantial—and this requirement often is not met in the real world. Moreover, some of this information is very costly to obtain. As a result, any single decision maker is unlikely to bear the cost of obtaining it. On the other hand, such information would be valuable to numerous decisions makers if it were collected and widely distributed. It is for this reason that, by collecting and disseminating information, governments play an important role in improving the functioning of markets, correcting this form of market failure. For example, the federal government provides regular agricultural market forecasts, including prediction of future supplies, demands, and prices. These estimates enable farmers to make more enlightened decisions on what to produce and when and where to market it. Similarly, by making projections of consumer spending, investment demand, and the GNP, government provides information which will facilitate business and household planning. Through this better planning, a more smoothly functioning economic system will result.

B. Problems and Policies Regarding Immobility

In addition to a lack of knowledge, and often combined with it, is the problem of immobility. This is a second friction that interferes with the smooth working of the price system. Simple models of the economy such as ours usually ignore not only time but also spatial considerations. Some immobility of resources is due to lack of knowledge about alternatives and can be reduced by spread of information. Labor market surveys frequently find that workers in one plant do not even know the wage scale for similar work in a plant across the street. Ignorance of wage rates in other parts of the city and other parts of the economy is considerably more widespread. Unionism and government employment exchanges reduce this ignorance, but it continues to be very extensive. Business managers, especially of small retail establishments, also are frequently ignorant of alternatives open to them.

While ignorance reduces the mobility of factors of production so that price changes fail to bring quick adjustment, immobility is also caused by the cost of overcoming distance. Coal mining has to take place at the coal seam. Production that is dependent on the use of coal requires weighing the cost of assembling other factors of production at the coal site against the cost of moving the extracted coal to some other site. Capital also has cost restrictions to its free movement. Usually the cost is prohibitive to dismantle the capital equipment of a factory and ship it to a new location.

A worker faces an economic cost in moving with his family to a new location. In addition, he faces a psychic cost in leaving relatives, friends, and familiar surroundings. (There is even a psychic cost in leaving fellow employees and a known relationship with supervisors for the unknown in a plant across the street.) The worker must weigh both psychic and economic costs in considering whether to respond to a higher wage somewhere else.

A further restriction on the mobility of factors of production relates to specialization. Skilled workers are loath to shift to a different kind of job because they lose the investment of time and money involved in learning their skill. The loss is regarded as not only the outlay for instruction but also the income forgone while being instructed. A worker may prefer periodic unemployment to abandoning these sunk costs and bearing the cost of retraining. The result is a surplus of labor in some localities and occupations, as well as a surplus attached to some industries. Seniority, pension rights, and the like also increase the reluctance to move.

Capital equipment is even more highly specialized than labor, and it does not shift in its existing form from a declining industry to an expanding industry. Since many capital goods are durable and are depreciated over 10 to 20 years, the shift of capital occurs over similar periods of time as firms decide about replacing it. This does not resemble the instantaneous adjustment posited in our model. Of course, when the whole system is expanding, all of the additions to capital stock can flow into expanding industries, easing the adjustment process.

Often government efforts to improve information are combined with efforts to reduce immobility in the economy. For example, all states maintain employment centers that give labor market information to unemployed workers or to workers seeking to change jobs. This information makes movement among alternatives more likely than it otherwise would be. Similarly, the U.S. Department of Labor provides assistance to migrant workers, aiding them to locate those regions with the highest potential employment opportunities.

In a very real sense, civil rights legislation has tended to reduce the immobility present in the U.S. economy. It has done so by opening up to black people and other minorities a number of alternatives in housing markets, employment markets, and markets for goods and services previously closed to them by artificial constraints. This legislation has probably had a more far-reaching impact on the existence of immobility than any public sector action in the last few decades. As such, it has made a significant contribution in the effort to increase the performance of the U.S. market system.

For much the same reason, the Equal Rights Amendment would have important economic consequences. It is designed to provide to women and minorities equal access to jobs and positions of responsibility. Like civil rights legislation, it too would increase the mobility of resources in the economy.

C. Problems and Policies Regarding Irrationality

Even if the frictions associated with imperfect information and immobilities were eliminated, the price system would fail to function in the manner depicted by our ideal market economy. In our model we assumed that all of the market participants are rational—that businesses would consistently attempt to maximize profits and households would attempt to maximize utility. But in the real economy the price system will work out its results in response to dollar "votes" even if they are based on irrational behavior.

Some critics of the theory of household demand argue that it is based on an outmoded hedonistic theory of psychology. It is true that behavior cannot be explained simply as a weighing of pleasure and pain. Psychological explanation of behavior recognizes more complexity today. In consumer behavior, there are compulsive buyers as well as impulsive buyers, and many kinds of expenditure are habitual. Yet the essence of the economic model is defensible because it is not dependent on a psychological theory; it is dependent only on observable facts of which we can be reasonably sure.

It is an observable fact that people choose among alternatives, that choice is constrained by limited income, and that the choices made usually reflect a fairly stable although roughly articulated preference system. Customers can be seen in any grocery store, momentarily indecisive about whether to put a product in their baskets. Surely they are weighing advantages and disadvantages. Income is a constraint, even if borrowing against future income is included. When habits are broken with changes in income or changes in associations, new choices are made in the formation of new habit patterns. If the individual does not weigh alternatives in considering the purchase of a new car, the banker from whom he seeks to borrow will see to it that he considers at least some of them, just to be assured of repayment of the loan.

There is sufficient stability in the pattern of consumer expenditures that the Survey Research Center at the University of Michigan has had good results forecasting purchases of consumer durables by questioning a sample of consumers as to their intentions. Income, prices, and expectations prove to play important roles in consumer purchasing decisions, as does the amount of existing assets and indebtedness. These are just what we would expect from out understanding of the theory of consumer demand. In constructing such models, the economist attempts to produce conceptual frameworks that give precision to these relationships. The difficulty of acquiring data for an empirical indifference map or demand curve may make further refinement of these two concepts improbable, and the two-dimensional character limits their empirical usefulness in any case. However, this does not destroy the usefulness of the concepts in understanding the rational process which underlies the functioning of the price system. Empirical studies do support the relevance of the variables and the relationships deduced in this brand of economic theory.

Irrationality in consumer behavior usually means to economists that consumers do not weigh choices to maximize utility. That some do not, or that all sometimes do not, may still leave intact the proposition that in the aggregate the relations inferred by economists among employment, income, prices, net assets, and expectations are operational concepts. Because they do not produce perfectly predictable results, economists would be delighted if other motives were discovered to improve our predictions, particularly in aggregate consumer behavior.

Irrational behavior of business management might be associated with actions not based on profit maximization. Nepotism, which is widespread in business, falls into this category whenever there is a negative answer to the question: Was the family relative hired by the firm at least as well qualified for the job as the best nonrelated person who could be employed? Other possible motives of business managers, such as output maximization, power maximization, or political equilibrium (within the firm), have been studied in research on the theory of the firm, but as yet no multimotive theory has taken full form.[7]

While the problem of irrationality does not destroy the meaning and applicability of the economist's models, it does require that they be framed and interpreted in a broader and less rigid way than the simple logical structure which we have presented. And while real-world behavior which is apparently inconsistent with any sort of "maximizing" effort is troublesome and is a "market failure," it is not clear what public policy can do to correct it.

On occasion, governments have attempted to restrict behavior which some people thought to be irrational. Early in this century, the federal government prohibited the production and sale of alcoholic beverages. Part of the rationale of those who supported prohibition was to keep people from doing things which were not in their own best interest—which were "irrational." The effort by government to reduce use of tobacco can be interpreted in a similar way, although the required health warning on packages can be viewed as simply improving the information on which people make their decisions. Another example is the law requiring the installation and use of seat belts in automobiles. Public opposition to such government coercion led Congress to set timetables for installation of involuntary restraints such as belts which automatically grasp

---

7. For an example of such studies, see R. M. Cyert and J. G. March, *Behavioral Theory of the Firm* (Englewood Cliffs, N.J.: Prentice-Hall, 1963).

the rider or air bags which inflate automatically. Irrational behavior will not be tolerated here!

III.   PUBLIC GOODS AND PUBLIC ACTION

In a market-directed economy most goods are produced by private firms and are bought and sold in markets in the private sector. When both implicit and explicit costs are included, the costs to the producer generally encompass society's opportunity costs in producing and distributing the good. Likewise, the competitive price charged for the good approximates its relative worth to society. Such goods are marketable in the sense that the producer is able to cover costs by requiring the purchaser to pay for the privilege of enjoying the benefits of the product. The market price tends to equate the *sacrifices* (costs) required of society to bring forth the last unit of the good with the *satisfactions* from its purchase and consumption. As we have seen, because of this equality, the optimum combination of goods is produced and in the most efficient fashion.

In chapter 1, we noted that there are some socially desirable goods and services that private firms do not find it profitable to produce. These are goods or services which provide benefits that are not marketable to individual purchasers. In many cases these benefits are not marketable because the good or service must automatically be provided to more than one member of society simultaneously if it is to be offered to any of them. These goods are referred to as *public goods*. Sometimes public goods are automatically made available to several members of society, but not all. The posting of signs on a highway is an example. The benefits cannot be denied to anyone who travels the road. In other cases, all citizens automatically benefit when a good or service is produced. For example, when a society provides national defense, the benefits accrue to all of its citizens.

Because a business firm cannot extract an appropriate price from someone who automatically receives the benefits of a public good, the firm does not receive the correct signals from the market. As a result of not being able to charge an appropriate amount, the firm will produce too little of the good or service—or perhaps none at all. This, then, is the market failure.

Consider the example of a cloud seeding firm which is able to increase rainfall in an area experiencing a water shortage. Any potential beneficiary of the modified weather would refuse to pay anything like what the additional rainfall was worth to him or her. Indeed, the buyer would be likely to express an unwillingness to pay anything at all for it. The buyer would reason: "If I simply sit tight and refuse to pay, I may get the benefit of the rainfall anyway if other people in the area pay the firm—after all, it is a public good." However, if each potential buyer reasons this way (and presumably each will), the increase in rainfall will not be provided by the private firm. (This syndrome is known as the *free rider* problem.) Public goods can only be provided in the right quantity, if at all, by collective action, usually through a government. Only through collective action can the availability of worthwhile public goods be assured.

It is for this reason that governments maintain armies, law courts, and police forces. While there are additional reasons related to justice and equity that argue for the collective provision of these goods, national defense and law and order are clearly public goods.

For a similar reason, fire protection, public health services, and sewage disposal are also publicly produced. Collective action in these cases is required because both fire and disease are "contagious" phenomena. The people who benefit from protection against spreading fires or disease cannot be charged an appropriate price for the protection by a firm which might provide the service. As a result, the service is publicly provided. As with the example of the cloud seeding firm, beneficiaries of fire protection or public health services cannot be denied the benefits of these services even if they refuse to pay anything for them. Because these beneficiaries cannot be excluded from the benefits, and because society has been unwilling to allow only those who are willing and able to pay for the benefits to receive them, fire protection and sewage disposal have been provided by the public sector.

IV. SPILLOVER EFFECTS ("EXTERNALITIES") AND COLLECTIVE ACTION

In addition to the failure of markets because some goods are public goods, a second reason that private markets may not function efficiently is the existence of *spillover* or *external* effects. When certain things are produced and sold privately, some people are required to incur costs for which they are not reimbursed or they receive benefits for which they do not have to pay. As a result, *private costs and gains may not coincide with total social costs and benefits.* When this divergence of private and social effects occurs, either too much or too little of the good will be produced and resource misallocation results.

For example a meat-packing firm may cover a residential neighborhood with an obnoxious odor. Citizens are not compensated for this spillover cost which is imposed on them. Nor does the meat-packing firm record this cost so that it can be reflected in the price of meat or in other firm decisions. Similarly, when your next-door neighbor plays his phonograph loudly and it annoys you, you are the object of a spillover cost; when the coal-burning industry in a community fills the sky with coal dust smog, residents of the community are the objects of a spillover cost; when the next semitruck pulls onto the highway with the effect of delaying your arrival and that of other highway motorists, a spillover cost is imposed on you and your fellow drivers. You cannot avoid this cost if you are on the freeway, and there is no market so that you can be compensated for the delay imposed. In each of these cases, the person harmed is forced to bear identifiable costs for which he is *not* compensated. These people would be willing to pay something to avoid bearing the spillover cost. Also, in none of these cases are the spillover costs recorded in the accounts of the business or individuals which generate them. As a result, no action is taken to minimize these costs. Moreover, because only a portion of all costs are considered by decision makers, they undertake an excess amount of that activity which generates these spillovers. As a result, resources are misallocated and economic waste results.

Spillover benefits, like spillover costs, abound in the real world. These external benefits occur when one party's action conveys an unavoidable gain to someone else for which payment is not required. When a business hires and trains an otherwise unskilled worker, it is likely that the firm will not recover the full value of the worker's training, especially if the worker changes jobs. To the extent that the investment is not recovered, other people—the next employer and others—are awarded spillover benefits because of the training provided by the first employer. Similarly, if one property owner landscapes his property, plants trees and flowers, and resods his lawn, his neighbors experience some of the benefit in the form of a pleasant view for which they are not required to pay. They are the recipients of a spillover benefit.

When spillover costs and spillover benefits exist, inefficiencies are created in the economy. Producers and consumers who create these spillovers do not take them into account when they make their decisions. As a result, the market fails to reflect them and prices become distorted. Such spillovers, then, have serious *efficiency* consequences for the economy.

In addition to these resource allocation or efficiency effects, spillovers also have *equity* effects. When spillovers exist, some people get hurt and others get helped through no action of their own. From society's point of view, it makes a difference who is being helped or hurt because of spillover effects. Hence, in addition to efficiency effects, the distributional impacts of spillovers must also be considered.

A. The Economics of Spillovers

As our models have demonstrated, the free market reaches an equilibrium where the supply and demand curves intersect. At this equilibrium, the price of the commodity or service is determined, as is the quantity of it which will be produced and exchanged. This equilibrium equates the willingness of buyers to pay for the good—reflected in the demand curve—with the cost of producing the good—reflected in the supply curve. Thus, at, and only at, the equilibrium price P_1 in Figure 8-1, the amount which buyers are willing to pay for the last or marginal unit of X just equals the cost of producing that last unit: marginal benefit equals marginal cost. If all of the benefits of the good were included in the demand curve and if all of its costs were included in the supply curve, this equilibrium would be ideal. To produce one more unit beyond Q_1 would entail more cost than the value of the benefits it would create; to stop producing before Q_1 would leave some gains unexploited. For example, if production were stopped at Q_0 society would not secure the excess of gains over costs (ab) from producing the next unit.

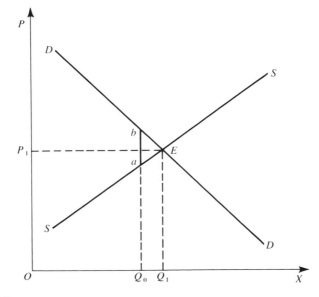

Figure 8-1

As we have illustrated, however, not all of the gains and costs are included in the market demand and supply curves when spillovers are present. For spillover *benefits*, there is a willingness to pay *in addition* to that which is captured in the demand curve. In Figure 8-2, for example, units of education are plotted on the x axis and dollars per unit are plotted on the y axis. The willingness of potential buyers to pay for education is included in the demand curve (*DD*). At very high prices, they are willing to buy less education than at lower prices. Their willingness to pay reflects their evaluation of the worth of education *to them*—higher incomes over their lifetime, the satisfaction gained from broad knowledge and educational experience, and so on. The costs of providing education are shown in the supply curve (*SS*): at lower prices, fewer units of education would be supplied than at higher prices. In a free market, Q_1 units of education would be produced and exchanged.

Education, however, involves spillover benefits. Other people receive a benefit in addition to the purchasers of education. The general population benefits if John Doe gets educated because an educated John Doe is less likely to be a juvenile delinquent; John Doe's family benefits because they are less likely to have to support him if

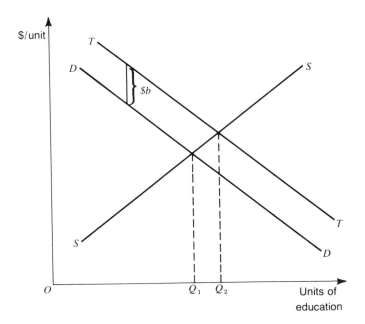

Figure 8-2

he becomes sick or unemployed; the nation as a whole benefits because an educated citizenry provides economic growth opportunities and social stability which would not otherwise exist. If these spillover benefits are added to the willingness to pay which is expressed in the market (the demand curve *DD*), the total willingness to pay (*TT*) is determined. As it is drawn, there exists a spillover benefit of $b per unit of education, no matter how much of it is produced.

This spillover benefit of $b per unit is ascertained in the same way that the demand curve was derived. For the demand curve, all of the purchasers of the good were asked how much they would be willing to pay for each of a number of quantities of the good. For the spillover benefits, all of the people who *indirectly* find themselves better off because a good is produced are asked how much they would be willing to pay to obtain the spillover benefit. In Figure 8-2, this amount is $b per unit.

As can now be seen, the existence of the spillover benefit results in an insufficient output if the market is free to function unobstructed. While the free market equilibrium would yield an output of Q_1 it is in the interest of society to have Q_2 units of education produced. At Q_1 the next unit of output yields benefits in excess of costs, and, hence, it is in the interest of society to have Q_2 units of education produced. *Where spillover benefits exist, the free market produces an output which is smaller than the socially optimum output.* And, as a result, social welfare is not maximized. Only if output is carried to Q_2 are marginal costs equated with *total* marginal benefits. Only then is the full contribution of education to social welfare attained.

The reverse of this situation occurs where spillover costs are present. This is shown in Figure 8-3. When there are spillover costs, the supply curve fails to capture all of the social costs of producing the output. Consider, for example, the case of the meat processor who pollutes a river. While the supply curve (*SS*) captures all of the private costs of processing meat, the water pollution costs which spill over onto those who use the river for recreation or fishing are not captured. These costs may take the form of reduced catches for fishermen or decreased swimming and boating opportunities for recreationists. If these spillover costs are added to the private costs, the total social cost of processing meat (*TT*) is obtained. As shown in Figure 8-3, this includes a spillover cost of $c per unit of meat produced. Again, in this case, the free unobstructed market fails to get the optimum quantity of output produced. From society's point of view, Q_2 is the optimum output level, but the free market generates a greater output of Q_1 units. *In the case of spillover costs, the free market output is greater than the optimum output that takes account of all social costs and gains.* All units of output beyond Q_2 involve marginal social costs in excess of marginal social benefits. And, because social costs exceed benefits for units of output beyond Q_2, social welfare is reduced.

The existence of spillovers, then, implies an "incorrect" or nonoptimal level of output if the free market is permitted to operate unobstructed. In the case of spillover benefits, buyers acting on the basis of their own private gains, convey to the market a demand (*DD*) which is less than that which would have been conveyed if total social gains (*TT*) had been reflected (Figure 8-2). In the case of spillover costs, sellers, acting on the basis of their own private costs, supply an output (*SS*) which is greater than the willingness to supply would have been if total social costs had been reflected in the seller's costs (Figure 8-3). In both instances, the wrong output (from society's point of view) results because individual decision makers behave on the basis of *private* costs and gains, which deviate from *total social* costs and gains. In the case of spillover benefits, too few of society's resources are allocated to the free market production of

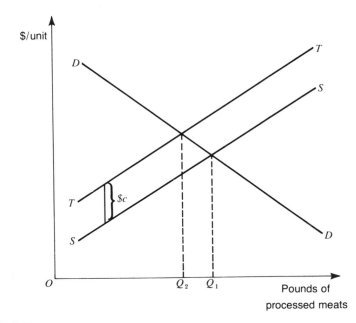

Figure 8-3

the good in question (and, hence, too many resources are allocated to the other goods produced in the economy). The opposite occurs in the case of free market production of goods with spillover costs. There, too many of society's resources are allocated to the good in question. In both of these cases, there is misallocation of resources, economic inefficiency, and a free market performance which fails to conform to the social optimum. In both cases, social welfare could be increased through collective action designed to correct inadequate market performance.

B. Spillovers and Public Policies: Illustrative Cases

A claim for some sort of collective action can be made whenever evidence of spillovers is present. In most spillover cases, however, neither the need for collective action nor the nature of the most effective public policy approach is clear. While some people argue that unrestricted private provision of certain outputs produces such undesirable spillover effects that public measures are called for, others argue that the social cost of public sector action and the concomitant discouragement of private enterprise is greater than the alleged social benefit from government provision. "Public sector failure," it is asserted, often becomes as large a problem as the market failure it was meant to correct. A few examples will give the flavor of this dilemma which lies at the basis of numerous policy debates.

1. Water Resource Development: The Role of Benefit-Cost Analysis. When the government constructs a dam on a river to, say, protect people living downstream from floods, it is acting to correct market failure. The provision of the dam may be socially worthwhile in that the social benefits in the form of flood damage reduction may exceed the costs of building and maintaining the dam. Private business would fail to undertake the provision of flood control because of the difficulty of recovering costs from the people living downstream who are benefited. The provision of flood protection has some of the nonmarketable characteristics of public goods and, consequently, the private sector fails to generate an optimum level of production.

Similarly, some of the other "outputs" of water resource development may have public good or externality characteristics. How does one economically collect from picnickers and boaters for the improved boating and picnic facilities created by the reservoir behind a dam? Or, how does one economically charge the barges which move goods on the river for the beneficial side effect of a more reliable river channel which is created in constructing a flood control dam? Moreover, should the government not produce and sell hydroelectric power at the flood control damsite once the dam is already there? To fail to do so might mean failure to take advantage of a low-cost production opportunity. Or again, once the reservoir is there, should not the government use its facilities for low-cost crop irrigation or municipal water supply?

When goods involving these spillover effects are present, the efficient resolution often involves production by the public sector. Even in those cases where production is left in the private sector, public action may be necessary either to ensure the socially optimum amount of production or to correct for undesirable inefficiencies.

Consider, for example, the decision to permit a private power company to build a power production dam on a river in lieu of a public dam. Will the company undertake to provide recreation, irrigation, and navigation facilities when these are socially efficient undertakings? Will it consider that it is producing flood control benefits in addition to power when it designs the dam? In each of these cases the answer is *no*, if the output is in the form of an externality or spillover and hence unsalable in a market.

Thus, if the social benefit of these nonmarketable services exceeds the cost of providing them, which it often does, and if the development of the river by a private firm precludes the development of these other purposes, which it often does, then private development of the stream denies society the benefit of these worthwhile yet external or spillover benefits. Indeed, private development, by failing to provide these services, imposes a cost on society. If society is to enjoy the benefits of these products, the government must undertake the multipurpose development of the water resource.[8]

The converse of this may exist if private development carries along with it enormous spillover *costs*. This is the case in a recent proposal to construct a huge hydroelectric dam on the Snake River in the Pacific Northwest. The construction of this dam would flood out the nation's deepest natural gorge—Hell's Canyon—destroying permanently its use for wilderness experience, scenic beauty, and other environmental values. These "outputs" of the canyon are public goods and their destruction by private development would create irreversible spillover costs which are not registered by the private

---

8. See John V. Krutilla and Otto Eckstein, *Multiple-Purpose River Development* (Baltimore: Johns Hopkins Press for Resources for the Future, Inc., 1958), for an excellent discussion of the external costs and benefits resulting from alternative plans for river development.

producer. In such a case, collective action may be required to keep a private project from being undertaken. It should be noted that this same conclusion would hold if the "developer" were a public agency rather than a private firm. Public agencies often have objectives which are limited in much the same way as those of private producers.

If it is accepted that government intervention may be required to correct the private sector's failure to take into account spillover costs and benefits, how can it be determined if the proposed public sector action is economically justified? This is not an easy question, but methods for evaluating proposed government actions have been, and are being, devised. The most widely used technique is known as *benefit-cost analysis*. In it, the dollar value today of all of a action's future benefits to society is evaluated and compared with the value today of all costs or sacrifices that society must incur in taking the action. If the benefits exceed the costs, the benefit-cost ratio is greater than 1—the mark of an efficient government action. If the benefits are less than the costs, the ratio is less than 1 and the action would entail a misallocation of resources.

Although it is difficult and extremely tricky to measure many of the social costs and benefits resulting from government actions, a number of appropriate techniques have been developed. The present value of the stream of power generation benefits, for example, can be estimated reasonably from the generating capacity planned plus estimates of the future growth of demand for power. Irrigation benefits can be calculated in the same way. Benefits from flood control are estimated from historical data of flood expectancy and estimates of future property value in the flood plain. Likewise, by projecting barge traffic on improved streams and comparing transportation costs by barge with the least expensive alternative method of transportation, estimates of navigation benefits can be obtained. In recent years rather successful techniques have been devised for empirically estimating the recreational benefits of water projects.

In the Hell's Canyon case, the task was to compare the net benefits of using the river for the production of electric power with the costs in the form of lost opportunities for future wilderness and environmental uses of the canyon. The research done on this proposed project indicated that even if very low values were placed on the environmental uses of the canyon and even if the growth of wilderness use was assumed to be very slow, the net power benefits were less than the environmental costs, and the private development should be prohibited by collective action.

Notwithstanding the progress that has been made in improving the accuracy of benefit-cost computations, the government continues to construct many inefficient projects or to make other decisions in which the social costs exceed social benefits. A major reason for this result is clear: an individual state or region need not be concerned with the efficiency of a project constructed within its bounds—it reaps the lion's share of the benefits while the nation as a whole bears the cost. Owing to the political power of its congressmen or senators or lobby groups, a region with such a relatively inefficient project may be able to secure federal appropriations for the project even though it fails to pass the benefit-cost test.[9]

2. Air and Water Pollution Control: Rule Enforcement vs. Economic Incentives. The preceding example deals with public sector decisions involving the construction of projects—or the prohibition of project construction—as a means to deal with public goods or spillover effects. In addition to such government actions, there are other policy measures which have been used to correct such market failures. One of these strategies has been referred to as *rule making and enforcement*; another involves the imposition of charges so as to establish appropriate *economic incentives*. Consider the external effects of air and water pollution which were mentioned earlier. These involve the creation of external or spillover costs by a private firm or government as it goes about its business. In each of these cases the private market fails to take into account all of the costs which a particular action entails. Consequently, in each case it is necessary to go outside the "automatic" price system to correct the market failure and to ensure that the costs to society are assigned to the relevant production process. Often the public sector has chosen policies other than government ownership and production to remedy this sort of market failure.

The most common method has been simply to legislate against the nuisance. Smoke abatement ordinances set standards for smoke density and soot content which require firms to shift to a different grade of coal or to install mechanisms that will trap offensive materials. Federal water and air pollution legislation imposes standards which limit the amount and the character of waste that can be dumped into public waters or the atmosphere. An alternative method of imposing social cost on the relevant production process is to charge the production unit an amount estimated to be the cost

---

9. See Robert Haveman and Robert Hamrin, eds., *The Political Economy of Federal Policy* (New York: Harper and Row, 1973) for a number of examples of how political power can be employed to override efficient policy measures.

inflicted on the rest of society from its actions—the external or spillover cost. This concept is embodied in recent proposals for *effluent charges* on firms and cities that use public waterways for waste disposal. The point is that external as well as private costs should be reflected in the price paid by the consumers of the product whose production imposes the cost, if resources are to be allocated efficiently. This sort of pricing—or economic incentives—strategy has been preferred by most economists over the rule-making and rule-enforcement strategy which is the basis of current pollution control policy.[10]

C. Conservation and Preservation: The Problem of Future Generations

External or spillover costs and benefits have a time dimension, too. When our generation uses certain resources in the production of something giving present satisfaction, it denies their use to generations yet unborn. Our use of the resources is a cost to these future generations. In order to assess this cost we turn to the rate of interest, which is the price that is supposed to allocate production between the present and the future. Since capital is created to produce goods in the future, it must be productive enough to cover an interest cost as well as return the amount paid for the resources which created it. When the interest rate is high, only those capital goods which produce a high return of return over cost will be created. Fewer resources will be devoted to production of capital, hence to future consumption, than when the interest rate is lower.

This function of allocating between present and future is submerged when the interest rate is manipulated for other purposes. When it is regulated by monetary authorities, the rate is set to cope with some contemporary problem such as inflation or a gold outflow. Even when it is set by the relatively free play of supply and demand in the market for loanable funds, the long-term rate probably reflects a time horizon of less than two generations (say, 50 years). To the extent that this is true, the consequences of our actions on people living far in the future are not appropriately taken into account. This phenomenon may require public sector action for the conservation or preservation of basic natural resources, as well as to influence the rate of growth in the stock of capital.

---

10. See A. M. Freeman, R. Haveman, and A. V. Kneese, *The Economics of Environmental Policy* (New York: John Wiley & Sons, 1973); and A.V. Kneese and C. Schultze, *Pollution, Prices, and Policy* (Washington, D.C.: The Brookings Institution, 1975).

When resources are free (or very cheap) and their supply appears to be inexhaustible, the costs of conservation practices often appear unrecoverable. For this reason productive land was maltreated through most of the nineteenth century in the United States. Today, we may be doing much the same thing with the resources of the ocean or with land resources which could be maintained as open space in rapidly growing metropolitan areas.

In much the same way, the free play of the price system is destroying the redwood forests of the West Coast. Redwood is superb lumber for many purposes, and lumbermen can make high profits by cutting it. But continued cutting may be creating contemporary social costs by destroying a unique and beautiful part of the nation's natural environment. Even if all of the contemporary social costs had to be covered by the lumbermen, the timber felling would likely continue. However, future generations are likely to have an interest in these stands, whether for lumber uses or for the esthetic value of viewing trees that were standing before the voyages of Columbus. If current decisions also had to consider these effects, perhaps cutting today should be prohibited. Such future generation effects are likely to be ignored unless there is social intervention.

This conclusion, of course, presumes that future generations will have the same general set of values as the present generation. If it is just as likely that future generations will dislike open space in urban areas or standing redwoods as it is that they will appreciate them, our discussion would have little relevance.

Many other examples will come to mind in which the cost and revenue considerations of the price system may fail to secure the optimal distribution of use of the resources between present and future generations. The cost of our error falls on future generations if we undervalue the future relative to the present. The price system then fails to operate fully in the society's interest both because it fails to produce some goods that are socially desirable and because it produces too many or too little of still others. If the interests of future generations are to be appropriately weighed, collective action must be used to modify and temper the operation of the market system.

As the concern for weighing social costs and benefits moves into the arena of differing value judgments, it becomes more and more important to devise ways for effective expression of social choice. Voting based on well-informed judgment may be effective only in clusters of people small enough that the voters can enter into public discussion. Referenda as effective devices seem to be limited to the town or small city. Perhaps ways can be devised to make voting better informed and more effective as an expression of the "will of the people" in larger communities. Our experience with referenda to finance local schools indicates that we have a long way to go. As an alternative, representative samples of the population might be polled, providing an effective device for expression of social choice that would lead to maximum consumer satisfaction.[11]

V. THE DISTRIBUTION OF INCOME, THE MARKET SYSTEM, AND PUBLIC POLICY

Every society must choose some mechanism by which to organize its production and to allocate its resources. There are numerous mechanisms which are candidates for this function. They range from pure communism on one extreme, through socialism, state planning, and mixed free enterprise and planning to a pure market system at the other extreme. All of these economic systems have merits and demerits, and it is after weighing them that society must make its choice.

The case for the market system is basically an economic efficiency case. It can be claimed that substantial welfare gains will accrue to a society that relies on the operation of the market mechanism. This claim is based on the following propositions.

1. Each individual knows best what will maximize his or her satisfaction.
2. The aggregate of these individual maxima will produce maximum satisfaction for the society.
3. The price system provides the best mechanism for making individual satisfactions known and for allocating resources in responses to individual demands.

In this chapter we have recognized problems with all of these propositions. Market power, stemming in part from technology, erodes the ability of the market system to allocate resources efficiently. Similarly, imperfect knowledge, immobilities, and other "frictions" keep real-world markets from functioning smoothly and adjusting rapidly. As a result, the ability of the system to allocate resources efficiently is weakened. Finally, public goods and spillover effects result in a failure of the market system to produce certain worthwhile goods and to produce too many or too few of other goods.

---

11. For a discussion of means for effective expression of social choice see A. Downs, *An Economic Theory of Democracy* (New York: Harper & Bros., 1956).

All of these characteristics lead to "market failure." Because of them, the real-world market system does not efficiently allocate resources or provide for maximum social welfare. Efforts are made to supplement it with other modes of choice. Many of these involve some form of government action.

If we prevent or offset control of supply and demand, if we reduce irrationality and immobility by education and communication, if we find ways to assign external costs and benefits accurately and to measure social choice in the government provision of public goods, then would the price system produce market values that coincide with social values?

Alas, there is another major qualification. The market system determines what will be produced, how it will be produced, and who will earn the income generated in response to the pattern of demands which are brought to the market. In turn, the pattern of demands depends on *who has money to spend* and *what they wish to spend it on*. That is, the market outcome depends on the *initial distribution of income*.

In this sense, then, the income distribution is built into the operation of the market system. The initial distribution of income determines the way in which the what? how? and for whom? questions are going to be answered. And, in turn, the answer to the for whom? question determines the distribution of income. It is a closed circle.

The key to this circle lies in the market system's answer to the for whom? question. As we saw in chapter 6, in a perfect market system, members of society receive *incomes* (wages, interest, profits, rent) *in accord with their contribution to the output* of the economy. This principle—income according to contribution—is the market system principle of income distribution. *If* the market system does not have serious "market failures," *and if* the members of society raise the market system income distribution principle to an ethical principle, the distributional outcome of the market system will, by definition, be acceptable.

For several reasons, most people are not willing to grant a high ethical status to the principle of "income according to contribution." This principle ignores the basic question of who owns the human and physical capital which yield the services of factors of production, and how these people came to own these assets. It would be one thing if all of the owners came to possess their education, skills, land, property, and brains through their own efforts. If this were the case, it could be claimed that these owners should be allowed to reap the rewards of their efforts by keeping the income which their factor services earn in the market.

It is seldom the case, however, that asset ownership is solely related to effort. The most obvious exception is found in the factor of land or natural resources. By and large, this factor was not "produced" by the present-day owner; in many cases, he or she obtained it through inheritance. Private ownership of land, inheritance, and the right to the return from these cannot be justified by the principle of "reward according to contribution."

The situation is not so much different in the case of "human capital." Most labor suppliers are not solely responsible for the education and training which have created their highly valued labor services. In many cases, the person was publicly educated, in which case the society in general paid (and hence is responsible) for most of the training and accumulated skill. Moreover, the person's physical and mental capacities are to some degree inherited. Where discrimination on the basis of race, religion, or sex exists, people of equal innate capacities may receive unequal education, training and, hence, incomes. "Connections" with important people controlling key jobs are not the same for one person as for another. For all of these reasons, it is difficult to subscribe to the principle of "reward according to contribution" as an unqualified high moral or ethical principle.

There are other concerns which erode the ethical basis of the market system's principle of income distribution. For example, what should we do about the handicapped, those with mental and emotional problems, and those with low skills, who cannot contribute to production, or who cannot contribute enough to live at subsistence or some identifiable level of human dignity? Equity calls for receipt of income above what such people are able to produce. Clearly, the problems of poverty and what to do about it are related to the ethic of income distribution.

Because the economic system does not work smoothly, what about those whose incomes are reduced or eliminated by malfunction of the system rather than their own inability? The problems of economic instability and unemployment also are related to the ethic of income distribution.

The point of all of this, then, is that the *distribution of income must be determined by an explicit social decision*, an explicit value judgment. There are no unqualified principles to guide this judgment, and there is nothing sacred about the "income according to contribution" principle. It is but one of many possible social value judgments.

To be sure, in many cases, gaining more equity or equality may require some sacrifice of economic efficiency. The nature of this sacrifice must be known, and then, knowing it, society must decide what combination of equality and efficiency to select.[12] Both contribute to the level of social well-being. After all, we judge economic systems by the level of human well-being which they yield, and not simply by the efficiency with which they allocate resources.

In the United States, the market system produces a very unequal distribution of income. In the first column of Table 8-1, we show how many American people would be in poverty if only the income from wages, interest, profits, and rent—the returns from supplying factor services to the market—were counted. In 1965, 40.8 million American people would have fallen below the poverty line if only market earnings counted. This number decreased by about 1 million—to 39.4 million—in 1972, indicating that the market system is not yielding very much more equality over time in the distribution of its incomes. Moreover, by 1976 the number of market income poor increased to over 44 million, a notable worsening in the effect of the market on economic inequality. In both 1975 and 1976, the number of people with market system incomes below the poverty line was about 20 percent of the total number of Americans.

The American citizenry has determined that such inequality is unacceptable. To alter this situation a large number of social welfare programs have been legislated, many with the purpose of raising these "market system poor" people above the poverty line. Indeed, in 1976, over $310 billion was being spent on this social welfare system. In Table 8-2, we show the broad outlines of this system for both 1965, 1972, and 1976. As can be seen there, this system has grown enormously in recent years—from $75 billion in 1965, to four times this amount in 1976.

This effort to reduce market system poverty has had some success. In the second column of Table 8-1, we show the number of poor persons in the various years, after the government *cash income* benefits have been added to market system income. These numbers are about two-thirds as big as the numbers in the first column. This indicates that the cash benefits of government programs have lifted about one-third of the market system poor above the poverty line. Moreover, these programs have given the remaining poor substantial income, although not enough to raise them out of poverty.

In addition to cash benefits, the public programs shown in Table 8-2 give large noncash benefits to poor people. These are sometimes

---

12. See Arthur Okun, *Equality and Efficiency: The Great Debate* (Washington, D.C.: The Brookings Institution, 1975).

Table 8-1
Poverty Levels With and Without Public Program Cash Benefits

YEAR	NUMBER OF POOR PERSONS COUNTING ONLY MARKET INCOME (millions)	NUMBER OF POOR PERSONS COUNTING BOTH MARKET INCOME AND PUBLIC PROGRAM CASH BENEFITS (millions)	NUMBER OF POOR PERSONS COUNTING MARKET INCOME AND PUBLIC PROGRAM CASH AND IN-KIND BENEFITS (millions)
1965	40.8	29.9	N.A.
1968	35.8	25.1	19.8
1970	37.8	25.5	19.0
1972	39.4	24.5	12.9
1974	42.4	24.3	16.4
1976	44.5	25.0	14.1

Source: Sheldon Danziger and Robert Plotnick, *Has the War on Poverty Been Won?* (New York: Academic Press, 1981).

called *in-kind income*. It has been estimated that if the value of these benefits were added to the cash income of the poor, about another one-third of the poor people would be raised out of poverty. These estimates are shown in the third column of Table 8-1 and suggest that government programs have reduced poverty from 45 to 14 million people in the United States in 1976.

The purpose of this discussion is simply to illustrate that the

Table 8-2
Government Social Welfare Expenditures, by Program Category: 1965, 1972, and 1976

PROGRAM CATEGORY	1965 (billions)	1972 (billions)	1976 (billions)
Social Security and welfare	$36.6	$ 80.1	$149.8
Nutrition	0.9	3.7	8.2
Housing	0.3	1.8	3.0
Health	5.6	24.6	48.0
Welfare and social services	1.4	5.3	6.3
Employment and manpower	0.7	3.9	a
Education	27.1	62.2	88.1
Other	2.2	3.2	7.5
Total	$74.8	$184.8	$310.9

Source: Sheldon Danziger and Robert Plotnick, *Has the War On Poverty Been Won?* (New York: Academic Press, 1981).
a Combined with "Other."

market system principle of "income according to contribution" does not have to be accepted for the market system to function. Society can make a decision to use public policy to alter the distribution of income in order to reduce poverty and to equalize incomes among people. And having done so, the market system can operate to produce goods and allocate resources in line with the pattern of market demands which the revised income distribution generates.

One final note: One should not leave this discussion with the feeling that we have moved a long way toward equality in the United States. We have not. In Table 8-3, the percentage distribution of family income (including market system income and cash benefits from public programs) is shown for 1950, 1970, and 1976. It indicates that 20 percent of the families with the higest income had 42 percent of the total income in the United States, while the lowest 20 percent had only about 5 percent. *Indeed, the richest 5 percent of families had nearly three times the amount of income as the lowest 20 percent.* The table also indicates that the degree of inequality has not changed very much since World War II. A good deal remains to be done if poverty is to be eliminated and extreme inequality reduced.

VI. CONCLUSION AND SUMMARY

This volume has attempted to explain how prices and markets may be used to organize economic activity in society. When the price system functions well, it generally leads to an efficient allocation of resources, which is an important economic goal of society.

The discussion in this chapter indicates that economic affairs in reality do not conform nicely to our theory, and even if they did, there would be areas in which efficient allocation of resources would not necessarily occur. The reader might well ask why he has

Table 8-3
Percentage Distribution of Family Income

	1950	1970	1976
Lowest 20 percent	4.5	5.5	5.4
Second 20 percent	12.0	12.0	11.8
Third 20 percent	17.4	17.4	17.6
Fourth 20 percent	23.5	23.5	24.1
Highest 20 percent	42.6	41.6	41.1
Total	100.0	100.0	100.0
Top 5 percent	17.0	14.4	15.6

been led through the theoretical structure if this is true. Our apologia runs through the volume—in the preface, toward the end of chapter 1, toward the end of chapter 2, and so on. Even so, it may bear repeating after this liberal dose of critical comment.

Some of our criticisms reflect the fact that the political and economic institutions of society have major structural problems. The criticisms point out directions for further striving toward a better institutional structure. Other criticisms stem from the fact that our theory falls short of reflecting reality and fails, in many circumstances, to predict economic behavior accurately. While our theory has many inadequacies, it is, nevertheless, the best we have at present and it does, we would argue, substantially add to understanding. It has helped us to define an important social goal, economic efficiency. It has provided us with sets of concepts and relationships that help us to formulate important economic problems in precise terms. It has been of significant help in evaluating public policy proposals. Although at times there has been insufficient recognition of the limitations of the theory for policy, at other times an understanding of the theory would have led to proper policy applications and closer attainment of the economic goals of society.

Hence, while insufficient in itself, our theory is an essential building block in the construction of more adequate tools for understanding social and economic behavior. Moreover, it provides substantial assistance in understanding the nature of individual choice in economic affairs.

Index